The Works

OF

ROBERT BURNS;

WITH

AN ACCOUNT OF HIS LIFE,

AND

A CRITICISM ON HIS WRITINGS.

TO WHICH ARE PREFIXED,

SOME OBSERVATIONS ON THE CHARACTER AND CONDITION OF

THE SCOTTISH PEASANTRY.

IN FOUR VOLUMES.
VOL. II.

THE SIXTH EDITION.

LONDON:
PRINTED FOR T. CADELL AND W. DAVIES, STRAND;
AND W. CREECH, AT EDINBURGH;
BY J. M'CREERY, BLACK-HORSE-COURT, FLEET-STREET.

1809.

ADVERTISEMENT.

It is impossible to dismiss this Volume of the Correspondence of our Bard, without some anxiety as to the reception it may meet with. The experiment we are making has not often been tried; perhaps on no occasion has so large a portion of the recent and unpremeditated effusions of a man of genius been committed to the press.

Of the following letters of Burns, a considerable number were transmitted for publication, by the individuals to whom they were addressed; but very few have been printed entire. It will easily be believed, that, in a series of letters, written without the least view to publication, various passages were found unfit for the press, from different considerations. It will also be readily supposed, that our Poet, writing nearly at the same time, and under the same feelings to different individuals, would sometimes fall into the same train of sentiment and forms of expression. To avoid, therefore, the tediousness of such repetitions, it has been found necessary to mutilate many of the individual letters, and sometimes to exscind parts of great delicacy—the unbridled effusions of panegyric and regard. But though many of the letters are printed from originals furnished by the persons to whom they were addressed, others are printed from first draughts, or sketches, found among the papers of our Bard. Though in general no man committed his thoughts to his correspondents with less consideration or effort than Burns, yet it appears that in some instances he was dissatisfied with his first essays, and wrote out his communications in a fairer character, or perhaps in more studied language. In the chaos of his manuscripts, some of the original sketches were found: and as these sketches, though less perfect, are fairly to be considered as the offspring of his mind, where they

they have seemed in themselves worthy of a place in this volume, we have not hesitated to insert them, though they may not always correspond exactly with the letters transmitted, which have been lost or withheld.

Our author appears at one time to have formed an intention of making a collection of his letters for the amusement of a friend. Accordingly he copied an inconsiderable number of them into a book, which he presented to Robert Riddel, of Glenriddel, Esq. Among these was the account of his life, addressed to Dr. Moore, and printed in the first volume. In copying from his imperfect sketches, (it does not appear that he had the letters actually sent to his correspondents before him) he seems to have occasionally enlarged his observations, and altered his expressions. In such instances his emendations have been adopted; but in truth there are but five of the letters thus selected by the poet, to be found in the present volume, the rest being thought of inferior merit, or otherwise unfit for the public eye.

In printing this volume, the Editor has
found

found some corrections of grammar necessary; but these have been very few, and such as may be supposed to occur in the careless effusions, even of literary characters, who have not been in the habit of carrying their compositions to the press. These corrections have never been extended to any habitual modes of expression of the Poet, even where his phraseology may seem to violate the delicacies of taste, or the idiom of our language, which he wrote in general with great accuracy. Some difference will indeed be found in this respect in his earlier and in his later compositions; and this volume will exhibit the progress of his style, as well as the history of his mind. In the Fourth Edition, several new letters were introduced, and some of inferior importance were omitted.

CONTENTS OF VOL. II.

LETTERS.

No.   Page

I. To Mr. JOHN MURDOCH, 15th Jan. 1783. Burns's former teacher; giving an account of his present studies, and temper of mind,   1

II. Extracts from MSS. Observations on various subjects, ...   5

III. To Mr. AIKEN. 1786. Written under distress of mind, ... 16

IV. To Mrs. DUNLOP. Thanks for her notice. Praise of her ancestor, Sir William Wallace, 21

V. To Mrs. STEWART of Stair. Inclosing a poem on Miss A———, ... 23

VI. Proclamation in the name of the Muses, . . 26

VII. Dr. BLACKLOCK to the Rev. G. LOWRIE. Encouraging the Bard to visit Edinburgh, and print a new edition of his poems there, 29

VIII. From the Rev. Mr. LOWRIE. 22d December, 1786. Advice to the Bard how to conduct himself in Edinburgh, ... 32

IX. To Mr. CHALMERS. 27th Dec. 1786. Praise of Miss Burnet of Monboddo, ... 34

CONTENTS.

No.		Page
X.	To the Earl of EGLINGTON. *Jan.* 1787. *Thanks for his patronage,*	36
XI.	To Mrs DUNLOP. 15*th Jan.* 1787. *Account of his situation in Edinburgh,*	38
XII.	To Dr. MOORE. 1787. *Grateful acknowledgments of Dr. M.'s notice of him in his letters to Mrs. Dunlop,*	42
XIII.	From Dr. MOORE. 23*d Jan.* 1787. *In answer to the foregoing, and inclosing a sonnet on the Bard, by Miss Williams,*	44
XIV.	To the Rev. G. LOWRIE. *Thanks for advice—reflections on his situation—compliment paid to Miss L——, by Mr. Mackenzie,*	47
XV.	To Dr. MOORE. 15*th Feb.* 1787,	50
XVI.	From Dr. MOORE, 28*th Feb.* 1787. *Sends the Bard a present of his " View of Society and Manners," &c.*	52
XVII.	To the Earl of GLENCAIRN. 1787. *Grateful acknowledgment of kindness,*	55
XVIII.	To the Earl of BUCHAN. *In reply to a letter of advice,*	57
XIX.	*Extract concerning the monument erected for Fergusson by our Poet,*	60
XX.	To ——. *Accompanying the foregoing,*	62
XXI.	Extract from ——. 8*th March,* 1787. *Good advice,*	64
XXII.	To Mrs. DUNLOP. 22*d March,* 1787. *Respecting his prospects on leaving Edinburgh,*	68
XXIII.	To the Same. 15*th April,* 1787. *On the same subject,*	71

CONTENTS.

No.		Page
XXIV.	To Dr. MOORE, 23d *April*, 1787. *On the same subject,*	73
XXV.	Extract to Mrs. DUNLOP. 30*th April. Reply to Criticisms,*	75
XXVI.	To the Rev. Dr. BLAIR. 3*d May. Written on leaving Edinburgh. Thanks for his kindness,*	77
XXVII.	From Dr. BLAIR. 4*th May. In reply to the preceding,*	79
XXVIII.	From Dr. MOORE. 23*d May,* 1787. *Criticism and good advice,*	83
XXIX.	To Mr. WALKER, *at Blair of Athole. Inclosing the Humble Petition of Bruar-water to the Duke of Athole,*	87
XXX.	To Mr. G. BURNS. 17*th Sept. Account of his tour through the Highlands,*	89
XXXI.	From Mr. RAMSAY *of Ochtertyre.* 22*d Oct. Inclosing Latin Inscriptions with Translations, and the Tale of Omeron Cameron,*	92
XXXII.	Mr. RAMSAY to the Rev. W. YOUNG. 22*d Oct. introducing our Poet,*	102
XXXIII.	Mr. RAMSAY to Dr. BLACKLOCK. 27*th Oct. Anecdotes of Scottish Songs for our Poet,*	105
XXXIV.	From Mr. JOHN MURDOCH, *in London.* 28*th Oct. In answer to No.* I.	107
XXXV.	From Mr. ———. *Gordon Castle,* 31*st Oct.* 1787. *Acknowledging a song sent to Lady Charlotte Gordon,*	110

CONTENTS.

No.		Page
XXXVI.	From the Rev. J. SKINNER. 14*th*. Nov. 1787. *Some Account of Scottish Poems,*	112
XXXVII.	From Mrs. ———. 30*th Nov. Inclosing Erse songs, with the music,*	117
XXXVIII.	To the Earl of GLENCAIRN. *Requests his assistance in getting into the Excise,*	120
XXXIX.	To —— DALRYMPLE, Esq. *Congratulation on his becoming a poet.—Praise of Lord Glencairn,*	122
XL.	To Sir JOHN WHITEFOORD. Dec. 1787. *Thanks for Friendship—Reflections on the poetical character,*	124
XLI.	To Mrs. DUNLOP. 21*st. Jan.* 1788. *Written on recovery from sickness,*	127
XLII.	Extract to the Same. 12*th Feb.* 1788. *Defence of himself,*	129
XLIII.	To the Same. 7*th March,* 1788. *Who had heard that he had ridiculed her,*	130
XLIV.	To Mr. CLEGHORN, 31*st March,* 1788. *Mentioning his having composed the first stanza of the Chevalier's Lament,*	132
XLV.	From Mr. CLEGHORN. 27*th April. In reply to the above. The Chevalier's Lament in full, in a Note,*	134
XLVI.	To Mrs. DUNLOP. 28*th April. Giving an account of his prospects,*	137
XLVII.	From the Rev. J. SKINNER. 28*th April,* 1788, *Enclosing two songs, one by himself, the other by a Buchan ploughman; the songs printed at large,*	139

No.		Page
XLVIII.	To Professor D. STEWART. *3d May. Thanks for his friendship,*	146
XLIX.	Extract to Mrs. DUNLOP. *4th May. Remarks on Dryden's Virgil, and Pope's Odyssey,*	147
L.	To the Same. *27th May. General Reflections,*	149
LI.	To the Same, *at Mr. Dunlop's, Haddington. 13th June, 1788. Account of his marriage,*	152
LII.	To Mr. P. HILL. *With a present of cheese,*	155
LIII.	To Mrs. DUNLOP. *2d August, 1788. With lines on a hermitage,*	160
LIV.	To the Same. *10th August. Farther account of his marriage,*	164
LV.	To the Same. *16th August. Reflections on human life,*	167
LVI.	To R. GRAHAM, *of Fintry, Esq. A petition in verse for a situation in the Excise,*	171
LVII.	To Mr. P. HILL. *1st Oct. 1788. Criticism on a poem, entitled, "An Address to Lochlomond,"*	176
LVIII.	To Mrs. DUNLOP, *at Moreham Maines, 13th November,*	181
LIX.	To *****, *8th Nov. Defence of the Family of the Stuarts. Baseness of insulting fallen greatness,*	183
LX.	To Mrs. DUNLOP. *17th December, with the soldier's song—"Go fetch to me a pint o' wine,"*	188

CONTENTS.

No. Page

LXI. To Miss DAVIES, *a young Lady who had heard he had been making a ballad on her, inclosing that ballad,* 191

LXII. From Mr. G. BURNS. *1st Jan.* 1789. *Reflections suggested by the day,* . . 194

LXIII. To Mrs. DUNLOP. *1st Jan. Reflections suggested by the day,* 195

LXIV. To Dr. MOORE. *4th Jan. Account of his situation and prospects,* . . 198

LXV. To Professor D. STEWART. *Inclosing poems for his criticism,* 202

LXVI. To Bishop GEDDES. *3d Feb. Account of his situation and prospects,* . 205

LXVII. From the Rev. P. CARFRAE. *2d Jan.* 1789. *Requesting advice as to the publishing Mr. Mylne's poems,* . . 208

LXVIII. To Mrs. DUNLOP. *4th March. Reflections after a visit to Edinburgh,* 211

LXIX. To the Rev. P. CARFRAE. *In answer to No.* LXVII. 215

LXX. To Dr. MOORE. *23d March. Inclosing a poem,* 218

LXXI. To Mr. HILL. *2d April. Apostrophe to Frugality,* 221

LXXII. To Mrs. DUNLOP. *4th April,* 1789. *With a sketch of an epistle in verse to the Right Hon. C. J. Fox,* . . . 225

LXXIII. To Mr. CUNNINGHAM. *4th May. With the first draught of the poem on a wounded Hare,* 228

CONTENTS.

No.		Page
LXXIV.	From Dr. GREGORY. 2d June. Criticism of the poem on a wounded Hare,	231
LXXV.	To Mr. M'AULEY of Dumbarton. 4th June. Account of his situation,	235
LXXVI.	To Mrs. DUNLOP, 21st June. Reflections on Religion,	237
LXXVII.	From Dr. MOORE. 10th June. 1789. Good advice,	240
LXXVIII.	From Miss J. LITTLE. 12th July. A poetess in humble life, with a poem in praise of our Bard,	243
LXXIX.	From Mr. ******, 5th August. Some account of Fergusson,	248
LXXX.	To Mr. ******. In answer,	250
LXXXI.	To Miss WILLIAMS. Inclosing a criticism on a poem of hers,	253
LXXXII.	From Miss WILLIAMS. In reply to the foregoing,	255
LXXXIII.	To Mrs. DUNLOP. 6th Sept. 1789. Praise of Zeluco.	257
LXXXIV.	From Dr. BLACKLOCK. 24th Aug. An epistle in verse,	261
LXXXV.	To Dr. BLACKLOCK. 21st Oct. Poetical reply to the above,	263
LXXXVI.	To R. GRAHAM, Esq. 9th Dec. Inclosing some electioneering ballads,	267
LXXXVII.	To Mrs DUNLOP. 13th Dec. 1789. Serious and interesting reflections,	270

No		Page
LXXXVIII.	To Sir JOHN SINCLAIR. *Account of a book society among the farmers in Nithsdale,*	274
LXXXIX.	To CHARLES SHARPE, Esq. *of Hoddam. Under a fictitious signature, inclosing a ballad,* 1790 or 1791,	279
XC.	To Mr. G. BURNS. 11*th Jan.* 1790. *With a prologue, spoken on the Dumfries theatre,*	283
XCI.	To Mrs DUNLOP. 25*th Jan. Some account of Falconer, author of the Shipwreck,*	286
XCII.	From Mr CUNNINGHAM. 28*th Jan.* 1790. *Inquiries after our Bard,*	291
XCIII.	To Mr. CUNNINGHAM. 13*th Feb. In reply to the above,*	293
XCIV.	To Mr. HILL. 2*d March. Orders for books,*	298
XCV.	To Mrs. DUNLOP. 10*th April. Remarks on the Lounger, and on the writings of Mr. Mackenzie,*	301
XCVI.	From Mr. CUNNINGHAM. 25*th May. Account of the death of Miss Burnet of Monboddo,*	306
XCVII.	To Dr. MOORE. 14*th July,* 1790. *Thanks for a present of Zeluco,*	308
XCVIII.	To Mrs. DUNLOP. 8*th Aug. Written under wounded pride,*	311
XCIX.	To Mr. CUNNINGHAM. 8*th Aug. Aspirations after independence,*	313

No.		Page
C.	From Dr. BLACKLOCK. 1st Sept. 1790. Poetical letter of friendship,	315
CI.	Extract from Mr. CUNNINGHAM. 14th Oct. Suggesting subjects for our poet's muse,	317
CII.	To Mrs. DUNLOP. Nov. 1790. Congratulations on the birth of her grandson,	319
CIII.	To Mr. CUNNINGHAM. 23d Jan. 1791. With an elegy on Miss Burnet of Monboddo,	322
CIV.	To Mr. HILL. 17th Jan. Indignant apostrophe to Poverty,	325
CV.	From A. F. TYTLER, Esq. 12th March. Criticism on Tam o' Shanter	328
CVI.	To A. F. Tytler, Esq. In reply to the above,	332
CVII.	To Mrs DUNLOP. 7th Feb. 1791. Inclosing his elegy on Miss Burnet,	334
CVIII.	To Lady W. M. CONSTABLE. Acknowledging a present of a snuff-box,	337
CIX.	To Mrs. GRAHAM of Fintry. Inclosing " Queen Mary's Lament,"	338
CX.	From the Rev. G. BAIRD. 8th of Feb. 1781. Requesting assistance in publishing the poems of Michael Bruce,	340
CXI.	To the Rev. G. BAIRD. In reply to the above,	343
CXII.	To Dr. MOORE. 28th of Feb. 1791. Inclosing Tam o' Shanter, &c.	345
CXIII.	From Dr. MOORE. 29th March. With remarks on Tam o' Shanter, &c.	349

No.		Page
CXIV.	To the Rev. A. ALISON. 14th Feb. Acknowledging his present of the "Essays on the Principles of Taste," with remarks on the book,	353
CXV.	To Mr. CUNNINGHAM. 12th March. With a Jacobite song, &c.	355
CXVI.	To Mrs. DUNLOP. 11th April. Comparison between female attractions in high and humble life,	358
CXVII.	To Mr. ———. Reflections on his own indolence,	361
CXVIII.	To Mr. CUNNINGHAM. 11th June. Requesting his interest for an oppressed friend,	362
CXIX.	From the Earl of BUCHAN. 17th June, 1791. Inviting over our Bard to the Coronation of the Bust of Thomson on Ednam Hill,	365
CXX.	To the Earl of BUCHAN. In reply,	367
CXXI.	From the Earl of BUCHAN. 16th Sept. 1791. Proposing a subject for our poet's muse,	369
CXXII.	To Lady E. CUNNINGHAM. Inclosing "The Lament for James Earl of Glencairn,"	371
CXXIII.	To Mr. AINSLIE. State of his mind after inebriation,	373
CXXIV.	From Sir JOHN WHITEFOORD. 16th Oct. Thanks for "The Lament on James, Earl of Glencairn,"	375
CXXV.	From A. F. TYTLER, Esq. 27th Nov. 1791. Criticism on the Whistle and the Lament,	377

CONTENTS.

No.		Page
CXXVI.	To Miss DAVIES. *Apology for neglecting her commands—moral reflections,*	381
CXXVII.	To Mrs. DUNLOP. *17th Dec. Inclosing "The Song of Death,"*	384
CXXVIII.	To Mrs. DUNLOP. *5th Jan. 1792. Acknowledging the present of a cup,*	387
CXXIX.	To Mr. WILLIAM SMELLIE. *22d Jan. Introducing Mrs. Riddel,*	389
CXXX.	To Mr. W. NICOL. *20th Feb. Ironical thanks for advice.*	392
CXXXI.	To Mr. CUNNINGHAM. *3d March, 1792. Commissions his arms to be cut on a seal—moral reflections,*	395
CXXXII.	To Mrs. DUNLOP. *22d August. Account of his meeting with Miss L—— B——, and inclosing a song on her,*	398
CXXXIII.	To Mr. CUNNINGHAM. *10th Sept. Wild apostrophe to a Spirit!*	402
CXXXIV.	To Mrs. DUNLOP, *24th Sept. Account of his family,*	409
CXXXV.	To Mrs. DUNLOP. *Letter of condolence under affliction,*	412
CXXXVI.	To Mrs. DUNLOP, *6th Dec. 1792. With a poem, entitled, "The Rights of Woman,*	414
CXXXVII.	To Miss B***** *of York, 21st March 1793. Letter of friendship,*	419
CXXXVIII.	To Miss C****. *August, 1793. Character and temperament of a poet,*	421
CXXXIX.	To JOHN M'MURDO, Esq. *Dec. 1793. Repaying money,*	424
CXL.	To Mrs. R******. *Advising her what play to bespeak at the Dumfries Theatre,*	426

No.		Page
CXLI.	To a Lady, *in favour of a Player's Benefit,*	428
CXLII.	Extract to Mr. ———, 1794. *On his prospects in the Excise,*	430
CXLIII.	To Mrs. R*****,	432
CXLIV.	To the Same. *Describes his melancholy feelings,*	434
CXLV.	To the Same. *Lending Werter,*	436
CXLVI.	To the Same. *On a return of interrupted friendship,*	437
CXLVII.	To the Same. *On a temporary estrangement,*	438
CXLVIII.	To JOHN SYME, Esq. *Reflections on the happiness of Mr. O——,*	440
CXLIX.	To Miss —— ——. *Requesting the return of MSS lent to a deceased friend,*	442
CL.	To Mr. CUNNINGHAM. 25th Feb. 1794. *Melancholy reflections—cheering prospects of a happier world,*	445
CLI.	To Mrs. R*****. *Supposed to be written from " The dead to the living,"*	449
CLII.	To Mrs. DUNLOP. 15th Dec. 1795. *Reflections on the situation of his family if he should die—praise of the poem entitled " The Task,"*	452
CLIII.	To the Same, *in London.* 20th Dec. 1795,	458
CLIV.	To Mrs. R*****. 20th Jan. 1796. *Thanks for the Travels of Anacharsis,*	462
CLV.	To Mrs. DUNLOP. 31st Jan. 1796. *Account of the Death of his Daughter, and of his own ill health,*	463

CONTENTS.

No. Page

CLVI. To Mrs. R*****. *4th June, 1796. Apology for not going to the birth-night assembly,* 465

CLVII. To Mr. Cunningham. *7th July, 1796. Account of his illness and of his poverty—anticipation of his death,* . . 466

CLVIII. To Mrs. Burns.—*Sea-bathing affords little relief.* 468

CLIX. To Mrs. Dunlop. *12th July, 1796. Last farewell.* 469

INDEX TO THE POETRY,

IN THE ALPHABETICAL ORDER OF THE FIRST LINES.

VOL. II.

	Page
By yon Castle wa' at the close of the day,	356
Dear Burns, thou brother of my heart,	261
Fair fa' the honest rustic swain,	244
Farewell thou fair day, thou green earth, and ye skies,	385
Go fetch to me a pint o' wine,	190
How does my dear friend, much I languish to hear,	315
How wisdom and folly meet, mix, and unite,	225
I look to the west when I gae to rest,	357
Inhuman man! curse on thy barb'rous art,	229
Life ne'er exulted in so rich a prize,	323
Like the fair plant that from our touch withdraws,	214
My Mary, dear departed shade!	272
No sculptur'd marble here, nor pompous lay,	63
No song nor dance bring I from yon great city,	284
Of all the numerous ills that hurt our peace,	8
O that I had ne'er been married,	453
O that my father had ne'er on me smil'd,	289
O, why should old age so much wound us? O,	143

Some

	Page
Some sing of sweet Mally, some sing of fair Nelly,	140
Still anxious to secure your partial favour,	454
The parent's heart that nestled fond in thee,	335
The small birds rejoice in the green leaves returning,	135
Thou whom chance may hither lead,	161
'Tis this, my friend, that streaks our morning bright,	259
When nature her great masterpiece design'd,	172
While Europe's eye is fix'd on mighty things,	417
While soon " the garden's flaunting flowers" decay,	46
Wow, but your letter made me vauntie!	263

LETTERS,

&c.

No. I.

To Mr. JOHN MURDOCH,

SCHOOLMASTER,

STAPLES INN BUILDINGS, LONDON.

Lochlee, 15th January, 1783.

DEAR SIR,

As I have an opportunity of sending you a letter, without putting you to that expense which any production of mine would but ill repay, I embrace it with pleasure, to tell you that I have not forgotten, nor ever will forget, the many obligations I lie under to your kindness and friendship.

I do not doubt, Sir, but you will wish to know what has been the result of all the pains of an indulgent father, and a masterly teacher; and I wish I could gratify your curiosity with such a recital as you would be pleased with; but that is what I am afraid will not be the case. I have, indeed, kept pretty clear of vicious habits; and in this respect, I hope, my conduct will not disgrace the education I have gotten; but as a man of the world, I am most miserably deficient.— One would have thought, that, bred as I have been, under a father who has figured pretty well as *un homme des affaires*, I might have been what the world calls a pushing, active fellow; but, to tell you the truth, Sir, there is hardly any thing more my reverse. I seem to be one sent into the world to see, and observe; and I very easily compound with the knave who tricks me of my money, if there be any thing original about him which shews me human nature in a different light from any thing I have seen before. In short, the joy of my heart is to " study men, their manners, and their ways;" and for this darling subject, I cheerfully sacrifice every other consideration. I am quite indolent about those great concerns that set the bustling busy sons of care agog; and if I have to answer for the present hour, I am very easy with regard to any thing further. Even the last, worst shift of the
unfortunate

unfortunate and the wretched, does not much terrify me: I know that even then my talent for what country folks call " a sensible crack," when once it is sanctified by a hoary head, would procure me so much esteem, that even then—I would learn to be happy.* However, I am under no apprehensions about that; for, though indolent, yet, so far as an extremely delicate constitution permits, I am not lazy; and in many things, especially in tavern matters, I am a strict economist; not indeed for the sake of the money, but one of the principal parts in my composition is a kind of pride of stomach, and I scorn to fear the face of any man living: above every thing, I abhor as hell, the idea of sneaking in a corner to avoid a dun—possibly some pitiful, sordid wretch, who in my heart I despise and detest. 'Tis this, and this alone, that endears economy to me. In the matter of books, indeed, I am very profuse. My favorite authors are of the sentimental kind, such as *Shenstone*, particularly his *Elegies; Thomson; Man of Feeling*, a book I prize next to the Bible; *Man of the World; Sterne*, especially his *Sentimental Journey; M‘Pherson's Ossian*, &c. These are the glorious models after which I endeavour

---

* The last shift alluded to here, must be the condition of an itinerant beggar. E.

deavour to form my conduct; and 'tis incongruous, 'tis absurd, to suppose that the man whose mind glows with sentiments lighted up at their sacred flame—the man whose heart distends with benevolence to all the human race—he " who can soar above this little scene of things," can he descend to mind the paltry concerns about which the terræfilial race fret, and fume, and vex themselves? O how the glorious triumph swells my heart! I forget that I am a poor insignificant devil, unnoticed and unknown, stalking up and down fairs and markets, when I happen to be in them, reading a page or two of mankind, and " catching the manners living as they rise," whilst the men of business jostle me one very side as an idle encumberance in their way.—But I dare say I have by this time tired your patience; so I shall conclude with begging you to give Mrs. Murdoch—not my compliments, for that is a mere commonplace story, but my warmest, kindest wishes for her welfare; and accept of the same for yourself, from,

Dear Sir,

Yours, &c.

No. II.

[The following is taken from the MS Prose presented by our Bard to Mr. Riddel.]

On rummaging over some old papers, I lighted on a MS of my early years, in which I had determined to write myself out, as I was placed by fortune among a class of men to whom my ideas would have been nonsense. I had meant that the book should have lain by me, in the fond hope that, some time or other, even after I was no more, my thoughts would fall into the hands of somebody capable of appreciating their value. It sets off thus:

Observations, Hints, Songs, Scraps of Poetry, &c. by R. B.—a man who had little art in making money, and still less in keeping it; but was however, a man of some sense, a great deal of honesty, and unbounded good will to every creature, rational and irrational. As he was but little indebted to scholastic education, and bred at a plough tail, his performances must be strongly tinctured with his unpolished rustic way of life; but as I believe they are really his *own*, it may be some entertainment to a curious observer of human nature, to see how a ploughman thinks and feels, under the pressure of love, ambition, anxiety, grief, with the like cares and passions, which, however diversified by the *modes* and *manners* of life, operate pretty much alike, I believe, on all the species.

" There are numbers in the world who do not want sense to make a figure, so much as an opinion of their own abilities, to put them upon recording their observations, and allowing them the same importance which they do to those which appear in print."

Shenstone.

" Pleasing, when youth is long expired, to trace
  The forms our pencil, or our pen designed!
Such was our youthful air, and shape, and face,
  Such the soft image of our youthful mind."

Ibid.

April,

April, 1783.

Notwithstanding all that has been said against love, respecting the folly and weakness it leads a young inexperienced mind into; still I think it in a great measure deserves the highest encomiums that have been passed on it. If any thing on earth deserves the name of rapture or transport, it is the feelings of green eighteen, in the company of the mistress of his heart, when she repays him with an equal return of affection.

. . . .

August.

There is certainly some connection between love, and music, and poetry; and therefore, I have always thought a fine touch of nature, that passage in a modern love composition:

> " As tow'rd her cot he jogg'd along,
> Her name was frequent in his song."

For my own part, I never had the least thought or inclination of turning poet, till I got once heartily in love; and then rhyme and song were, in a manner, the spontaneous language of my heart.

September.

September.

I entirely agree with that judicious philosopher, Mr. Smith, in his excellent *Theory of Moral Sentiments*, that remorse is the most painful sentiment that can embitter the human bosom. Any ordinary pitch of fortitude may bear up tolerably well under those calamities, in the procurement of which we ourselves have had no hand; but when our own follies, or crimes, have made us miserable and wretched, to bear up with manly firmness, and at the same time have a proper penitential sense of our misconduct, is a glorious effort of self-command.

Of all the numerous ills that hurt our peace,
That press the soul, or wring the mind with anguish,
Beyond comparison the worst are those
That to our folly or our guilt we owe.
In every other circumstance, the mind
Has this to say—" It was no deed of mine;"
But when to all the evil of misfortune
This sting is added—" Blame thy foolish self!"
Or worser far, the pangs of keen remorse;
The torturing, gnawing consciousness of guilt—
Of guilt, perhaps, where we've involved others;
The young, the innocent, who fondly lov'd us,
Nay, more, that very love their cause of ruin!
O burning hell! in all thy store of torments,
There's not a keener lash!
Lives there a man so firm, who, while his heart

Feels

Feels all the bitter horrors of his crime,
Can reason down its agonizing throbs;
And, after proper purpose of amendment,
Can firmly force his jarring thoughts to peace?
O, happy! happy! enviable man!
O glorious magnanimity of soul!

. . . .

March, 1784.

I have often observed, in the course of my experience of human life, that every man, even the worst, has something good about him; though very often nothing else than a happy temperament of constitution inclining him to this or that virtue. For this reason, no man can say in what degree any other person, besides himself, can be, with strict justice, called *wicked.* Let any of the strictest character for regularity of conduct among us, examine impartially how many vices he has never been guilty of, not from any care or vigilance, but for want of opportunity, or some accidental circumstance intervening; how many of the weaknesses of mankind he has escaped, because he was out of the line of such temptation; and, what often, if not always, weighs more than all the rest, how much he is indebted to the world's good opinion, because the world does not know all:

all: I say, any man who can thus think, will scan the failings, nay, the faults and crimes, of mankind around him, with a brother's eye.

I have often courted the acquaintance of that part of mankind commonly known by the ordinary phrase of *blackguards*, sometimes farther than was consistent with the safety of my character; those who, by thoughtless prodigality or headstrong passions, have been driven to ruin. Though disgraced by follies, nay sometimes " stained with guilt, * * * * * * * *," I have yet found among them, in not a few instances, some of the noblest virtues, magnanimity, generosity, disinterested friendship, and even modesty.

. . . .

April.

As I am what the men of the world, if they knew such a man, would call a whimsical mortal, I have various sources of pleasure and enjoyment, which are, in a manner, *peculiar* to myself, or some here and there such other out-of-the-way person. Such is the peculiar pleasure I take in the season of winter, more than the rest of the year. This I believe, may be be partly owing to my misfortunes giving my mind a melancholy cast: but there is something even in the

"Mighty tempest, and the hoary waste
Abrupt and deep, stretch'd o'er the buried earth,"—

which raises the mind to a serious sublimity, favourable to every thing great and noble. There is scarcely any earthly object gives me more—I do not know if I should call it pleasure—but something which exalts me, something which enraptures me—than to walk in the sheltered side of a wood, or high plantation, in a cloudy winter-day, and hear the stormy wind howling among the trees, and raving over the plain. It is my best season for devotion: my mind is wrapt up in a kind of enthusiasm to *Him*, who, in the pompous language of the Hebrew bard, "walks on the wings of the wind." In one of these seasons, just after a train of misfortunes, I composed the following:

The wintry west extends his blast, &c.
See vol. iii. *p.* 171.

Shenstone

Shenstone finely observes, that love-verses, writ without any real passion, are the most nauseous of all conceits; and I have often thought that no man can be a proper critic of love-composition, except he himself, in one or more instances, have been a warm votary of this passion. As I have been all along a miserable dupe to love, and have been led into a thousand weaknesses and follies by it, for that reason I put the more confidence in my critical skill, in distinguishing foppery, and conceit, from real passion and nature. Whether the following song will stand the test, I will not pretend to say, because it is my own; only I can say it was, at the time, genuine from the heart.

Behind yon hills, &c.
See vol. iii. *p.* 278.

. . . .

I think the whole species of young men may be naturally enough divided into two grand classes, which I shall call the *grave*, and the *merry;* though, by the bye, these terms do not with propriety enough express my ideas. The grave I shall cast into the usual division of those who are goaded on by the love of money, and those

those whose darling wish is to make a figure in the world. The merry are, the men of pleasure of all denominations; the jovial lads, who have too much fire and spirit to have any settled rule of action; but, without much deliberation follow the strong impulses of nature: the thoughtless, the careless, the indolent—in particular *he*, who, with a happy sweetness of natural temper, and a cheerful vacancy of thought, steals through life—generally, indeed, in poverty and obscurity; but poverty and obscurity are only evils to him who can sit gravely down and make a repining comparison between his own situation and that of others; and lastly, to grace the quorum, such are, generally, those whose heads are capable of all the towerings of genius, and whose hearts are warmed with all the delicacy of feeling.

. . . .

As the grand end of human life is to cultivate an intercourse with that *Being* to whom we owe life, with every enjoyment that can render life delightful; and to maintain an integritive conduct towards our fellow-creatures; that so, by forming piety and virtue into habit, we may be fit members for that society of the pious and the good, which reason and revelation
tion

tion teach us to expect beyond the grave: I do not see that the turn of mind and pursuits of any son of poverty and obscurity, are in the least more inimical to the sacred interests of piety and virtue, than the, even lawful, bustling and straining after the world's riches and honors; and I do not see but that he may gain Heaven as well, (which, by the bye, is no mean consideration) who steals through the vale of life, amusing himself with every little flower that fortune throws in his way; as he who, straining straight forward, and perhaps bespattering all about him, gains some of life's little eminences; where, after all, he can only see, and be seen, a little more conspicuously, than what, in the pride of his heart, he is apt to term the poor, indolent devil he has left behind him.

. . . .

There is a noble sublimity, a heart-melting tenderness, in some of our ancient ballads, which shew them to be the work of a masterly hand: and it has often given me many a heart-ache to reflect, that such glorious old bards—bards who very probably owed all their talents to native genius, yet have described the exploits of heroes, the pangs of disappointment, and the meltings of love, with such fine strokes of nature—that
their

their very names (O how mortifying to a bard's vanity!) are now "buried among the wreck of things which were."

O ye illustrious names unknown! who could feel so strongly and describe so well; the last, the meanest of the muses train—one who, though far inferior to your flights, yet eyes your path, and with trembling wing would sometimes soar after you—a poor rustic bard unknown, pays this sympathetic pang to your memory! Some of you tell us, with all the charms of verse, that you have been unfortunate in the world—unfortunate in love: he too has felt the loss of his little fortune, the loss of friends, and, worse than all, the loss of the woman he adored. Like you, all his consolation was his muse: she taught him in rustic measures to complain. Happy could he have done it with your strength of imagination and flow of verse! May the turf lie lightly on your bones! and may you now enjoy that solace and rest which this world rarely gives to the heart, tuned to all the feelings of poesy and love!

. . . .

This is all worth quoting in my MSS, and more than all.

R. B.

No. III.

To Mr. AIKEN.

[*The Gentleman to whom the* COTTER'S SATURDAY NIGHT *is addressed.*]

Ayrshire, 1786.

SIR,

I was with Wilson, my printer, t'other day, and settled all our by-gone matters between us. After I had paid him all demands, I made him the offer of the second edition, on the hazard of being paid out of the *first and readiest*, which he declines. By his account, the paper of a thousand copies would cost about twenty-seven pounds, and the printing about fifteen or sixteen: he offers to agree to this for the printing, if I will advance for the paper; but this,

this you know, is out of my power; so farewel hopes of a second edition till I grow richer! an epocha, which, I think, will arrive at the payment of the British national debt.

There is scarcely any thing hurts me so much in being disappointed of my second edition, as not having it in my power to shew my gratitude to Mr. Ballantyne, by publishing my poem of *The Brigs of Ayr*. I would detest myself as a wretch, if I thought I were capable, in a very long life, of forgetting the honest, warm, and tender delicacy with which he enters into my interests. I am sometimes pleased with myself in my grateful sensations; but I believe, on the whole, I have very little merit in it, as my gratitude is not a virtue, the consequence of reflection, but sheerly the instinctive emotion of a heart too inattentive to allow worldly maxims and views to settle into selfish habits.

I have been feeling all the various rotations and movements within, respecting the excise. There are many things plead strongly against it; the uncertainty of getting soon into business, the consequences of my follies, which may perhaps make it impracticable for me to stay at home; and besides, I have for some time been pining under secret wretchedness, from causes which you pretty well know—the pang of disappointment, the sting of pride, with some wandering stabs of remorse, which never fail to settle on my vitals like vultures, when attention is not called away by the calls of society or the vagaries of the muse. Even in the hour of social mirth, my gaiety is the madness of an intoxicated criminal under the hands of the executioner. All these reasons urge me to go abroad; and to all these reasons I have only one answer—the feelings of a father. This, in the present mood I am in, overbalances every thing that can be laid in the scale against it.

* * * * * *

You may perhaps think it an extravagant fancy, but it is a sentiment which strikes home to my very soul: though sceptical, in some points, of our current belief, yet, I think, I have every evidence for the reality of a life beyond the stinted bourne of our present existence; if so, then how should I, in the presence of that tremendous Being, the Author of existence, how should I meet the reproaches of those who stand to me in the dear relation of children, whom I deserted in the smiling innocency of helpless infancy? O, thou great, unknown Power! thou Almighty God! who has lighted up reason in

my

my breast, and blessed me with immortality! I have frequently wandered from that order and regularity necessary for the perfection of thy works, yet thou hast never left me nor forsaken me!

* * * * * *

Since I wrote the foregoing sheet, I have seen something of the storm of mischief thickening over my folly-devoted head. Should you, my friends, my benefactors, be successful in your applications for me, perhaps it may not be in my power in that way to reap the fruit of your friendly efforts. What I have written in the preceding pages is the settled tenor of my present resolution; but should inimical circumstances forbid me closing with your kind offer, or, enjoying it, only threaten to entail farther misery—

* * * * * *

To tell the truth, I have little reason for complaint, as the world, in general, has been kind to me, fully up to my deserts. I was, for some time past, fast getting into the pining distrustful snarl of the misanthrope. I saw myself alone, unfit for the struggle of life, shrinking at every rising cloud in the chance-directed atmosphere of fortune, while, all defenceless, I looked about in vain for a cover. It never occurred to me, at least never with the force it deserved, that this world is a busy scene, and man a creature destined for a progressive struggle; and that, however I might possess a warm heart and inoffensive manners, (which last, by the bye, was rather more than I could well boast) still, more than these passive qualities, there was something to be *done*. When all my school-fellows and youthful compeers, (those misguided few excepted who joined, to use a Gentoo phrase, the *hallachores* of the human race) were striking off with eager hope and earnest intent on some one or other of the many paths of busy life, I was " standing idle in the market place," or only left the chase of the butterfly from flower to flower, to hunt fancy from whim to whim.

* * * * * * *

You see, Sir, that if to *know* one's errors were a probability of *mending* them, I stand a fair chance; but, according to the reverend Westminster divines, though conviction must precede conversion, it is very far from always implying it.*

* * * * * * *

No. IV.

---

* This letter was evidently written under the distress of mind occasioned by our Poet's separation from Mrs. Burns.   E.

No. IV.

To Mrs. DUNLOP *of* Dunlop.

Ayrshire, 1786.

MADAM,

I AM truly sorry I was not at home yesterday, when I was so much honoured with your order for my copies, and incomparably more by the handsome compliments you are pleased to pay my poetic abilities. I am fully persuaded that there is not any class of mankind so feelingly alive to the titillations of applause as the sons of Parnassus; nor is it easy to conceive how the heart of the poor bard dances with rapture, when those whose character in life gives them a right to be polite judges, honour him with their approbation. Had you been thoroughly acquainted with me, Madam, you could not have touched my darling heart-chord

more

more sweetly than by noticing my attempts to celebrate our illustrious ancestor, the *Saviour of his Country.*

" Great patriot-hero! ill-requited chief!"

The first book I met with in my early years, which I perused with pleasure, was *The Life of Hannibal:* the next was *The History of Sir William Wallace:* for several of my earlier years I had few other authors; and many a solitary hour have I stole out, after the laborious vocations of the day, to shed a tear over their glorious but unfortunate stories. In those boyish days I remember in particular being struck with that part of Wallace's story where these lines occur—

" Syne to the Leglen wood, when it was late,
To make a silent and a safe retreat."

I chose a fine summer Sunday, the only day my line of life allowed, and walked half a dozen of miles to pay my respects to the Leglen wood, with as much devout enthusiasm as ever pilgrim did to Loretto: and, as I explored every den and dell where I could suppose my heroic countryman to have lodged, I recollect (for even then I was a rhymer) that my heart glowed with a wish to be able to make a song on him in some measure equal to his merits.

No. V.

No. V.

To Mrs. STEWART of Stair.

1786.

MADAM,

THE hurry of my preparations for going abroad has hindered me from performing my promise so soon as I intended. I have here sent you a parcel of songs, &c. which never made their appearance, except to a friend or two at most. Perhaps some of them may be no great entertainment to you; but of that I am far from being an adequate judge. The song to the tune of *Ettrick Banks*, you will easily see the impropriety of exposing much, even in manuscript. I think, myself, it has some merit, both as a tolerable description of one of Nature's sweetest scenes, a July evening; and one of the finest pieces of Nature's work-manship,

manship, the finest, indeed, we know any thing of, an amiable, beautiful young woman;* but I have no common friend to procure me that permission, without which I would not dare to spread the copy.

I am quite aware, Madam, what task the world would assign me in this letter. The obscure bard, when any of the great condescend to take notice of him, should heap the altar with the incense of flattery. Their high ancestry, their own great and godlike qualities and actions, should be recounted with the most exaggerated description. This, Madam, is a task for which I am altogether unfit. Besides a certain disqualifying pride of heart, I know nothing of your connections in life, and have no access to where your real character is to be found—the company of your compeers: and more, I am afraid that even the most refined adulation is by no means the road to your good opinion.

One feature of your character I shall ever with grateful pleasure remember—the reception I got when I had the honour of waiting on you at Stair. I am little acquainted with politeness;
but

---

* Miss A********.

but I know a good deal of benevolence of temper and goodness of heart. Surely, did those in exalted stations know how happy they could make some classes of their inferiors by condescension and affability, they would never stand so high, measuring out with every look the height of their elevation, but condescend as sweetly as did Mrs. Stewart of Stair.*

---

* The song inclosed is that given in the Life of our Poet; beginning,

'Twas e'en—the dewy fields were green, &c.

The lass o' Ballochmyle.

See the Index to Vol. 1.
E.

No. VI.

In the Name of the NINE.   *Amen.*

WE, ROBERT BURNS, by virtue of a Warrant from NATURE, bearing date the Twenty-fifth day of January, Anno Domini one thousand seven hundred and fifty-nine,* POET-LAUREAT and BARD IN CHIEF in and over the Districts and Countries of KYLE, CUNNINGHAM and CARRICK, of old extent, To our trusty and well-beloved WILLIAM CHALMERS and JOHN M'ADAM, Students and Practitioners in the ancient and mysterious Science of CONFOUNDING RIGHT and WRONG.

RIGHT

---

* His birth-day.   E.

RIGHT TRUSTY,

Be it known unto you, That whereas, in the course of our care and watchings over the Order and Police of all and sundry the MANUFACTURERS, RETAINERS, and VENDERS of POESY; Bards, Poets, Poetasters, Rhymers, Jinglers, Songsters, Ballad-singers, &c. &c. &c. &c. &c. male and female—We have discovered a certain * * *, nefarious, abominable, and wicked SONG or BALLAD, a copy whereof We have here inclosed; Our WILL THEREFORE IS, that YE pitch upon and appoint the most execrable Individual of that most execrable Species, known by the appellation, phrase, and nickname, of THE DEIL'S YELL NOWTE:* and, after having caused him to kindle a fire at the CROSS of AYR, ye shall, at noontide of the day, put into the said wretch's merciless hands the said copy of the said nefarious and wicked Song, to be consumed by fire in the presence of all Beholders, in abhorrence of, and terrorem to, all such COMPOSITIONS and COMPOSERS. And this in no wise leave ye undone, but have it executed in every point as this OUR MANDATE bears, before the twenty-fourth current, when IN PERSON We hope to applaud your faithfulness and zeal,

GIVEN

---

* Old Bachelors.

GIVEN at MAUCHLINE, this twentieth day of November, Anno Domini one thousand seven hundred and eighty-six.*

GOD SAVE THE BARD!

---

* Inclosed was the ballad, probably Holy Willie's Prayer.   E.

No. VII.

No. VII.

Dr. BLACKLOCK,

TO

The Reverend Mr. G. LOWRIE.

REVEREND AND DEAR SIR,

I OUGHT to have acknowledged your favour long ago, not only as a testimony of your kind remembrance, but as it gave me an opportunity of sharing one of the finest, and, perhaps, one of the most genuine entertainments, of which the human mind is susceptible. A number of avocations retarded my progress in reading the poems; at last, however, I have finished that pleasing perusal. Many instances have I seen of Nature's force and beneficence exerted under numerous and formidable disadvantages; but none equal to hat with which you have been kind enough to

present

present me. There is a pathos and delicacy in his serious poems, a vein of wit and humour in those of a more festive turn, which cannot be too much admired, nor too warmly approved; and I think I shall never open the book without feeling my astonishment renewed and increased. It was my wish to have expressed my approbation in verse; but whether from declining life, or a temporary depression of spirits, it is at present out of my power to accomplish that agreeable intention.

Mr. Stewart, Professor of Morals in this University, had formerly read me three of the poems, and I had desired him to get my name inserted among the subscribers: but whether this was done, or not, I never could learn. I have little intercourse with Dr. Blair, but will take care to have the poems communicated to him by the intervention of some mutual friend. It has been told me by a gentleman, to whom I shewed the performances, and who sought a copy with diligence and ardour, that the whole impression is already exhausted. It were, therefore, much to be wished, for the sake of the young man, that a second edition, more numerous than the former, could immediately be printed; as it appears certain that its intrinsic merit, and the exertion of the author's friends,
might

might give it a more universal circulation than any thing of the kind which has been published within my memory.*

---

* The reader will perceive that this is the letter which produced the determination of our Bard to give up his scheme of going to the West Indies, and to try the fate of a new edition of his Poems in Edinburgh. A copy of this letter was sent by Mr. Lowrie to Mr. G. Hamilton, and by him communicated to Burns, among whose papers it was found.

For an account of Mr. Lowrie and his family see the letter of Gilbert Burns to the Editor, in the Appendix to Vol. III.

E.

No. VIII.

No. VIII.

From the Reverend MR. LOWRIE.

22nd December, 1786.

DEAR SIR,

I LAST week received a letter from Dr. Blacklock, in which he expresses a desire of seeing you. I write this to you, that you may lose no time in waiting upon him, should you not yet have seen him.

* * * * * * *

I rejoice to hear, from all corners, of your rising fame, and I wish and expect it may tower still higher by the new publication. But, as a friend, I warn you to prepare to meet with your share of detraction and envy—a train that
always

always accompany great men. For your comfort I am in great hopes that the number of your friends and admirers will increase, and that you have some chance of ministerial, or even * * * * patronage. Now, my friend, such rapid success is very uncommon: and do you think yourself in no danger of suffering by applause and a full purse? Remember Solomon's advice, which he spoke from experience, " stronger is he that conquers," &c. Keep fast hold of your rural simplicity and purity, like Telemachus, by Mentor's aid, in Calypso's isle, or even in that of Cyprus. I hope *you* have also Minerva with you. I need not tell you how much a modest diffidence and invincible temperance adorn the most shining talents, and elevate the mind, and exalt and refine the imagination, even of a poet.

I hope you will not imagine I speak from suspicion or evil report. I assure you I speak from love and good report, and good opinion, and a strong desire to see you shine as much in the sun-shine as you have done in the shade, and in the practice as you do in the theory of virtue. This is my prayer, in return for your elegant composition in verse. All here join in compliments and good wishes for your further prosperity.

No. IX.

To Mr. CHALMERS.

Edinburgh, 27th December, 1786.

MY DEAR FRIEND,

I confess I have sinned the sin for which there is hardly any forgiveness—ingratitude to friendship—in not writing you sooner; but, of all men living, I had intended to send you an entertaining letter; and by all the plodding stupid powers that in nodding conceited majesty preside over the dull routine of business—a heavily-solemn oath this!—I am, and have been ever since I came to Edinburgh, as unfit to write a letter of humour as to write a commentary on the *Revelations*.

* * * * *

To make you some amends for what, before you reach this paragraph, you will have suffered, ed, I inclose you two poems I have carded and spun since I passed Glenbuck. One blank in the address to Edinburgh, " Fair B———," is the heavenly Miss Burnet, daughter to Lord Monboddo, at whose house I have had the honour to be more than once. There has not been any thing nearly like her, in all the combinations of beauty, grace, and goodness, the great Creator has formed, since Milton's Eve on the first day of her existence.

I have sent you a parcel of subscription-bills; and have written to Mr. Ballantine and Mr. Aiken, to call on you for some of them, if they want them. My direction is—Care of Andrew Bruce, merchant, Bridge-street.

No. X.

To the EARL of EGLINTON.

Edinburgh, January, 1787.

MY LORD,

As I have but slender pretensions to philosophy, I cannot rise to the exalted ideas of a citizen of the world; but have all those national prejudices which, I believe, glow peculiarly strong in the breast of a Scotchman. There is scarcely any thing to which I am so feelingly alive, as the honour and welfare of my country; and, as a poet, I have no higher enjoyment than singing her sons and daughters. Fate had cast my station in the veriest shades of life; but never did a heart pant more ardently, than mine, to be distinguished: though, till very lately, I looked in vain on every side for a ray of light. It is easy, then, to guess

how

how much I was gratified with the countenance and approbation of one of my country's most illustrious sons, when Mr. Wauchope called on me yesterday on the part of your Lordship. Your munificence, my Lord, certainly deserves my very grateful acknowledgments; but your patronage is a bounty peculiarly suited to my feelings. I am not master enough of the etiquette of life, to know whether there be not some impropriety in troubling your Lordship with my thanks; but my heart whispered me to do it. From the emotions of my inmost soul I do it. Selfish ingratitude, I hope, I am incapable of; and mercenary servility, I trust, I shall ever have so much honest pride as to detest.

No.

No. XI.

To Mrs. DUNLOP.

Edinburgh, 15th January, 1787.

MADAM,

Yours of the 9th current, which I am this moment honor'd with, is a deep reproach to me for ungrateful neglect. I will tell you the real truth, for I am miserably awkward at a fib: I wished to have written to Dr. Moore before I wrote to you; but though, every day since I received yours of Dec. 30th, the idea, the wish to write to him, has constantly pressed on my thoughts, yet I could not for my soul set about it. I know his fame and character, and I am one of " the sons of little men." To write him a mere matter-of-fact affair, like a merchant's order, would be disgracing the little character I have; and to write the author of *The View of Society*

Society and Manners a letter of sentiment—I declare every artery runs cold at the thought. I shall try, however, to write to him to-morrow or next day. His kind interposition in my behalf I have already experienced, as a gentleman waited on me the other day, on the part of Lord Eglinton, with ten guineas, by way of subscription for two copies of my next edition.

The word you object to in the mention I have made of my glorious countryman and your immortal ancestor, is indeed borrowed from Thomson; but it does not strike me as an improper epithet. I distrusted my own judgment on your finding fault with it, and applied for the opinion of some of the Literati here, who honour me with their critical strictures, and they all allow it to be proper. The song you ask I cannot recollect, and I have not a copy of it. I have not composed any thing on the great Wallace, except what you have seen in print, and the inclosed, which I will print in this edition.* You will see I have mentioned some others of the name. When I composed my *Vision* long ago, I had attempted a description of Koyle, of which

---

* Stanzas in the *Vision*, vol. iii. beginning page 103, " By stately tower or palace fair," and ending with the first Duan.   E.

which the additional stanzas are a part, as it originally stood. My heart glows with a wish to be able to do justice to the merits of the *Saviour of his Country*, which sooner or later, I shall at least attempt.

You are afraid I shall grow intoxicated with my prosperity as a poet. Alas! Madam, I know myself and the world too well. I do not mean any airs of affected modesty; I am willing to believe that my abilities deserved some notice; but in a most enlightened, informed age and nation, when poetry is and has been the study of men of the first natural genius, aided with all the powers of polite learning, polite books, and polite company—to be dragged forth to the full glare of learned and polite observation, with all my imperfections of awkward rusticity and crude unpolished ideas on my head—I assure you, Madam, I do not dissemble when I tell you I tremble for the consequences. The novelty of a poet in my obscure situation, without any of those advantages which are reckoned necessary for that character, at least at this time of day, has raised a partial tide of public notice, which has borne me to a height where I am absolutely, feelingly certain my abilities are inadequate to support me; and too surely do I see that time when the same tide will leave me, and recede,

perhaps,

perhaps, as far below the mark of truth. I do not say this in the ridiculous affectation of self-abasement and modesty. I have studied myself, and know what ground I occupy; and, however a friend or the world may differ from me in that particular, I stand for my own opinion, in silent resolve, with all the tenaciousness of property. I mention this to you, once for all, to disburthen my mind, and I do not wish to hear or say more about it.—But

" When proud fortune's ebbing tide recedes,"

you will bear me witness, that, when my bubble of fame was at the highest, I stood, unintoxicated, with the inebriating cup in my hand, looking forward with rueful resolve to the hastening time when the blow of Calumny should dash it to the ground, with all the eagerness of vengeful triumph.

* * * * * * *

Your patronising me, and interesting yourself in my fame and character as a poet, I rejoice in; it exalts me in my own idea; and whether you can or cannot aid me in my subscription is a trifle. Has a paltry subscription-bill any charms to the heart of a bard, compared with the patronage of the descendant of the immortal Wallace?

No.

No. XII.

To Dr. MOORE.

1787.

SIR,

Mrs. Dunlop has been so kind as to send me extracts of letters she has had from you, where you do the rustic bard the honour of noticing him and his works. Those who have felt the anxieties and solicitudes of authorship, can only know what pleasure it gives to be noticed in such a manner by judges of the first character. Your criticisms, Sir, I receive with reverence; only, I am sorry they mostly came too late: a peccant passage or two, that I would certainly have altered, were gone to the press.

The hope to be admired for ages is, in by far the greater part of those even who are authors

of

of repute, an unsubstantial dream. For my part, my first ambition was, and still my strongest wish is, to please my compeers, the rustic inmates of the hamlet, while ever-changing language and manners shall allow me to be relished and understood. I am very willing to admit that I have some poetical abilities; and as few, if any writers, either moral or poetical, are intimately acquainted with the classes of mankind among whom I have chiefly mingled, I may have seen men and manners in a different phasis from what is common, which may assist originality of thought. Still I know very well the novelty of my character has by far the greatest share in the learned and polite notice I have lately had; and in a language where Pope and Churchill have raised the laugh, and Shenstone and Gray drawn the tear—where Thomson and Beattie have painted the landscape, and Littleton and Collins described the heart, I am not vain enough to hope for distinguished poetic fame.

No.

No. XIII.

From Dr. MOORE.

Clifford-street, January 23d, 1787.

SIR,

I HAVE just received your letter, by which I find I have reason to complain of my friend Mrs. Dunlop for transmitting to you extracts from my letters to her, by much too freely and too carelessly written for your perusal. I must forgive her, however, in consideration of her good intention, as you will forgive me, I hope, for the freedom I use with certain expressions, in consideration of my admiration of the poems in general. If I may judge of the author's disposition from his works, with all the other good qualities of a poet, he has not the *irritable* temper ascribed to that race of men by

one

one of their own number, whom you have the happiness to resemble in ease and *curious felicity* of expression. Indeed the poetical beauties, however original and brilliant, and lavishly scattered, are not all I admire in your works; the love of your native country, that feeling sensibility to all the objects of humanity, and the independent spirit which breathes through the whole, give me a most favourable impression of the poet, and have made me often regret that I did not see the poems, the certain effect of which would have been my seeing the author last summer, when I was longer in Scotland than I have been for many years.

I rejoice very sincerely at the encouragement you receive at Edinburgh, and I think you peculiarly fortunate in the patronage of Dr. Blair, who, I am informed, interests himself very much for you. I beg to be remembered to him: nobody can have a warmer regard for that gentleman than I have, which, independent of the worth of his character, would be kept alive by the memory of our common friend, the late Mr. George B———e.

Before I received your letter, I sent inclosed in a letter to ———, a sonnet by Miss Williams, a young poetical lady, which she wrote on reading

ing your Mountain-daisy; perhaps it may not displease you.*

I have been trying to add to the number of your subscribers, but find many of my acquaintance are already among them. I have only to add, that with every sentiment of esteem, and the most cordial good wishes,

I am,
Your obedient humble servant,
J. MOORE.

No.

---

* The sonnet is as follows:

WHILE soon " the garden's flaunting flowers" decay,
   And scattered on the earth neglected lie,
The " Mountain-daisy," cherished by the ray
   A poet drew from heaven, shall never die.
Ah, like that lonely flower the poet rose!
   'Mid penury's bare soil and bitter gale;
He felt each storm that on the mountain blows,
   Nor ever knew the shelter of the vale.
By genius in her native vigour nurst,
   On nature with impassion'd look he gazed;
Then through the cloud of adverse fortune burst
   Indignant, and in light unborrow'd blazed.
Scotia! from rude affliction shield thy bard,
His heaven-taught numbers Fame herself will guard.

E.

No. XIV.

TO THE

Reverend G. LOWRIE, *of* NEWMILLS.

NEAR KILMARNOCK.

Edinburgh, 5th February, 1787.

REVEREND AND DEAR SIR,

WHEN I look at the date of your kind letter, my heart reproaches me severely with ingratitude in neglecting so long to answer it. I will not trouble you with any account, by way of apology, of my hurried life and distracted attention: do me the justice to believe that my delay by no means proceeded from want of respect. I feel, and ever shall feel, for you, the mingled sentiments of esteem for a friend, and reverence for a father.

I thank

I thank you, Sir, with all my soul, for your friendly hints; though I do not need them so much as my friends are apt to imagine. You are dazzled with newspaper accounts and distant reports; but in reality, I have no great temptation to be intoxicated with the cup of prosperity. Novelty may attract the attention of mankind awhile; to it I owe my present eclat: but I see the time not far distant, when the popular tide, which has borne me to a height of which I am, perhaps, unworthy, shall recede with silent celerity, and leave me a barren waste of sand, to descend at my leisure to my former station. I do not say this in the affectation of modesty; I see the consequence is unavoidable, and am prepared for it. I had been at a good deal of pains to form a just, impartial estimate of my intellectual powers before I came here; I have not added, since I came to Edinburgh, any thing to the account; and I trust I shall take every atom of it back to my shades, the coverts of my unnoticed, early years.

In Dr. Blacklock, whom I see very often, I have found, what I would have expected in our friend, a clear head and an excellent heart.

By far the most agreeable hours I spend in Edinburgh

Edinburgh must be placed to the account of Miss Lowrie and her piano forté. I cannot help repeating to you and Mrs. Lowrie a compliment that Mr. Mackenzie, the celebrated "Man of Feeling," paid to Miss Lowrie, the other night, at the concert. I had come in at the interlude, and sat down by him, till I saw Miss Lowrie in a seat not very distant, and went up to pay my respects to her. On my return to Mr. Mackenzie, he asked me who she was; I told him 'twas the daughter of a reverend friend of mine in the west country. He returned, there was something very striking, to his idea, in her appearance. On my desiring to know what it was, he was pleased to say, "She has a great deal of the elegance of a wellbred lady about her, with all the sweet simplicity of a country girl."

My compliments to all the happy inmates of Saint Margaret's.

I am, dear Sir,

Yours most gratefully,

ROBT. BURNS.

No. XV.

To Dr. MOORE.

Edinburgh, 15th February, 1787.

SIR,

PARDON my seeming neglect in delaying so long to acknowledge the honour you have done me, in your kind notice of me, January 23d. Not many months ago I knew no other employment than following the plough, nor could boast any thing higher than a distant acquaintance with a country clergyman. Mere greatness never embarrasses me: I have nothing to ask from the great, and I do not fear their judgment: but genius, polished by learning, and at its proper point of elevation in the eye of the world, this of late I frequently meet with, and tremble at its approach. I scorn the affectation of seeming modesty to cover self-conceit. That

That I have some merit, I do not deny; but I see, with frequent wringings of heart, that the novelty of my character, and the honest national prejudice of my countrymen, have borne me to a height altogether untenable to my abilities.

For the honor Miss W. has done me, please, Sir, return her, in my name, my most grateful thanks. I have more than once thought of paying her in kind, but have hitherto quitted the idea in hopeless despondency. I had never before heard of her; but the other day I got her poems, which, for several reasons, some belonging to the head, and others the offspring of the heart, gave me a great deal of pleasure. I have little pretensions to critic lore: there are, I think, two characteristic features in her poetry—the unfettered wild flight of native genius, and the querulous, *sombre* tenderness of " time-settled sorrow."

I only know what pleases me, often without being able to tell why.

No. XVI.

From Dr. MOORE.

Clifford-Street, 28*th February,* 1787.

DEAR SIR,

Your letter of the 15th gave me a great deal of pleasure. It is not surprising that you improve in correctness and taste, considering where you have been for some time past. And I dare swear there is no danger of your admitting any polish which might weaken the vigour of your native powers.

I am glad to perceive that you disdain the nauseous affectation of decrying your own merit as a poet, an affectation which is displayed with most ostentation by those who have the greatest share of self-conceit, and which only

adds

adds undeceiving falsehood to disgusting vanity. For you to deny the merit of your poems would be arraigning the fixed opinion of the public.

As the new edition of my *View of Society* is not yet ready, I have sent you the former edition, which I beg you will accept as a small mark of my esteem. It is sent by sea to the care of Mr. Creech; and, along with these four volumes for yourself, I have also sent my *Medical Sketches*, in one volume, for my friend Mrs. Dunlop of Dunlop: this you will be so obliging as to transmit, or if you chance to pass soon by Dunlop, to give to her.

I am happy to hear that your subscription is so ample, and shall rejoice at every piece of good fortune that befals you; for you are a very great favourite in my family; and this is a higher compliment than perhaps you are aware of. It includes almost all the professions, and of course is a proof that your writings are adapted to various tastes and situations. My youngest son, who is at Winchester school, writes to me that he is translating some stanzas of your *Hallow E'en* into Latin verse, for the benefit of his comrades. This union of taste partly proceeds, no doubt, from the cement of
Scottish

Scottish partiality, with which they are all somewhat tinctured. Even *your translator*, who left Scotland too early in life for recollection, is not without it.

* * * * * * *

I remain, with great sincerity,

Your obedient servant,

J. MOORE.

No.

No. XVII.

To the Earl *of* GLENCAIRN.

MY LORD,
      Edinburgh, 1787.

I wanted to purchase a profile of your lordship, which I was told was to be got in town: but I am truly sorry to see that a blundering painter has spoiled a " human face divine." The inclosed stanzas I intended to have written below a picture or profile of your lordship, could I have been so happy as to procure one with any thing of a likeness.

As I will soon return to my shades, I wanted to have something like a material object for my gratitude; I wanted to have it in my power to say to a friend, There is my noble patron, my generous benefactor. Allow me, my lord, to publish these verses. I conjure your lordship by the honest throe of gratitude, by the generous wish of benevolence, by all the powers and
         feelings

feelings which compose the magnanimous mind, do not deny me this petition.* I owe much to your lordship; and what has not in some other instances always been the case with me, the weight of the obligation is a pleasing load. I trust I have a heart as independent as your lordship's, than which I can say nothing more: and I would not be beholden to favours that would crucify my feelings. Your dignified character in life, and manner of supporting that character, are flattering to my pride; and I would be jealous of the purity of my grateful attachment where I was under the patronage of one of the much favoured sons of fortune.

Almost every poet has celebrated his patrons, particularly when they were names dear to fame, and illustrious in their country; allow me, then, my lord, if you think the verses have intrinsic merit, to tell the world how much I have the honour to be

Your lordship's highly indebted,

and ever grateful humble servant.

No.

---

* It does not appear that the Earl granted this request, nor have the verses alluded to been found among the MSS.   E.

No. XVIII.

To the Earl of BUCHAN.

MY LORD,

The honour your lordship has done me, by your notice and advice in yours of the 1st instant, I shall ever gratefully remember:

" Praise from thy lips 'tis mine with joy to boast,
 They best can give it who deserve it most."

Your lordship touches the darling chord of my heart, when you advise me to fire my muse at Scottish story and Scottish scenes. I wish for nothing more than to make a leisurely pilgrimage through my native country; to sit and muse on those once hard-contended fields, where Caledonia, rejoicing, saw her bloody lion borne through broken ranks to victory and fame;

fame; and, catching the inspiration, to pour the deathless names in song. But, my lord, in the midst of these enthusiastic reveries, a long-visaged, dry, moral-looking phantom strides across my imagination, and pronounces these emphatic words.

" I Wisdom, dwell with Prudence. Friend, I do not come to open the ill-closed wounds of your follies and misfortunes, merely to give you pain: I wish through these wounds to imprint a lasting lesson on your heart. I will not mention how many of my salutary advices you have despised: I have given you line upon line and precept upon precept; and while I was chalking out to you the straight way to wealth and character, with audacious effrontery you have zig-zagged across the path, contemning me to my face: you know the consequences. It is not yet three months since home was so hot for you that you were on the wing for the western shore of the Atlantic, not to make a fortune, but to hide your misfortune.

" Now that your dear-lov'd Scotia puts it in your power to return to the situation of your forefathers, will you follow these Will-o'-Wisp meteors of fancy and whim, till they bring you once more to the brink of ruin? I grant that
the

the utmost ground you can occupy is but half a step from the veriest poverty; but still it is half a step from it. If all that I can urge be ineffectual, let her who seldom calls to you in vain, let the call of pride prevail with you. You know how you feel at the iron-gripe of ruthless oppression: you know how you bear the galling sneer of contumelious greatness. I hold you out the conveniences, the comforts of life, independence and character, on the one hand; I tender you servility, dependence, and wretchedness, on the other. I will not insult your understanding by bidding you make a choice."*

This, my lord, is unanswerable. I must return to my humble station, and woo my rustic muse in my wonted way at the plough-tail. Still, my lord, while the drops of life warm my heart, gratitude to that dear-loved country in which I boast my birth, and gratitude to those her distinguished sons who have honoured me so much with their patronage and approbation, shall, while stealing through my humble shades, ever distend my bosom, and at times, as now, draw forth the swelling tear.

No.

---

* Copied from the Bee, vol. ii. p. 319, and compared with the Author's MSS. E.

No. XIX.

Ext. Property in favour of Mr. ROBERT BURNS, *to erect and keep up a Headstone in memory of Poet* FERGUSSON, 1787.

. . . .

Session-house within the Kirk of Canongate, the twenty-second day of February, one thousand seven hundred eighty-seven years.

Sederunt of the managers of the Kirk and Kirk-yard Funds of Canongate.

WHICH day, the treasurer to the said funds produced a letter from Mr. Robert Burns, of date the sixth current, which was read, and appointed to be engrossed in their sederunt-book, and of which letter the tenor follows: " To the Honourable Bailies of Canongate, Edinburgh. Gentlemen, I am sorry to be told that the remains of Robert Fergusson, the so justly celebrated poet, a man whose talents,

for

for ages to come, will do honour to our Caledonian name, lie in your church-yard, among the ignoble dead, unnoticed and unknown.

" Some memorial to direct the steps of the lovers of Scottish song, when they wish to shed a tear over the " narrow house" of the bard who is no more, is surely a tribute due to Fergusson's memory; a tribute I wish to have the honour of paying.

" I petition you then, Gentlemen, to permit me to lay a simple stone over his revered ashes, to remain an unalienable property to his deathless fame. I have the honour to be, Gentlemen, your very humble servant, *(sic subscribitur)*.
ROBERT BURNS."

Thereafter the said managers, in consideration of the laudable and disinterested motion of Mr. Burns, and the propriety of his request, did, and hereby do, unanimously, grant power and liberty to the said Robert Burns to erect a headstone at the grave of the said Robert Fergusson, and to keep up and preserve the same to his memory in all time coming. Extracted forth of the records of the managers by
WILLIAM SPROTT, Clerk.

No.

No. XX.

To ————.

MY DEAR SIR,

You may think, and too justly, that I am a selfish ungrateful fellow, having received so many repeated instances of kindness from you, and yet never putting pen to paper to say —thank you; but if you knew what a devil of a life my conscience has led me on that account, your good heart would think yourself too much avenged. By the bye, there is nothing in the whole frame of man which seems to me so unaccountable as that thing called conscience. Had the troublesome yelping cur powers efficient to prevent a mischief, he might be of use; but at the beginning of the business, his feeble efforts are to the workings of passion as the infant frosts of an autumnal morning to the
unclouded

unclouded fervour of the rising sun: and no sooner are the tumultuous doings of the wicked deed over, than, amidst the bitter native consequences of folly, in the very vortex of our horrors, up starts conscience, and harrows us with the feelings of the d*****.

I have inclosed you, by way of expiation, some verse and prose, that, if they merit a place in your truly entertaining miscellany, you are welcome to. The prose extract is literally as Mr. Sprott sent it me.

The Inscription of the Stone is as follows:

HERE LIES ROBERT FERGUSSON, POET.

Born September 5th, 1751—Died, 16th October, 1774.

> No sculptur'd marble here, nor pompous lay,
> " No storied urn nor animated bust,"
> This simple stone directs pale Scotia's way
> To pour her sorrows o'er her poet's dust.

On the other side of the Stone is as follows:

" By special grant of the Managers to Robert Burns, who erected this stone, this burial-place is to remain for ever sacred to the memory of Robert Fergusson."

No.

No. XXI.

Extract of a Letter from ————

8th March, 1787.

I AM truly happy to know you have found a friend in *********; his patronage of you does him great honour. He is truly a good man; by far the best I ever knew, or perhaps ever shall know, in this world. But I must not speak all I think of him, lest I should be thought partial.

So you have obtained liberty from the magistrates to erect a stone over Fergusson's grave? I do not doubt it; such things have been, as Shakespeare says, " in the olden-time:"

" The poet's fate is here in emblem shewn,
　He ask'd for bread, and he received a stone."

It is, I believe, upon poor Butler's tomb that this is written. But how many brothers of Parnassus, as well as poor Butler and poor Fergusson, have asked for bread, and been served with the same sauce!

The magistrates *gave you liberty*, did they? O generous magistrates! ******* celebrated over the three kingdoms for his public spirit, gives a poor poet liberty to raise a tomb to a poor poet's memory! most generous! ******* once upon a time gave that same poet the mighty sum of eighteen pence for a copy of his works. But then it must be considered that the poet was at this time absolutely starving, and besought his aid with all the earnestness of hunger; and, over and above, he received a ******** worth, at least one-third of the value, in exchange, but which, I believe, the poet afwards very ungratefully expunged.

Next week I hope to have the pleasure of seeing you in Edinburgh; and as my stay will be for eight or ten days, I wish you or ***** would take a snug, well-aired bed-room for me, where I may have the pleasure of seeing you over a morning cup of tea. But, by all accounts, it will be a matter of some difficulty to see you at all, unless your company is bespoke a week before hand. There is a great rumour here concerning your great intimacy with the Duchess of ———, and other ladies of distinction. I am really told that " cards " to invite fly by thousands each night;" and, if you had one, I suppose there would also be " bribes to your old secretary." It seems you are resolved to make hay while the sun shines, and avoid, if possible, the fate of poor Fergusson, * * * * * * * * *Quærenda pecunia primum est, virtus post nummos,* is a good maxim to thrive by: you seemed to despise it while in this country; but probably some philosopher in Edinburgh has taught you better sense.

Pray, are you yet engraving as well as printing?—Are you yet seized

"With itch of picture in the front,
With bays and wicked rhyme upon't?"

But I must give up this trifling, and attend to matters that more concern myself; so, as the Aberdeen wit says, *adieu dryly, we sal drink phan we meet.**

---

* The above extract is from a letter of one of the ablest of our Poet's correspondents, which contains some
interesting

interesting anecdotes of Fergusson, that we should have been happy to have inserted, if they could have been authenticated. The writer is mistaken in supposing the magistrates of Edinburgh had any share in the transaction respecting the monument erected for Fergusson by our Bard; this, it is evident, passed between Burns and the Kirk Session of the Canongate. Neither at Edinburgh, nor any where else, do magistrates usually trouble themselves to inquire how the house of a poor poet is furnished, or how his grave is adorned.   E.

No. XXII.

To Mrs. DUNLOP.

Edinburgh, March 22, 1787.

MADAM,

I READ your letter with watery eyes. A little, very little while ago, *I had scarce a friend but the stubborn pride of my own bosom*; now I am distinguished, patronised, befriended by you. Your friendly advices, I will not give them the cold name of criticisms, I receive with reverence. I have made some small alterations in what I before had printed. I have the advice of some very judicious friends among the Literati here, but with them I sometimes find it necessary to claim the privilege of thinking for myself. The noble Earl of Glencairn, to whom I owe more than to any man, does me the honour of giving me his strictures: his hints, with respect to impropriety or indelicacy, I follow implicitly.

You kindly interest yourself in my future views and prospects: there I can give you no light; it is all

" Dark as was chaos ere the infant sun
Was roll'd together, or had try'd his beams
Athwart the gloom profound."

The appellation of a Scottish bard is by far my highest pride; to continue to deserve it is my most exalted ambition. Scottish scenes and Scottish story are the themes I could wish to sing. I have no dearer aim than to have it in my power, unplagued with the routine of business, for which, heaven knows! I am unfit enough, to make leisurely pilgrimages through Caledonia; to sit on the fields of her battles; to wander on the romantic banks of her rivers; and to muse by the stately towers or venerable ruins, once the honoured abodes of her heroes.

But these are all Utopian thoughts: I have dallied long enough with life; 'tis time to be in earnest. I have a fond, an aged mother to care for: and some other bosom ties perhaps equally tender. Where the individual only suffers by the consequences of his own thoughtlessness, indolence, or folly, he may be excusable: nay, shining abilities, and some of the nobler virtues,

may

may half-sanctify a heedless character: but where God and nature have entrusted the welfare of others to his care; where the trust is sacred, and the ties are dear, that man must be far gone in selfishness, or strangely lost to reflection, whom these connections will not rouse to exertion.

I guess that I shall clear between two and three hundred pounds by my authorship; with that sum I intend, so far as I may be said to have any intention, to return to my old acquaintance, the plough, and, if I can meet with a lease by which I can live, to commence farmer. I do not intend to give up poetry: being bred to labour secures me independence; and the muses are my chief, sometimes have been my only, enjoyment. If my practice second my resolution, I shall have principally at heart the serious business of life: but, while following my plough, or building up my shocks, I shall cast a leisure glance to that dear, that only feature of my character, which gave me the notice of my country, and the patronage of a Wallace.

Thus, honoured Madam, I have given you the bard, his situation, and his views, native as they are in his own bosom.

* * * * * * * * * *

No.

No. XXIII.

TO THE SAME.

Edinburgh, 15*th April*, 1787.

MADAM,

THERE is an affectation of gratitude which I dislike. The periods of Johnson and the pauses of Sterne may hide a selfish heart. For my part, Madam, I trust I have too much pride for servility, and too little prudence for selfishness. I have this moment broken open your letter, but

> " Rude am I in speech,
> And therefore little can I grace my cause
> In speaking for myself—"

so I shall not trouble you with any fine speeches and hunted figures. I shall just lay my hand on my heart, and say, I hope I shall ever have the truest, the warmest, sense of your goodness.

I come

I come abroad in print for certain on Wednesday. Your orders I shall punctually attend to; only, by the way, I must tell you that I was paid before for Dr. Moore's and Miss W.'s copies, through the medium of Commissioner Cochrane in this place; but that we can settle when I have the honour of waiting on you.

Dr. Smith* was just gone to London the morning before I received your letter to him.

No.

---

* Adam Smith.

No. XXIV.

To Dr. MOORE.

Edinburgh, 23d April, 1787.

I received the books, and sent the one you mentioned to Mrs. Dunlop. I am ill-skilled in beating the coverts of imagination for metaphors of gratitude. I thank you, Sir, for the honour you have done me; and to my latest hour will warmly remember it. To be highly pleased with your book, is what I have in common with the world; but to regard these volumes as a mark of the author's friendly esteem, is a still more supreme gratification.

I leave Edinburgh in the course of ten days or a fortnight; and, after a few pilgrimages over some of the classic ground of Caledonia, *Cowden Knowes, Banks of Yarrow, Tweed, &c.*
I shall

I shall return to my rural shades, in all likelihood never more to quit them. I have formed many intimacies and friendships here, but I am afraid they are all of too tender a construction to bear carriage a hundred and fifty miles. To the rich, the great, the fashionable, the polite, I have no equivalent to offer; and I am afraid my meteor appearance will by no means entitle me to a settled correspondence with any of you, who are the permanent lights of genius and literature.

My most respectful compliments to Miss W. If once this tangent flight of mine were over, and I were returned to my wonted leisurely motion in my old circle, I may probably endeavour to return her poetic compliment in kind.

No.

No. XXV.

EXTRACT OF A LETTER

To Mrs. DUNLOP.

———

Edinburgh, 30th April, 1787.

———Your criticisms, Madam, I understand very well, and could have wished to have pleased you better. You are right in your guess that I am not very amenable to counsel. Poets, much my superiors, have so flattered those who possessed the adventitious qualities of wealth and power, that I am determined to flatter no created being either in prose or verse.

I set as little by princes, lords, clergy, critics, &c. as all these respective gentry do by my bardship. I know what I may expect from the world by and by—illiberal abuse, and perhaps contemptuous neglect.

I am

I am happy, Madam, that some of my own favourite pieces are distinguished by your particular approbation. For my Dream, which has unfortunately incurred your loyal displeasure, I hope in four weeks, or less, to have the honor of appearing at Dunlop, in its defence, in person.

No.

No. XXVI.

TO

The Reverend Dr. HUGH BLAIR.

Lawn-Market, Edinburgh, 3d May, 1787.

REVEREND AND MUCH-RESPECTED SIR,

I LEAVE Edinburgh to-morrow morning, but could not go without troubling you with half a line, sincerely to thank you for the kindness, patronage, and friendship you have shewn me. I often felt the embarrassment of my singular situation; drawn forth from the veriest shades of life to the glare of remark; and honored by the notice of those illustrious names of my country, whose works, while they are applauded to the end of time, will ever instruct and mend the heart. However the meteor-like novelty of my appearance in the world might attract notice, and honor me with the

acquaintance

acquaintance of the permanent lights of genius and literature, those who are truly benefactors of the immortal nature of man; I knew very well, that my utmost merit was far unequal to the task of preserving that character when once the novelty was over. I have made up my mind, that abuse, or almost even neglect, will not surprise me in my quarters.

I have sent you a proof impression of Beugo's work for me, done on Indian paper, as a trifling but sincere testimony with what heart-warm gratitude I am, &c.

No.

No. XXVII.

From Dr. BLAIR.

Argyle-Square, Edinburgh, 4th May, 1787.

DEAR SIR,

I WAS favoured this forenoon with your very obliging letter, together with an impression of your portrait, for which I return you my best thanks. The success you have met with I do not think was beyond your merits; and if I have had any small hand in contributing to it, it gives me great pleasure. I know no way in which literary persons, who are advanced in years, can do more service to the world, than in forwarding the efforts of rising genius, or bringing forth unknown merit from obscurity. I was the first person who brought out to the notice of the world the poems of Ossian; first, by the *Fragments of ancient Poetry* which I published, and afterwards, by

my

my setting on foot the undertaking for collecting and publishing the *Works of Ossian;* and I have always considered this as a meritorious action of my life.

Your situation, as you say, was indeed very singular; and, in being brought out all at once from the shades of deepest privacy, to so great a share of public notice and observation, you had to stand a severe trial. I am happy that you have stood it so well; and, as far as I have known or heard, though in the midst of many temptations, without reproach to your character and behaviour.

You are now, I presume, to retire to a more private walk of life; and, I trust, will conduct yourself there with industry, prudence, and honour. You have laid the foundation for just public esteem. In the midst of those employments, which your situation will render proper, you will not, I hope, neglect to promote that esteem, by cultivating your genius, and attending to such productions of it as may raise your character still higher. At the same time, be not in too great a haste to come forward. Take time and leisure to improve and mature your talents; for, on any second production you give the world, your fate, as a poet, will very much

much depend. There is, no doubt, a gloss of novelty which time wears off. As you very properly hint yourself, you are not to be surprised if, in your rural retreat, you do not find yourself surrounded with that glare of notice and applause which here shone upon you. No man can be a good poet without being somewhat of a philosopher. He must lay his account, that any one, who exposes himself to public observation, will occasionally meet with the attacks of illiberal censure, which it is always best to overlook and despise. He will be inclined sometimes to court retreat, and to disappear from public view. He will not affect to shine always, that he may at proper seasons come forth with more advantage and energy. He will not think himself neglected if he be not always praised. I have taken the liberty, you see, of an old man, to give advice and make reflections which your own good sense will, I dare say, render unnecessary.

As you mention your being just about to leave town, you are going, I should suppose, to Dumfries-shire, to look at some of Mr. Miller's farms. I heartily wish the offers to be made you there may answer; as I am persuaded you will not easily find a more generous and better hearted proprietor to live under than

Mr. Miller. When you return, if you come this way, I will be happy to see you, and to know concerning your future plans of life. You will find me, by the 22d of this month, not in my house in Argyle-square, but at a country-house at Restalrig, about a mile east from Edinburgh, near the Musselburgh road. Wishing you all success and prosperity, I am, with real regard and esteem,

Dear Sir,

Yours sincerely,

HUGH BLAIR.

No. XXVIII.

From Dr. MOORE.

Clifford-Street, May 23, 1787.

DEAR SIR,

I HAD the pleasure of your letter by Mr. Creech, and soon after he sent me the new edition of your poems. You seem to think it incumbent on you to send to each subscriber a number of copies proportionate to his subscription money; but, you may depend upon it, few subscribers expect more than one copy, whatever they subscribed. I must inform you, however, that I took twelve copies for those subscribers for whose money you were so accurate as to send me a receipt; and Lord Eglintoun told me he had sent for six copies for himself, as he wished to give five of them as presents.

Some of the poems you have added in this last

last edition are very beautiful, particularly the *Winter Night*, the *Address to Edinburgh*, *Green grow the Rashes*, and the two songs immediately following; the latter of which is exquisite. By the way, I imagine you have a peculiar talent for such compositions, which you ought to indulge.* No kind of poetry demands more delicacy or higher polishing. Horace is more admired on account of his *Odes* than all his other writings. But nothing now added is equal to your *Vision*, and *Cotter's Saturday Night*. In these are united fine imagery, natural and pathetic description, with sublimity of language and thought. It is evident that you already possess a great variety of expression and command of the English language, you ought, therefore, to deal more sparingly, for the future, in the provincial dialect:—why should you, by using *that*, limit the number of your admirers to those who understand the Scottish, when you can extend it to all persons of taste who understand the English language? In my opinion you should plan some larger work than any you have as yet attempted. I mean, reflect upon some proper subject, and arrange

---

* The fourth volume will bear testimony to the accuracy of Dr. Moore's judgment. E.

arrange the plan in your mind, without beginning to execute any part of it till you have studied most of the best English poets, and read a little more of history. The Greek and Roman stories you can read in some abridgment, and soon become master of the most brilliant facts, which must highly delight a poetical mind. You *should* also, and very soon *may*, become master of the heathen mythology, to which there are everlasting allusions in all the poets, and which in itself is charmingly fanciful. What will require to be studied with more attention, is modern history; that is, the history of France and Great Britain, from the beginning of Henry the Seventh's reign. I know very well you have a mind capable of attaining knowledge by a shorter process than is commonly used, and I am certain you are capable of making a better use of it, when attained, than is generally done.

I beg you will not give yourself the trouble of writing to me when it is *inconvenient*, and make no apology when you do write for having postponed it;—be assured of this, however, that I shall always be happy to hear from you. I think my friend Mr. —— told me that you had some poems in manuscript by you, of a satirical and humorous nature, (in which, by the way, I think

think you very strong) which your prudent friends prevailed on you to omit; particularly one called *Somebody's Confession;* if you will entrust me with a sight of any of these, I will pawn my word to give no copies, and will be obliged to you for a perusal of them.

I understand you intend to take a farm, and make the useful and respectable business of husbandry your chief occupation; this, I hope, will not prevent your making occasional addresses to the nine ladies who have shewn you such favour, one of whom visited you in the *auld clay biggin.* Virgil, before you, proved to the world that there is nothing in the business of husbandry inimical to poetry; and I sincerely hope that you may afford an example of a good poet being a successful farmer. I fear it will not be in my power to visit Scotland this season; when I do, I'll endeavour to find you out, for I heartily wish to see and converse with you. If ever your occasions call you to this place, I make no doubt of your paying me a visit, and you may depend on a very cordial welcome from this family.

I am, Dear Sir,
Your friend and obedient servant,
J. MOORE.

No. XXIX.

To Mr. WALKER, *Blair of Athole.*

Inverness, 5th September, 1787.

MY DEAR SIR,

I HAVE just time to write the foregoing,* and to tell you that it was, (at least most part of it) the effusion of an half-hour I spent at Bruar. I do not mean it was *extempore*, for I have endeavoured to brush it up as well as Mr. N———'s chat, and the jogging of the chaise, would allow. It eases my heart a good deal, as rhyme is the coin with which a poet pays his debts of honour or gratitude. What I owe

---

* *The humble petition of Bruar-Water to the Duke of Athole.* Vol. iii. p. 355.

owe to the noble family of Athole, of the first kind, I shall ever proudly boast; what I owe of the last, so help me God in my hour of need! I shall never forget.

The " little angel-band!" I declare I prayed for them very sincerely to-day at the Fall of Fyars. I shall never forget the fine family-piece I saw at Blair: the amiable, the truly noble duchess, with her smiling little seraph in her lap, at the head of the table: the lovely " olive plants," as the Hebrew bard finely says, round the happy mother; the beautiful Mrs. G——; the lovely, sweet Miss C. &c. I wish I had the powers of Guido to do them justice! My Lord Duke's kind hospitality—markedly kind indeed! Mr. G. of F——'s charms of conversation—Sir W. M——'s friendship. In short, the recollection of all that polite, agreeable company, raises an honest glow in my bosom.

No.

No. XXX.

To Mr. GILBERT BURNS.

Edinburgh, 17th September, 1787.

MY DEAR BROTHER,

I ARRIVED here safe yesterday evening after a tour of twenty-two days, and travelling near six hundred miles, windings included. My farthest stretch was about ten miles beyond Inverness. I went through the heart of the Highlands, by Crieff, Taymouth, the famous seat of Lord Breadalbane, down the Tay, among cascades and druidical circles of stones, to Dunkeld, a seat of the Duke of Athole; thence cross Tay, and up one of his tributary streams to Blair of Athole, another of the Duke's seats, where I had the honour of spending nearly two days with his Grace and family; thence

thence many miles through a wild country, among cliffs grey with eternal snows, and gloomy savage glens, till I crossed Spey and went down the stream through Strathspey, so famous in Scottish music, Badenoch, &c. till I reached Grant Castle, where I spent half a day with Sir James Grant and family; and then crossed the country for Fort George, but called by the way at Cawdor, the ancient seat of Macbeth; there I saw the identical bed in which, tradition says, king Duncan was murdered: lastly, from Fort George to Inverness.

I returned by the coast, through Nairn, Forres, and so on, to Aberdeen; thence to Stonehive, where James Burness, from Montrose, met me by appointment. I spent two days among our relations, and found our aunts, Jean and Isabel, still alive, and hale old women. John Caird, though born the same year with our father, walks as vigorously as I can; they have had several letters from his son in New York. William Brand is likewise a stout old fellow: but further particulars I delay till I see you, which will be in two or three weeks. The rest of my stages are not worth rehearsing: warm as I was from Ossian's country, where I had seen his very grave, what cared I for fishing towns or fertile carses? I slept at the famous

mous Brodie of Brodie's one night, and dined at Gordon Castle next day with the duke, duchess, and family. I am thinking to cause my old mare to meet me, by means of John Ronald, at Glasgow: but you shall hear farther from me before I leave Edinburgh. My duty, and many compliments from the north, to my mother, and my brotherly compliments to the rest. I have been trying for a birth for William, but am not likely to be successful.— Farewel!

No.

No. XXXI.

From Mr. R*****.

Ochtertyre, 22d October, 1787.

SIR,

'Twas only yesterday I got Colonel Edmondstoune's answer, that neither the words of *Down the burn Davie*, nor *Dainty Davie*, (I forgot which you mentioned) were written by Colonel G. Crawford. Next time I meet him, I will inquire about his cousin's poetical talents.

Inclosed are the inscriptions you requested, and a letter to Mr. Young, whose company and musical talents will, I am persuaded, be a feast to to you.* Nobody can give you better hints, as to your present plan than he. Receive also Omeron Cameron, which seemed to make such a deep

---

* These Inscriptions, so much admired by Burns, are below:

WRITTEN IN 1768.

For the Salictum† at Ochtertyre.

SALUBRITATIS voluptatisque causâ,
Hoc Salictum,
Paludem olim infidam,
Mihi meisque desicco et exorno.
Hic, procul negotiis strepituque,
Innocuis deliciis
Silvulas inter nascentes reptandi,
Apiumque labores suspiciendi,
Fruor.
Hic, si faxit Deus opt. max.
Prope hunc fontem pellucidum,
Cum quodam juventutis amico superstite,
Sæpe conquiescam, senex,
Contentus modicis, meoque lætus!
Sin aliter—
Ævique paululum supersit,
Vos silvulæ, et amici,
Cæteraque amoena,
Valete, diuque lætamini!

ENGLISHED

. . . .

† Salictum—Grove of Willows, Willow-ground.

a deep impression on your imagination, that I am not without hopes it will beget something to delight the public in due time: and, no doubt, the circumstances of this little tale might be varied or extended, so as to make part of a pastoral comedy. Age or wounds might have kept Omeron at home, whilst his countrymen

---

ENGLISHED.

To improve both air and soil,
I drain and decorate this plantation of willows,
Which was lately an unprofitable morass.
Here, far from noise and strife,
I love to wander,
Now fondly marking the progress of my trees,
Now studying the bee, its arts and manners
Here, if it pleases Almighty God,
May I often rest in the evening of life,
Near that transparent fountain,
With some surviving friend of my youth;
Contented with a competency,
And happy with my lot.
If vain these humble wishes,
And life draws near a close,
Ye trees and friends,
And whatever else is dear,
Farewel, and long may ye flourish!

. . . .

Above

countrymen were in the field. His station may be somewhat varied, without losing his simplicity and kindness * * * *. A group of characters, male and female, connected with the plot, might be formed from his family, or some neighbouring one of rank. It is not indispensable that the guest should be a man of high station; nor is the political quarrel in which

---

Above the Door of the House,

WRITTEN IN 1775.

MIHI meisque utinam contingat,
Prope Taichi marginem,
Avito in Agello,
Bene vivere fausteque mori!

ENGLISHED.

On the banks of the Teith,
In the small but sweet inheritance
Of my fathers,
May I and mine live in peace,
And die in joyful hope!

. . . .

These inscriptions, and the translations, are in the handwriting of Mr. Ramsay.   E.

which he is engaged of much importance, unless to call forth the exercise of generosity and faithfulness, grafted on patriarchal hospitality. To introduce state-affairs, would raise the style above comedy; though a small spice of them would season the converse of swains. Upon this head I cannot say more than to recommend the study of the character of Eumæus in the Odyssey, which, in Mr. Pope's translation, is an exquisite and invaluable drawing from nature, that would suit some of our country Elders of the present day.

There must be love in the plot, and a happy discovery; and peace and pardon may be the reward of hospitality, and honest attachment to misguided principles. When you have once thought of a plot, and brought the story into form, Dr. Blacklock, or Mr. H. Mackenzie, may be useful in dividing it into acts and scenes; for in these matters one must pay some attention to certain rules of the drama. These you could afterwards fill up at your leisure. But, whilst I presume to give a few well-meant hints, let me advise you to study the spirit of my namesake's dialogue,* which is
natural

---

* Allan Ramsay, in the Gentle Shepherd.

E.

natural without being low, and, under the trammels of verse, is such as country people, in these situations, speak every day. You have only to bring *down* your own strain a very little. A great plan, such as this, would concenter all your ideas, which facilitates the execution, and makes it a part of one's pleasure.

I approve of your plan of retiring from din and dissipation to a farm of very moderate size, sufficient to find exercise for mind and body, but not so great as to absorb better things. And if some intellectual pursuit be well chosen and steadily pursued, it will be more lucrative than most farms, in this age of rapid improvement.

Upon this subject, as your well-wisher and admirer, permit me to go a step further. Let those bright talents, which the Almighty has bestowed on you, be henceforth employed to the noble purpose of supporting the cause of truth and virtue. An imagination so varied and forcible as yours, may do this in many different modes: nor is it necessary to be always serious, which you have been to good purpose; good morals may be recommended in a comedy, or even in a song. Great allowances are due to the heat and inexperience of youth; —and few poets can boast, like Thomson, of never having written a line which, dying, they would wish to blot. In particular, I wish you to keep clear of the thorny walks of satire, which makes a man an hundred enemies for one friend, and is doubly dangerous when one is supposed to extend the slips and weaknesses of individuals to their sect or party. About modes of faith, serious and excellent men have always differed; and there are certain curious questions, which may afford scope to men of metaphysical heads, but seldom mend the heart or temper. Whilst these points are beyond human ken, it is sufficient that all our sects concur in their views of morals. You will forgive me for these hints.

Well! what think you of good Lady Clackmannan?* It is a pity she is so deaf, and speaks so indistinctly. Her house is a specimen of the mansions of our gentry of the last age, when hospitality and elevation of mind were conspicuous amidst plain fare and plain furniture. I shall be glad to hear from you at times, if it were no more than to shew that you take the effusions of an obscure man like me in good

---

* Mrs. Bruce of Clackmannan.   E.

good part. I beg my best respects to Dr. and Mrs. Blacklock.*

And am, Sir,

Your most obedient humble servant,

J. RAMSAY.

---

* TALE OF OMERON CAMERON.

IN one of the wars betwixt the Crown of Scotland and the Lords of the Isles, Alexander Stewart, Earl of Mar, (a distinguished character in the fifteenth century) and Donald Stewart, Earl of Caithness, had the command of the royal army. They marched into Lochabar, with a view of attacking a body of M'Donalds, commanded by Donald Balloch, and posted upon an arm of the sea which intersects that country. Having timely intelligence of their approach, the insurgents got off percipitately to the opposite shore in their curraghs, or boats covered with skins. The king's troops encamped in full security; but the M'Donalds, returning about midnight, surprised them, killed the Earl of Caithness, and destroyed or dispersed the whole army.

The Earl of Mar escaped in the dark, without any

but, as there was no meat in the house, he told his wife he would directly kill *Maol Odhar*,* to feed the stranger. " Kill our only cow!" said she, " our own and our little children's principal support!" More attentive, however, to the present call for hospitality, than to the remonstrances of his wife, or the future exigencies of his family, he killed the cow. The best and tenderest parts were immediately roasted before the fire, and plenty of *innirich*, or Highland soup, prepared to conclude their meal. The whole family and their guest ate heartily, and the evening was spent, as usual, in telling tales and singing songs beside a cheerful fire. Bed-time came; Omeron brushed the hearth, spread the cow-hide upon it, and desired the stranger to lie down. The Earl wrapped his plaid about him, and slept soundly on the hide, whilst the family betook themselves to rest in a corner of the same room.

Next morning they had a plentiful breakfast, and at his departure his guest asked Cameron, if he knew whom he had entertained? " You may probably," answered he, " be one of the King's officers; but whoever you are, you " came here in distress, and here it was my duty to pro-" tect you. To what my cottage afforded, you was most " welcome."—" Your guest, then," replied the other, " is " the Earl of Mar: and if hereafter you fall into any mis-" fortune, fail not to come to the castle of Kildrummie." —" My blessing be with you! noble stranger," said Omeron; " if I am ever in distress, you shall soon see me."

The royal army was soon after re-assembled; and the insurgents, finding themselves unable to make head against it,

. . . .

* Maol odhar, *i. e.* the brown humble cow.

it, dispersed. The M'Donalds, however, got notice that Omeron had been the Earl's host, and forced him to fly the country. He came with his wife and children to the gate of Kildrummie castle, and required admittance with a confidence which hardly corresponded with his habit and appearance. The porter told him rudely, his lordship was at dinner, and must not be disturbed. He became noisy and importunate: at last his name was announced. Upon hearing that it was Omeron Cameron, the Earl started from his seat, and is said to have exclaimed in a sort of poetical stanza, " I was a night in his house, and fared most plen-
" tifully; but naked of clothes was my bed. Omeron
" from Breugach is an excellent fellow." He was introduced into the great hall, and received with the welcome he deserved. Upon hearing how he had been treated, the Earl gave him a four merk land near the castle; and it is said there are still a number of Camerons descended of this Highland Eumæus.

No. XXXII.

From Mr. J. RAMSAY,

TO THE

Reverend W. YOUNG, *at* Erskine.

Ochtertyre, 22d *October*, 1787.

DEAR SIR,

Allow me to introduce Mr. Burns, whose poems, I dare say, have given you much pleasure. Upon a personal acquaintance, I doubt not, you will relish the man as much as his works, in which there is a rich vein of intellectual ore. He has heard some of our Highland *luinigs* or songs played, which delighted him so much that he has made words to one or two of them, which will render these more popular.

pular. As he has thought of being in your quarter, I am persuaded you will not think it labour lost to indulge the poet of nature with a sample of those sweet artless melodies, which only want to be *married* (in Milton's phrase) to congenial words. I wish we could conjure up the ghost of Joseph M'D. to infuse into our bard a portion of his enthusiasm for those neglected airs, which do not suit the fastidious musicians of the present hour. But if it be true that Corelli (whom I looked on as the Homer of music) is out of date, it is no proof of their taste;—this, however, is going out of my province. You can shew Mr. Burns the manner of singing these same *luinigs*; and, if he can humour it in words, I do not despair of seeing one of them sung upon the stage, in the original style, round a napkin.

I am very sorry we are likely to meet so seldom in this neighbourhood. It is one of the greatest drawbacks that attends obscurity, that one has so few opportunities of cultivating acquaintances at a distance. I hope, however, some time or other, to have the pleasure of beating up your quarters at Erskine, and of hauling you away to Paisley, &c. meanwhile I beg to be remembered to Messrs. Boog and Mylne.

If Mr. B. goes by ———, give him a billet on our friend Mr. Stuart, who, I presume, does not dread the frowns of his *diocesan*.

I am, Dear Sir,

Your most obedient humble servant,

J. RAMSAY.

No.

No. XXXIII.

From Mr. RAMSAY,

To Dr. BLACKLOCK.

Ochtertyre, 27th October, 1787.

DEAR SIR,

I RECEIVED yours by Mr. Burns, and give you many thanks for giving me an opportunity of conversing with a man of his calibre. He will, I doubt not, let you know what passed between us on the subject of my hints, to which I have made additions in a letter I sent him t'other day to your care.

* * * * * * *

You may tell Mr. Burns, when you see him, that

that Colonel Edmondstoune told me t'other day, that his cousin, Colonel George Crawford, was no poet, but a great singer of songs; but that his eldest brother Robert (by a former marriage) had a great turn that way, having written the words of *The Bush aboon Traquair*, and *Tweedside*. That the Mary to whom it was addressed was Mary Stewart, of the Castlemilk family, afterwards wife of Mr. John Relches. The Colonel never saw Robert Crawford, though he was at his burial fifty-five years ago. He was a pretty young man, and had lived long in France. Lady Ankerville is his niece, and may know more of his poetical vein. An epitaph-monger like me might moralize upon the vanity of life, and the vanity of those sweet effusions. But I have hardly room to offer my best compliments to Mrs. Blacklock; and am,

Dear Doctor,

Your most obedient humble servant,

J. RAMSAY.

No. XXXIV.

From Mr. JOHN MURDOCH.

London, 28th October, 1787.

MY DEAR SIR,

As my friend, Mr. Brown, is going from this place to your neighbourhood, I embrace the opportunity of telling you that I am yet alive, tolerably well, and always in expectation of being better. By the much-valued letters before me, I see that it was my duty to have given you this intelligence about three years and nine months ago; and have nothing to allege as an excuse, but that we poor, busy, bustling bodies in London, are so much taken up with the various pursuits in which we are here engaged, that we seldom think of any person, creature, place, or thing, that is absent.

sent. But this is not altogether the case with me; for I often think of you, and *Hornie*, and *Russel*, and an *unfathomed depth*, and *lowan brunstane*, all in the same minute, although you and they are (as I suppose) at a considerable distance. I flatter myself, however, with the pleasing thought, that you and I shall meet some time or other either in Scotland or England. If ever you come hither, you will have the satisfaction of seeing your poems relished by the Caledonians in London, full as much as they can be by those of Edinburgh. We frequently repeat some of your verses in our Caledonian society; and you may believe, that I am not a little vain that I have had some share in cultivating such a genius. I was not absolutely certain that you were the author, till a few days ago, when I made a visit to Mrs. Hill, Dr. M'Comb's eldest daughter, who lives in town, and who told me that she was informed of it by a letter from her sister in Edinburgh, with whom you had been in company when in that capital.

Pray let me know if you have any intention of visiting this huge, overgrown metropolis? It would afford matter for a large poem. Here you would have an opportunity of indulging your vein in the study of mankind, perhaps to a greater a greater degree than in any city upon the face of the globe; for the inhabitants of London, as you know, are a collection of all nations, kindreds, and tongues, who make it, as it were, the centre of their commerce.

* * * * * *

Present my respectful compliments to Mrs. Burns, to my dear friend Gilbert, and all the rest of her amiable children. May the Father of the universe bless you all with those principles and dispositions that the best of parents took such uncommon pains to instil into your minds from your earliest infancy! May you live as he did! if you do, you can never be unhappy. I feel myself grown serious all at once, and affected in a manner I cannot describe. I shall only add, that it is one of the greatest pleasures I promise myself before I die, that of seeing the family of a man whose memory I revere more than that of any person that ever I was acquainted with.

I am, my dear Friend,

Yours sincerely,

JOHN MURDOCH.

No. XXXV.

From Mr. ———.

Gordon Castle, 31st October, 1787.

SIR,

IF you were not sensible of your fault as well as of your loss, in leaving this place so suddenly, I should condemn you to starve upon *cauld kail* for *ae towmont* at least; and as for *Dick Latine*,* your travelling companion, without banning him *wi' a'* the curses contained in your letter, (which he'll *no* value a *bawbee)* I should give him nought but *Stra'bogie castocks* to chew for *sax ouks*, or ay until he was as sensible of his error as you seem to be of yours.

* * * * * * * *

Your

---

* Mr. Nicol.

Your song I shewed without producing the author; and it was judged by the duchess to be the production of Dr. Beattie. I sent a copy of it, by her Grace's desire, to a Mrs. M'Pherson in Badenoch, who sings *Morag* and all other Gaelic songs in great perfection. I have recorded it likewise, by Lady Charlotte's desire, in a book belonging to her ladyship, where it is in company with a great many other poems and verses, some of the writers of which are no less eminent for their political than for their poetical abilities. When the duchess was informed that you were the author, she wished you had written the verses in Scotch.

Any letter directed to me here will come to hand safely, and, if sent under the duke's cover it will likewise come free; that is, as long as the duke is in this country.

I am, Sir, yours sincerely.

No.

No. XXXVI.

FROM

The Reverend JOHN SKINNER.

Linsheart, 14*th November,* 1787.

SIR,

Your kind return without date, but of post-mark October 25th, came to my hand only this day; and, to testify my punctuality to my poetic engagement, I sit down immediately to answer it in kind. Your acknowledgment of my poor but just encomiums on your surprising genius, and your opinion of my rhyming excursions, are both, I think, by far too high. The difference between our two tracks of education and ways of life is entirely in your favour, and gives you the preference every manner of way. I know a classical education will not create a versifying taste, but it mightily improves and assists it; and though, where

both

both these meet, there may sometimes be ground for approbation, yet where taste appears single as it were, and neither cramped nor supported by acquisition, I will always sustain the justice of its prior claim to applause. A small portion of taste, this way, I have had almost from childhood, especially in the old Scottish dialect: and it is as old a thing as I remember, my fondness for *Christ-kirk o' the Green*, which I had by heart ere I was twelve years of age, and which, some years ago, I attempted to turn into Latin verse. While I was young, I dabbled a good deal in these things; but, on getting the black gown, I gave it pretty much over, till my daughters grew up, who, being all good singers, plagued me for words to some of their favourite tunes, and so extorted these effusions, which have made a public appearance beyond my expectations, and contrary to my intentions, at the same time that I hope there is nothing to be found in them uncharacteristic, or unbecoming the cloth, which I would always wish to see respected.

As to the assistance you propose from me in the undertaking you are engaged in,* I am

---

* A plan of publishing a complete collection of Scottish Songs, &c.   E.

sorry I cannot give it so far as I could wish, and you perhaps expect. My daughters, who were my only intelligencers, are all *foris-familiate*, and the old woman their mother has lost that taste. There are two from my own pen, which I might give you, if worth the while. One to the old Scotch tune of *Dumbarton's drums*.

The other perhaps you have met with, as your noble friend the Duchess has, I am told, heard of it. It was squeezed out of me by a brother parson in her neighbourhood, to accommodate a new Highland reel for the Marquis's birth-day, to the stanza of

" Tune your fiddles, tune them sweetly," &c.

If this last answer your purpose, you may have it from a brother of mine, Mr. James Skinner, writer, in Edinburgh, who, I believe, can give the music too.

There is another humorous thing, I have heard said to be done by the catholic priest Geddes, and which hit my taste much:

" There was a wee wifeikie, was coming frae the fair,
 Had gotten a little drapikie, which bred her meikle care,

It took upo' the wifie's heart, and she began to spew,
And co' the wee wifeikie, I wish I binna fou,
    I wish," &c. &c.

I have heard of another new composition, by a young ploughman of my acquaintance, that I am vastly pleased with, to the tune of *The humours of Glen,* which I fear won't do, as the music, I am told, is of Irish original. I have mentioned these, such as they are, to shew my readiness to oblige you, and to contribute my mite, if I could, to the patriotic work you have in hand, and which I wish all success to. You have only to notify your mind, and what you want of the above shall be sent you.

Mean time, while you are thus publickly, I may say, employed, do not sheath your own proper and piercing weapon. From what I have seen of yours already, I am inclined to hope for much good. One lesson of virtue and morality delivered in your amusing style, and from such as you, will operate more than dozens would do from such as me, who shall be told it is our employment, and be never more minded: whereas, from a pen like yours, as being one of the many, what comes will be admired. Admiration will produce regard, and regard will leave an impression, especially *when example goes along.*

>Now binna saying I'm ill bred,
>Else, by my troth, I'll no be glad;
>For cadgers, ye have heard it said,
>>And sic like fry,
>Maun ay be harland in their trade,
>>And sae maun I.

Wishing you, from my poet-pen, all success, and, in my other character, all happiness and heavenly direction,

I remain, with esteem,

Your sincere friend,

JOHN SKINNER.

No.

No. XXXVII.

From Mrs. ROSE.

Kilravock Castle, 30th November, 1787.

SIR,

I HOPE you will do me the justice to believe, that it was no defect in gratitude for your punctual performance of your parting promise, that has made me so long in acknowledging it, but merely the difficulty I had in getting the Highland songs you wished to have, accurately noted: they are at last inclosed; but how shall I convey along with them those *graces* they acquired from the melodious voice of one of the fair spirits of the hill of Kildrummie! *These* I must leave to your imagination to supply. It has powers sufficient to transport you to her side, to recal her accents, and to make them still vibrate in the ears
of

of memory. To her I am indebted for getting the inclosed notes. They are clothed with " *thoughts* that breathe, and *words* that burn." *These*, however, being in an *unknown* tongue to you, you must again have recourse to that same fertile imagination of yours to interpret them, and suppose a lover's description of the beauties of an adored mistress—Why did I say unknown? The language of love is an universal one, that seems to have escaped the confusion of Babel, and to be understood by all nations.

I rejoice to find that you were pleased with so many things, persons, and places, in your northern tour, because it leads me to hope you may be induced to revisit them again. That the old castle of Kilravock, and its inhabitants were amongst these, adds to my satisfaction. I am even vain enough to admit your very flattering application of the line of Addison's; at any rate, allow me to believe, that " friendship will maintain the ground she has occupied, in both our hearts," in spite of absence, and that when we do meet, it will be as acquaintance of a score of years standing; and on this footing consider me as interested in the future course of your fame so splendidly commenced. Any communications of the progress
of

of your muse will be received with great gratitude, and the fire of your genius will have power to warm, even us, frozen sisters of the north.

The fire-sides of Kilravock and Kildrummie unite in cordial regards to you. When you incline to figure either in your idea, suppose some of us reading your poems, and some of us singing your songs, and my little Hugh looking at your picture, and you'll seldom be wrong. We remember Mr. Nicol with as much good will as we can do any body who hurried Mr. Burns from us.

Farewel, Sir, I can only contribute the *widow's mite* to the esteem and admiration excited by your merits and genius; but this I give, as she did, with all my heart—being sincerely yours,

EL. ROSE.

No. XXXVIII.

To the Earl of GLENCAIRN.

MY LORD,

I KNOW your lordship will disapprove of my ideas in a request I am going to make to you, but I have weighed, long and seriously weighed, my situation, my hopes and turn of mind, and am fully fixed to my scheme if I can possibly effectuate it. I wish to get into the Excise; I am told that your Lordship's interest will easily procure me the grant from the Commissioners; and your lordship's patronage and goodness, which have already rescued me from obscurity, wretchedness, and exile, embolden me to ask that interest. You have likewise put it in my power to save the little tie of *home* that sheltered an aged mother, two brothers, and three sisters, from destruction. There, my lord, you have bound me over to the highest gratitude.

My brother's farm is but a wretched lease; but I think he will probably weather out the remaining seven years of it; and, after the assistance which I have given and will give him, to keep the family together, I think, by my guess, I shall have rather better than two hundred pounds, and instead of seeking what is almost impossible at present to find, a farm that I can certainly live by, with so small a stock, I shall lodge this sum in a banking-house, a sacred deposit, excepting only the calls of uncommon distress or necessitous old age: ********.

These, my lord, are my views: I have resolved from the maturest deliberation; and now I am fixed, I shall leave no stone unturned to carry my resolve into execution. Your lordship's patronage is the strength of my hopes; nor have I yet applied to any body else. Indeed my heart sinks within me at the idea of applying to any other of the Great who have honoured me with their countenance. I am ill qualified to dog the heels of greatness with the impertinence of solicitation, and tremble nearly as much at the thought of the cold promise as the cold denial: but to your lordship I have not only the honour, the comfort, but the pleasure of being

  Your lordship's much obliged
    and deeply indebted humble servant.
      No.

No. XXXIX.

To —— DALRYMPLE, Esq.

OF ORANGEFIELD.

Edinburgh, 1787.

DEAR SIR,

I suppose the devil is so elated with his success with you, that he is determined, by a *coup de main*, to complete his purposes on you all at once, in making you a poet. I broke open the letter you sent me: hummed over the rhymes; and, as I saw they were extempore, said to myself, they were very well: but when I saw at the bottom a name that I shall ever value with grateful respect, " I gapit wide but naething spak." I was nearly as much struck as the friends of Job, of affliction-bearing memory, when they sat down with him seven days and seven nights, and spake not a word.

* * * * * * *

I am naturally of a superstitious cast, and as soon

soon as my wonder-scared imagination regained its consciousness, and resumed its functions, I cast about what this mania of yours might portend. My foreboding ideas had the wide stretch of possibility; and several events, great in their magnitude, and important in their consequences, occurred to my fancy. The downfal of the conclave, or the crushing of the cork rumps; a ducal coronet to Lord George G———, and the protestant interest, or St. Peter's keys, to ******.

You want to know how I come on. I am just *in statu quo*, or, not to insult a gentleman with my Latin, in " auld use and wont." The noble Earl of Glencairn took me by the hand to-day, and interested himself in my concerns, with a goodness like that benevolent Being whose image he so richly bears. He is a stronger proof of the immortality of the soul than any that philosophy ever produced. A mind like his can never die. Let the worshipful squire H. L. or the reverend Mass J. M. go into their primitive nothing. At best, they are but ill-digested lumps of chaos, only one of them strongly tinged with bituminous particles and sulphureous effluvia. But my noble patron, eternal as the heroic swell of magnanimity, and the generous throb of benevolence, shall look on with princely eye at "the war of elements, the wreck of matter, and the crush of worlds."

No. XL.

To Sir JOHN WHITEFOORD.

December, 1787.

SIR,

Mr. M‘Kenzie, in Mauchline, my very warm and worthy friend, has informed me how much you are pleased to interest yourself in my fate as a man, and (what to me is incomparably dearer) my fame as a poet. I have, Sir, in one or two instances, been patronised by those of your character in life, when I was introduced to their notice by ****** friends to them, and honoured acquaintances to me; but you are the first gentleman in the country whose benevolence and goodness of heart has interested him for me, unsolicited and unknown. I am not master enough of the etiquette of these matters to know, nor did I stay to inquire, whether formal duty bade, or cold propriety

priety disallowed, my thanking you in this manner, as I am convinced, from the light in which you kindly view me, that you will do me the justice to believe this letter is not the manœuvre of the needy, sharping author, fastening on those in upper life who honour him with a little notice of him or his works. Indeed, the situation of poets is generally such, to a proverb, as may, in some measure, palliate that prostitution of heart and talents they have at times been guilty of. I do not think prodigality is, by any means, a necessary concomitant of a poetic turn; but I believe a careless, indolent inattention to œconomy, is almost inseparable from it; then there must be, in the heart of every bard of Nature's making, a certain modest sensibility, mixed with a kind of pride, that will ever keep him out of the way of those windfalls of fortune, which frequently light on hardy impudence and foot-licking servility. It is not easy to imagine a more helpless state than his, whose poetic fancy unfits him for the world, and whose character as a scholar gives him some pretensions to the *politesse* of life—yet is as poor as I am.

For my part, I thank Heaven my star has been kinder; learning never elevated my ideas above

above the peasant's shed, and I have an independent fortune at the plough-tail.

I was surprised to hear that any one, who pretended in the least to the *manners of the gentleman*, should be so foolish, or worse, as to stoop to traduce the morals of such a one as I am, and so inhumanly cruel, too, as to meddle with that late most unfortunate, unhappy part of my story. With a tear of gratitude, I thank you, Sir, for the warmth with which you interposed in behalf of my conduct. I am, I acknowledge, too frequently the sport of whim, caprice, and passion—but reverence to God, and integrity to my fellow creatures, I hope I shall ever preserve. I have no return, Sir, to make you for your goodness, but one—a return which, I am persuaded, will not be unacceptable—the honest, warm wishes of a grateful heart for your happiness, and every one of that lovely flock who stand to you in a filial relation. If ever calumny aim the poisoned shaft at *them*, may friendship be by to ward the blow!

No.

No. XLI.

To Mrs. DUNLOP.

Edinburgh, 21*st January*, 1788.

AFTER six weeks confinement, I am beginning to walk across the room. They have been six horrible weeks, anguish and low spirits made me unfit to read, write, or think.

I have a hundred times wished that one could resign life as an officer resigns a commission: for I would not *take in* any poor, ignorant wretch, by *selling out*. Lately I was a sixpenny private; and, God knows, a miserable soldier enough: now I march to the campaign, a starving cadet; a little more conspicuously wretched.

I am ashamed of all this; for though I do
want

want bravery for the warfare of life, I could wish, like some other soldiers, to have as much fortitude or cunning as to dissemble or conceal my cowardice.

As soon as I can bear the journey, which will be, I suppose, about the middle of next week, I leave Edinburgh, and soon after I shall pay my grateful duty at Dunlop-house.

No.

No. XLII.

EXTRACT OF A LETTER

TO THE SAME.

———

Edinburgh, 12th February, 1788.

SOME things in your late letters hurt me: not that *you say them*, but that *you mistake me*. Religion, my honoured Madam, has not only been all my life my chief dependence, but my dearest enjoyment. I have indeed been the luckless victim of wayward follies: but alas! I have ever been " more fool than knave." A mathematician without religion, is a probable character; an irreligious poet, is a monster.

* * * * * * * * *

No. XLIII.

To Mrs. DUNLOP.

Mossgiel, 7th March, 1788.

MADAM,

THE last paragraph in yours of the 30th February affected me most, so I shall begin my answer where you ended your letter. That I am often a sinner with any little wit I have, I do confess: but I have taxed my recollection to no purpose to find out when it was employed against you. I hate an ungenerous sarcasm a great deal worse than I do the devil; at least, as Milton describes him; and though I may be rascally enough to be sometimes guilty of it myself, I cannot endure it in others. You my honoured friend, who cannot appear in any light but you are sure of being respectable—you can afford to pass by an occasion to display
play

play your wit, because you may depend for fame on your sense; or if you choose to be silent, you know you can rely on the gratitude of many and the esteem of all; but, God help us who are wits or witlings by profession, if we stand not for fame there, we sink unsupported!

I am highly flattered by the news you tell me of Coila.* I may say to the fair painter who does me so much honour, as Dr. Beattie says to Ross the poet, of his muse Scota, from which, by the bye, I took the idea of Coila: ('Tis a poem of Beattie's in the Scots dialect, which perhaps you have never seen.)

> " Ye shak your head, but o' my fegs,
> Ye've set auld Scota on her legs:
> Lang had she lien wi' buffe and flegs,
>   Bombaz'd and dizzie,
> Her fiddle wanted strings and pegs,
>   Waes me, poor hizzie!"

No.

---

* A lady (daughter of Mrs. Dunlop) was making a picture from the description of Coila in the Vision. E.

No. XLIV.

To Mr. ROBERT CLEGHORN.

Mauchline, 31st March, 1788.

YESTERDAY, my dear Sir, as I was riding thro' a track of melancholy, joyless muirs, between Galloway and Ayrshire, it being Sunday, I turned my thoughts to psalms, and hymns, and spiritual songs; and your favourite air *Captain Okean,* coming at length in my head, I tried these words to it. You will see that the first part of the tune must be repeated.*

I am tolerably pleased with these verses; but, as I have only a sketch of the tune, I leave

---

* Here the Bard gives the first stanza of the *Chevalier's Lament.*   E.

leave it with you to try if they suit the measure of the music.

I am so harrassed with care and anxiety about this farming project of mine, that my muse has degenerated into the veriest prose wench that ever picked cinders or followed a tinker. When I am fairly got into the routine of business, I shall trouble you with a longer epistle; perhaps with some queries respecting farming; at present, the world sits such a load on my mind, that it has effaced almost every trace of the ———— in me.

My very best compliments and good wishes to Mrs. Cleghorn.

No.

No. XLV.

From Mr. ROBERT CLEGHORN.

Saughton Mills, 27th April, 1788.

MY DEAR BROTHER FARMER,

I WAS favoured with your very kind letter of the 31st ult. and consider myself greatly obliged to you for your attention in sending me the song to my favourite air, *Captain Okean*. The words delight me much; they fit the tune to a hair. I wish you would send me a verse or two more: and if you have no objection, I would have it in the Jacobite style. Suppose it should be sung after the fatal field of Culloden by the unfortunate Charles. Tenducci personates the lovely Mary Stuart in the song, *Queen Mary's Lamentation*. Why may not

not I sing in the person of her great-great-great-grandson?*

Any

---

* Our Poet took this advice. The whole of this beautiful song, as it was afterwards finished, is below:

THE CHEVALIER'S LAMENT.

THE small birds rejoice in the green leaves returning,
   The murmuring streamlet winds clear thro' the vale;
The hawthorn trees blow in the dews of the morning,
   And wild scatter'd cowslips bedeck the green dale:

But what can give pleasure, or what can seem fair,
While the lingering moments are number'd by care?
   No flowers gaily springing, nor birds sweetly singing,
Can soothe the sad bosom of joyless despair.

The deed that I dar'd could it merit their malice,
   A king and a father to place on his throne?
His right are these hills and his right are these vallies,
   Where the wild beasts find shelter, but I can find none.

But 'tis not my sufferings thus wretched, forlorn,
My brave gallant friends, 'tis your ruin I mourn:
   Your deeds prov'd so loyal in hot bloody trial,
Alas! can I make you no sweeter return!

E.

Any skill I have in country business you may truly command. Situation, soil, customs of countries may vary from each other, but *Farmer Attention* is a good farmer in every place. I beg to hear from you soon. Mrs. Cleghorn joins me in best compliments.

I am, in the most comprehensive sense of the word, your very sincere friend,

ROBERT CLEGHORN.

No. XLVI.

To Mrs. DUNLOP.

Mauchline, 28th April, 1788.

MADAM,

Your powers of reprehension must be great indeed, as I assure you they made my heart ache with penitential pangs, even though I was really not guilty. As I commence farmer at Whitsunday, you will easily guess I must be pretty busy! but that is not all. As I got the offer of the excise-business without solicitation; and as it costs me only six months attendance for instructions to entitle me to a commission, which commission lies by me, and at any future period, on my simple petition, can be resumed; I thought five-and-thirty pounds a-year was no bad dernier resort for a poor poet, if fortune, in her jade tricks, should kick him down from the little eminence to which she has lately helped him up.

For this reason, I am at present attending these instructions, to have them completed before Whitsunday. Still, Madam, I prepared, with the sincerest pleasure, to meet you at the Mount, and came to my brother's on Saturday night, to set out on Sunday; but for some nights preceding, I had slept in an apartment where the force of the winds and rains was only mitigated by being sifted through numberless apertures in the windows, walls, &c. In consequence, I was on Sunday, Monday, and part of Tuesday, unable to stir out of bed, with all the miserable effects of a violent cold.

You see, Madam, the truth of the French maxim *Le vrai n'est pas toujours le vrai-semblable;* your last was so full of expostulation, and was something so like the language of an offended friend, that I began to tremble for a correspondence which I had with grateful pleasure set down as one of the greatest enjoyments of my future life.

* * * * * * *

Your books have delighted me: *Virgil, Dryden,* and *Tasso,* were all equally strangers to me: but of this more at large in my next.

No. XLVII.

FROM

The Reverend JOHN SKINNER.

Linshart, 28th April, 1788.

DEAR SIR,

I RECEIVED your last with the curious present you have favoured me with, and would have made proper acknowledgments before now, but that I have been necessarily engaged in matters of a different complexion. And now that I have got a little respite, I make use of it to thank you for this valuable instance of your good-will, and to assure you that, with the sincere heart of a true Scotsman, I highly esteem both the gift and the giver: as a small testimony of which I have herewith sent you for your amusement, (and in a form which I hope
you

you will excuse for saving postage) the two songs I wrote about to you already. *Charming Nancy*, is the real production of genius in a ploughman of twenty years of age at the time of its appearing, with no more education than what he picked up at an old farmer-grandfather's fire-side, though now by the strength of natural parts, he is clerk to a thriving bleachfield in the neighbourhood. And I doubt not but you will find in it a simplicity and delicacy, with some turns of humour, that will please one of your taste; at least it pleased me when I first saw it, if that can be any recommendation to it. The other is entirely descriptive of my own sentiments; and you may make use of one or both as you shall see good.*

You

---

* CHARMING NANCY.

A song by a BUCHAN *Ploughman.*

Tune—" HUMOURS OF GLEN."

SOME sing of sweet Mally, some sing of fair Nelly,
   And some call sweet Susie the cause of their pain:
Some love to be jolly, some love melancholy,
   And some love to sing of the Humours of Glen.

But

You will oblige me by presenting my respects to your host, Mr. Cruikshank, who has given such high approbation to my poor *Latinity*; you may let him know, that as I have likewise

---

But my only fancy is my pretty Nancy,
   In venting my passion I'll strive to be plain,
I'll ask no more treasure, I'll seek no more pleasure,
   But thee my dear Nancy, gin thou wert my ain.

Her beauty delights me, her kindness invites me,
   Her pleasant behaviour is free from all stain,
Therefore, my sweet jewel, O do not prove cruel!
   Consent, my dear Nancy, and come be my ain:
Her carriage is comely, her language is homely,
   Her dress is quite decent when ta'en in the main;
She's blooming in feature, she's handsome in stature,
   My charming dear Nancy, O wert thou my ain!

Like Phœbus adorning the fair ruddy morning,
   Her bright eyes are sparkling, her brows are serene,
Her yellow locks shining, in beauty combining,
   My charming sweet Nancy, wilt thou be my ain?
The whole of her face is with maidenly graces
   Array'd like the gowans that grow in yon glen;
She's well shap'd and slender, true-hearted and tender,
   My charming sweet Nancy, O wert thou my ain!

likewise been a dabbler in Latin poetry, I have two things that I would, if he desires it, submit, not to his judgment, but to his amusement; the one, a translation of *Christ's Kirk o' the Green*, printed at Aberdeen some years ago; the other, *Batrachomyomachia Homeri latinis vestita cum additamentis*, given in lately to Chalmers, to print if he pleases. Mr. C. will know *Seria non semper delectant, non joca semper. Semper delectant seria mixta jocis.*

I have

I'll seek thro' the nation for some habitation,
  To shelter my jewel from cold, snow, and rain,
With songs to my deary, I'll keep her ay cheery,
  My charming sweet Nancy, gin thou wert my ain.
I'll work at my calling to furnish thy dwelling,
  With ev'ry thing needful thy life to sustain,
Thou shalt not sit single, but by a clear ingle,
  I'll marrow thee, Nancy, when thou art my ain.

I'll make true affection the constant direction
  Of loving my Nancy, while life doth remain:
Tho' youth will be wasting, true love shall be lasting,
  My charming sweet Nancy, gin thou wert my ain.
But what if my Nancy should alter her fancy,
  To favour another be forward and fain,
I will not compel her, but plainly I'll tell her,
  Begone, thou false Nancy, thou'se ne'er be my ain.

I have just room to repeat compliments and good wishes from,

Sir, your humble servant,

JOHN SKINNER.

THE OLD MAN'S SONG.

Tune—"Dumbarton's Drums."

BY THE REVEREND J. SKINNER.

O! why should old age so much wound us? O,
There is nothing in't all to confound us, O,
    For how happy now am I,
    With my old wife sitting by,
And our bairns and our oys all around us, O.

We began in the world wi' naething, O,
And we've jogg'd on, and toil'd for the ae thing, O;
    We made use of what we had,
    And our thankful hearts were glad,
When we got the bit meat and the claething, O.

We have liv'd all our life-time contented, O,
Since the day we became first acquainted, O;
    It's true we've been but poor,
    And we are so to this hour,
Yet we never yet repin'd nor lamented, O.

We ne'er thought of schemes to be wealthy, O,
By ways that were cunning or stealthy, O,
      But we always had the bliss,
      And what further could we wiss,
To be pleas'd wi' ourselves, and be healthy, O.

What tho' we canna boast of our guineas, O,
We have plenty of Jockies and Jeanies, O,
      And these, I'm certain, are
      More desirable by far,
Than a pocket full of poor yellow sleenies, O.

We have seen many wonder and ferlie, O,
Of changes that almost are yearly, O,
      Among rich folks up and down,
      Both in country and in town,
Who now live but scrimply and barely, O.

Then why should people brag of prosperity, O,
A straiten'd life we see is no rarity, O,
      Indeed we've been in want,
      And our living been but scant,
Yet we never were reduc'd to need charity, O.

In this house we first came together, O,
Where we've long been a Father and Mither, O,
      And, tho' not of stone and lime,
      It will last us a' our time,
And, I hope, we shall never need anither, O.

And when we leave this habitation, O,
We'll depart with a good commendation, O,
      We'll go hand in hand, I wiss,
      To a better house than this,
To make room for the next generation, O.

Then why should old age so much wound us? O,
There's nothing in it all to confound us, O,
    For how happy now am I,
    With my old wife sitting by,
And our bairns and our oys all around us, O.

No. XLVIII.

To Professor DUGALD STEWART.

Mauchline, 3d. May, 1788.

SIR,

I INCLOSE you one or two more of my bagatelles. If the fervent wishes of honest gratitude have any influence with that great unknown Being, who frames the chain of causes and events, prosperity and happiness will attend your visit to the continent, and return you safe to your native shore.

Wherever I am, allow me, Sir, to claim it as my privilege to acquaint you with my progress in my trade of rhymes; as I am sure I could say it with truth, that, next to my little fame, and the having it in my power to make life more comfortable to those whom nature has made dear to me, I shall ever regard your countenance, your patronage, your friendly good offices, as the most valued consequence of my late success in life.

No. XLIX.

EXTRACT OF A LETTER

To Mrs. DUNLOP.

Mauchline, 4th May, 1788.

MADAM,

DRYDEN's *Virgil* has delighted me. I do not know whether the critics will agree with me, but the *Georgics* are to me by far the best of Virgil. It is, indeed, a species of writing entirely new to me, and has filled my head with a thousand fancies of emulation: but, alas! when I read the *Georgics*, and then survey my own powers, 'tis like the idea of a Shetland poney, drawn up by the side of a thorough-bred hunter, to start for the plate. I own I am disappointed in the Æneid. Faultless correctness may please, and does highly please, the lettered critic: but to that awful character I have not the most distant pretensions. I do not know whether I do not hazard my pretensions to be a critic of any kind, when I say that I think Virgil, in many instances, a *servile* copier of Homer. If I had the *Odyssey* by me, I could parallel many passages where Virgil has evidently copied, but by no means improved Homer. Nor can I think there is any thing of this owing to the translators; for, from every thing I have seen of Dryden, I think him, in genius and fluency of language, Pope's master. I have not perused Tasso enough to form an opinion: in some future letter you shall have my ideas of him; though I am conscious my criticisms must be very inaccurate and imperfect, as there I have ever felt and lamented my want of learning most.

No. L.

TO THE SAME.

27th May, 1788.

MADAM,

I HAVE been torturing my philosophy to no purpose to account for that kind partiality of yours, which, unlike * * * * * * * * * * * has followed me in my return to the shade of life, with assiduous benevolence. Often did I regret, in the fleeting hours of my late Will-o'-Wisp appearance, that " here I had no continuing city;" and, but for the consolation of a few solid guineas, could almost lament the time that a momentary acquaintance with wealth and splendour put me so much out of conceit with the sworn companions of my road through life, insignificance and poverty.

* * * * * *

There

There are few circumstances relating to the unequal distribution of the good things of this life, that give me more vexation (I mean in what I see around me) than the importance the opulent bestow on their trifling family affairs, compared with the very same things on the contracted scale of a cottage. Last afternoon I had the honour to spend an hour or two at a good woman's fireside, where the planks, that composed the floor, were decorated with a splendid carpet, and the gay table sparkled with silver and china. 'Tis now about term-day, and there has been a revolution among those creatures, who, though in appearance partakers, and equally noble partakers, of the same nature with Madame, are from time to time, their nerves, their sinews, their health, strength, wisdom, experience, genius, time, nay a good part of their very thoughts, sold for months and years, * * * * * * * * * * * not only to the necessities, the conveniences, but the caprices of the important few.* We talked of the insignificant creatures; nay, notwithstanding their general stupidity

---

* Servants, in Scotland, are hired from term to term; *i. e.* from Whitsunday to Martinmas, &c.   E.

pidity and rascality, did some of the poor devils the honour to commend them. But light be the turf upon his breast who taught—" Reverence thyself." We looked down on the unpolished wretches, their impertinent wives and clouterly brats, as the lordly bull does on the little dirty ant-hill, whose puny inhabitants he crushes in the carelessness of his ramble, or tosses in the air in the wantonness of his pride.

* * * * * *

No. LI.

TO THE SAME,

AT MR. DUNLOP'S, HADDINGTON.

Ellisland, 13th June, 1788.

" Where'er I roam, whatever realms I see,
My heart, untravell'd, fondly turns to thee,
Still to my friend it turns with ceaseless pain,
And drags at each remove a lengthen'd chain."

GOLDSMITH.

THIS is the second day, my honoured friend, that I have been on my farm. A solitary inmate of an old smoky *Spence;* far from every object I love, or by whom I am beloved; nor any acquaintance older than yesterday, except *Jenny Geddes*, the old mare I ride on; while uncouth cares and novel plans hourly insult my
awkward

awkward ignorance and bashful inexperience. There is a foggy atmosphere native to my soul in the hour of care, consequently the dreary objects seem larger than the life. Extreme sensibility, irritated and prejudiced on the gloomy side by a series of misfortunes and disappointments, at that period of my existence when the soul is laying in her cargo of ideas for the voyage of life, is, I believe, the principal cause of this unhappy frame of mind:

" The valiant, in himself, what can he suffer?
Or what need he regard his *single* woes?" &c.

Your surmise, Madam, is just; I am indeed a husband.

* * * * * * * *

I found a once much-loved and still much-loved female, literally and truly cast out to the mercy of the naked elements; but as I enabled her to *purchase* a shelter; and there is no sporting with a fellow-creature's happiness or misery.

The most placid good-nature and sweetness of disposition; a warm heart, gratefully devoted with all its powers to love me; vigorous health and sprightly cheerfulness, set off to the best

best advantage by a more than commonly handsome figure; these, I think, in a woman, may make a good wife, though she should never have read a page but *the Scriptures of the Old and New Testament,* nor have danced in a brighter assembly than a penny-pay wedding.

* * * * * * *

No.

No. LII.

To Mr. P. HILL.

MY DEAR HILL,

I SHALL say nothing at all to your mad present—you have long and often been of important service to me, and I suppose you mean to go on conferring obligations until I shall not be able to lift up my face before you. In the mean time, as Sir Roger de Coverley, because it happened to be a cold day in which he made his will, ordered his servants great coats for mourning, so, because I have been this week plagued with an indigestion, I have sent you by the carrier a fine old ewe-milk cheese.

Indigestion is the devil: nay, 'tis the devil and all. It besets a man in every one of his senses. I lose my appetite at the sight of successful

cessful knavery, and sicken to loathing at the noise and nonsense of self-important folly. When the hollow-hearted wretch takes me by the hand, the feeling spoils my dinner; the proud man's wine so offends my palate that it choaks me in the gullet; and the *pulvilis'd*, feather'd, pert coxcomb, is so disgustful in my nostril, that my stomach turns.

If ever you have any of these disagreeable sensations, let me prescribe for you patience and a bit of my cheese. I know that you are no niggard of your good things among your friends, and some of them are in much need of a slice. There in my eye is our friend, Smellie; a man positively of the first abilities and greatest strength of mind, as well as one of the best hearts and keenest wits that I have ever met with; when you see him, as, alas! he too is smarting at the pinch of distressful circumstances, aggravated by the sneer of contumelious greatness—a bit of my cheese alone will not cure him; but if you add a tankard of brown stout, and superadd a magnum of right Oporto, you will see his sorrows vanish like the morning mist before the summer sun.

C——h, the earliest friend, except my only brother, that I have on earth, and one of the
worthiest

worthiest fellows that ever any man called by the name of friend, if a luncheon of my cheese would help to rid him of some of his superabundant modesty, you would do well to give it him.

David,* with his *Courant*, comes too, across my recollection, and I beg you will help him largely from the said ewe-milk cheese, to enable him to digest those—bedaubing paragraphs with which he is eternally larding the lean characters of certain great men in a certain great town. I grant you the periods are very well turned; so, a fresh egg is a very good thing, but when thrown at a man in a pillory, it does not at all improve his figure, not to mention the irreparable loss of the egg.

My facetious friend, D——r, I would wish also to be a partaker; not to digest his spleen, for that he laughs off, but to digest his last night's wine at the last field-day of the Crochallan corps.†

Among

---

* Printer of the Edinburgh Evening Courant.

† A club of choice spirits.

Among our common friends, I must not forget one of the dearest of them, Cunningham. The brutality, insolence, and selfishness of a world unworthy of having such a fellow as he is in it, I know sticks in his stomach; and if you can help him to any thing that will make him a little easier on that score, it will be very obliging.

As to honest J—— S———e, he is such a contented happy man, that I know not what can annoy him, except perhaps he may not have got the better of a parcel of modest anecdotes which a certain poet gave him one night at supper, the last time the said poet was in town.

Though I have mentioned so many men of law, I shall have nothing to do with them professedly.—The faculty are beyond my prescription. As to their *clients*, that is another thing; God knows, they have much to digest!

The clergy I pass by; their profundity of erudition, and their liberality of sentiment; their total want of pride, and their detestation of hypocrisy, are so proverbially notorious as to place them far, far above either my praise or censure.

I was

I was going to mention a man of worth, whom I have the honour to call friend, the Laird of Craigdarroch; but I have spoken to the landlord of the King's-arms inn here, to have, at the next county-meeting, a large ewe-milk cheese on the table, for the benefit of the Dumfriesshire whigs, to enable them to digest the Duke of Queensberry's late political conduct.

I have just this moment an opportunity of a private hand to Edinburgh, as perhaps you would not digest double postage.

No.

No. LIII.

To Mrs. DUNLOP.

Mauchline, 2nd August, 1788.

HONOURED MADAM,

Your kind letter welcomed me, yesternight, to Ayrshire. I am indeed seriously angry with you at the *quantum* of your *luck-penny*; but, vexed and hurt as I was, I could not help laughing very heartily at the noble lord's apology for the missed napkin.

I would write you from Nithsdale, and give you my direction there, but I have scarce an opportunity of calling at a post-office once in a fortnight. I am six miles from Dumfries, am scarcely ever in it myself, and, as yet, have little acquaintance in the neighbourhood. Besides, I am now very busy on my farm, building a dwelling-house; as at present I am almost an evangelical man in Nithsdale, for I have scarce " where to lay my head."

There are some passages in your last that brought tears in my eyes. " The heart knoweth its own sorrows, and a stranger intermeddleth not therewith." The repository of these " sorrows of the heart," is a kind of *sanctum sanctorum:* and 'tis only a chosen friend, and that too at particular sacred times, who dares enter into them.

> " Heaven oft tears the bosom-chords
> That nature finest strung."

You will excuse this quotation for the sake of the author. Instead of entering on this subject farther, I shall transcribe you a few lines I wrote in a hermitage belonging to a gentleman in my Nithsdale neighbourhood. They are almost the only favours the muses have conferred on me in that country.

> Thou whom chance may hither lead,
> Be thou clad in russet weed,
> Be thou deckt in silken stole,
> 'Grave these maxims on thy soul.
>
> Life is but a day at most,
> Sprung from night, in darkness lost:
> Hope not sunshine every hour:
> Fear not clouds will ever lour.

Happiness is but a name,
Make content and ease thy aim.
Ambition is a meteor-gleam:
Fame, an idle restless dream:
Peace, the tenderest flow'r of spring:
Pleasures, insects on the wing.
Those that sip the dew alone,
Make the butterflies thy own;
Those that would the bloom devour,
Crush the locusts, save the flower.
For the future be prepar'd,
Guard wherever thou canst guard;
But thy utmost duly done,
Welcome what thou canst not shun.
Follies past give thou to air,
Make their *consequence* thy care:
Keep the name of man in mind,
And dishonour not thy kind.
Reverence with lowly heart
Him whose wond'rous work thou art;
Keep his goodness still in view,
Thy trust and thy example too.
Stranger, go! heaven be thy guide!
Quod the Beadsman of Nith-side.

Since I am in the way of transcribing, the following were the production of yesterday as I jogged through the wild hills of New Cumnock. I intend inserting them, or something like them, in an epistle I am going to write to the gentleman on whose friendship my excise-hopes depend, Mr. Graham of Fintry, one of

the

the worthiest and most accomplished gentlemen, not only of this country, but, I will dare to say it, of this age. The following are just the first crude thoughts " unhousel'd, unanointed, unanneal'd."

* * * * * * *

Pity the tuneful muses' helpless train;
Weak, timid landsmen on life's stormy main:
The world were blest, did bliss on them depend;
Ah, that " the friendly e'er should want a friend!"
The little fate bestows they share as soon;
Unlike sage, proverb'd, wisdom's hard-wrung boon.
Let prudence number o'er each sturdy son
Who life and wisdom at one race begun;
Who feel by reason, and who give by rule;
(Instinct's a brute, and sentiment a fool!)
Who make poor *will do* wait upon *I should*;
We own they're prudent, but who owns they're good?

Ye wise ones, hence! ye hurt the social eye!
God's image rudely etch'd on base alloy!
But come * * * * * * *

Here the muse left me. I am astonished at what you tell me of Anthony's writing me. I never received it. Poor fellow! you vex me much by telling me that he is unfortunate. I shall be in Ayrshire ten days from this date. I have just room for an old Roman farewel!

No. LIV.

TO THE SAME.

Mauchline, 10*th August,* 1788.

MY MUCH HONOURED FRIEND,

Yours of the 24th June is before me. I found it, as well as another valued friend—my wife, waiting to welcome me to Ayrshire: I met both with the sincerest pleasure.

When I write you, Madam, I do not sit down to answer every paragraph of yours, by echoing every sentiment, like the faithful commons of Great Britain in Parliament assembled, answering a speech from the best of kings! I express myself in the fulness of my heart, and may perhaps be guilty of neglecting some of your kind inquiries; but not from your very odd reason, that I do not read your letters. All your epistles for several months have cost me nothing,

nothing, except a swelling throb of gratitude, or a deep-felt sentiment of veneration.

Mrs. Burns, Madam, is the identical woman

* * * * * * *

When she first found herself " as women wish to be who love their lords," as I loved her nearly to distraction, we took steps for a private marriage. Her parents got the hint; and not only forbade me her company and the house, but, on my rumoured West-Indian voyage, got a warrant to put me in jail till I should find security in my about-to-be paternal relation. You know my lucky reverse of fortune. On my eclatant return to Mauchline, I was made very welcome to visit my girl. The usual consequences began to betray her; and as I was at that time laid up a cripple in Edinburgh, she was turned, literally turned out of doors: and I wrote to a friend to shelter her till my return, when our marriage was declared. Her happiness or misery were in my hands; and who could trifle with such a deposit?

* * * * * * *

I can easily *fancy* a more agreeable companion for my journey of life, but, upon my honour, I have never *seen* the individual instance.

* * * * * * *

Circumstanced

Circumstanced as I am, I could never have got a female partner for life, who could have entered into my favourite studies, relished my favourite authors, &c. without probably entailing on me, at the same time, expensive living, fantastic caprice, perhaps apish affectation, with all the other blessed boarding-school acquirements, which *(pardonnez moi, Madame)* are sometimes to be found among females of the upper ranks, but almost universally pervade the misses of the would-be gentry.

* * * * * *

I like your way in your church-yard lucubrations. Thoughts that are the spontaneous result of accidental situations, either respecting health, place, or company, have often a strength, and always an originality, that would in vain be looked for in fancied circumstances and studied paragraphs. For me, I have often thought of keeping a letter, *in progression*, by me, to send you when the sheet was written out. Now I talk of sheets, I must tell you, my reason for writing to you on paper of this kind, is my pruriency of writing to you at large. A page of post is on such a dis-social, narrow-minded scale, that I cannot abide it; and double letters, at least in my miscellaneous reverie manner, are a monstrous tax in a close correspondence.

No. LV.

No. LV.

TO THE SAME.

Ellisland, 16*th August,* 1788.

I am in a fine disposition, my honoured friend, to send you an elegiac epistle; and want only genius to make it quite Shenstonian.

" Why droops my heart with fancied woes forlorn?
Why sinks my soul beneath each wintry sky?"

* * * * * * *

My increasing cares in this, as yet, strange country—gloomy conjectures in the dark vista of futurity—consciousness of my own inability for the struggle of the world—my broadened mark to misfortune in a wife and children:—I could indulge these reflections, till my humour should ferment into the most acid chagrin, that would corrode the very thread of life.

To counterwork these baneful feelings, I have

have sat down to write to you; as I declare, upon my soul, I always find *that* the most sovereign balm for my wounded spirit.

I was yesterday at Mr. ———'s to dinner, for the first time. My reception was quite to my mind: from the lady of the house, quite flattering. She sometimes hits on a couplet or two, *impromptu*. She repeated one or two to the admiration of all present. My suffrage as a professional man, was expected: I for once went agonizing over the belly of my conscience. Pardon me, ye, my adored household gods—Independence of spirit, and Integrity of soul! In the course of conversation, *Johnson's Musical Museum*, a collection of Scottish songs with the music, was talked of. We got a song on the harpsichord, beginning,

" Raving winds around her blowing."*

The air was much admired: the lady of the house asked me whose were the words; " Mine, Madam—they are indeed my very best verses;" she took not the smallest notice of them! The old Scottish proverb says well, " king's caff is better than ither folk's corn." I was going to
make

---

* *See vol.* iv. *p.* 277.

make a New Testament quotation about "casting pearls;" but that would be too virulent, for the lady is actually a woman of sense and taste.

* * * * * *

After all that has been said on the other side of the question, man is by no means a happy creature. I do not speak of the selected few, favoured by partial heaven; whose souls are tuned to gladness amid riches and honours, and prudence and wisdom. I speak of the neglected many, whose nerves, whose sinews, whose days are sold to the minions of fortune.

If I thought you had never seen it, I would transcribe for you a stanza of an old Scottish ballad, called *The life and age of man*; beginning thus:

" 'Twas in the sixteenth hunder year
  Of God and fifty-three,
Frae Christ was born, that bought us dear,
  As writings testifie."

I had an old grand-uncle, with whom my mother lived a while in her girlish years; the good old man, for such he was, was long blind ere he died, during which time, his highest enjoyment was to sit down and cry, while my mother

mother would sing the simple old song of *The life and age of man.*

It is this way of thinking, it is these melancholy truths, that make religion so precious to the poor miserable children of men—if it is a mere phanton, existing only in the heated imagination of enthusiasm,

" What truth on earth so precious as the lie ?"

My idle reasonings sometimes make me a little sceptical, but the necessities of my heart always give the cold philosophisings the lie. Who looks for the heart weaned from earth; the soul affianced to her God; the correspondence fixed with heaven; the pious supplication and devout thanksgiving, constant as the vicissitudes of even and morn; who thinks to meet with these in the court, the palace, in the glare of public life? No: to find them in their precious importance and divine efficacy, we must search among the obscure recesses of disappointment, affliction, poverty, and distress.

I am sure, dear Madam, you are now *more* than pleased with the *length* of my letters. I return to Ayrshire middle of next week: and it quickens my pace to think that there will be a letter from you waiting me there. I must be here again very soon for my harvest.

No.

No. LVI.

To R. GRAHAM, *of* FINTRY, Esq.

Sir,

When I had the honour of being introduced to you at Athole-house, I did not think so soon of asking a favour of you. When Lear, in Shakespeare, asks old Kent why he wished to be in his service, he answers, "Because you have that in your face which I could like to call master." For some such reason, Sir, do I now solicit your patronage. You know, I dare say, of an application I lately made to your Board to be admitted an officer of excise. I have, according to form, been examined by a supervisor, and to-day I gave in his certificate, with a request for an order for instructions. In this affair, if I succeed, I am afraid I shall but too much need a patronizing friend. Propriety of conduct as a man, and fidelity and attention as an officer, I dare engage for; but with any thing like business, except manual labour, I am totally unacquainted.

* * * * * *

I had

I had intended to have closed my late appearance on the stage of life in the character of a country farmer; but, after discharging some filial and fraternal claims, I find I could only fight for existence in that miserable manner, which I have lived to see throw a venerable parent into the jaws of a jail; whence death, the poor man's last and often best friend, rescued him.

I know, Sir, that to need your goodness is to have a claim on it: may I therefore beg your patronage to forward me in this affair, till I be appointed to a division, where, by the help of rigid œconomy, I will try to support that independence so dear to my soul, but which has been too often so distant from my situation.

. . . .

WHEN Nature her great master-piece design'd,
And fram'd her last, best work, the human mind,
Her eye intent on all the mazy plan,
She form'd of various parts the various man.

Then first she calls the useful many forth;
Plain plodding industry, and sober worth:
Thence peasants, farmers, native sons of earth,
And merchandise' whole genus take their birth:
Each

Each prudent cit a warm existence finds,
And all mechanics' many-apron'd kinds.
Some other rarer sorts are wanted yet,
The lead and buoy are needful to the net:
The *caput mortuum* of gross desires
Makes a material for mere knights and squires;
The martial phosphorus is taught to flow,
She kneads the lumpish philosophic dough,
Then marks th' unyielding mass with grave designs,
Law, physics, politics, and deep divines:
Last, she sublimes th' Aurora of the poles,
The flashing elements of female souls.

  The order'd system fair before her stood,
Nature, well-pleas'd, pronounc'd it very good;
But ere she gave creating labour o'er,
Half-jest, she try'd one curious labour more.
Some spumy, fiery, *ignis fatuus* matter;
Such as the slightest breath of air might scatter;
With arch-alacrity and conscious glee
(Nature may have her whim as well as we,
Her Hogarth-art perhaps she meant to show it)
She forms the thing, and christens it—a poet.
Creature, tho' oft the prey of care and sorrow,
When blest to-day unmindful of to-morrow.
A being form'd t' amuse his graver friends,
Admir'd and prais'd— and there the homage ends:
A mortal quite unfit for Fortune's strife,
Yet oft the sport of all the ills of life;
Prone to enjoy each pleasure riches give,
Yet haply, wanting wherewithal to live;
Longing to wipe each tear, to heal each groan,
Yet frequent all unheeded in his own.

                                                But

But honest Nature is not quite a Turk,
She laugh'd at first, then felt for her poor work.
Pitying the propless climber of mankind,
She cast about a *standard tree* to find;
And, to support his helpless woodbine state,
Attach'd him to the *generous truly great*,
A title, and the only one I claim,
To lay strong hold for help on bounteous Graham.

Pity the tuneful muses' hapless train,
Weak, timid landsmen on life's stormy main!
Their hearts no selfish stern absorbent stuff,
That never gives—tho' humbly takes enough;
The little fate allows, they share as soon,
Unlike sage, proverb'd, wisdom's hard-wrung boon.
The world were blest did bliss on them depend,
Ah, that " the friendly e'er should want a friend!"
Let prudence number o'er each sturdy son,
Who life and wisdom at one race begun,
Who feel by reason, and who give by rule,
(Instinct's a brute and sentiment a fool!)
Who make poor *will do* wait upon *I should*—
We own they're prudent, but who feels they're good?
Ye wise ones, hence! ye hurt the social eye!
God's image rudely etch'd on base alloy!
But come ye who the godlike pleasure know,
Heaven's attribute distinguish'd—to bestow!
Whose arms of love would grasp the human race:
Come *thou* who giv'st with all a courtier's grace:
Friend of my life, true patron of my rhymes!
Prop of my dearest hopes for future times.
Why shrinks my soul half-blushing, half-afraid,
Backward, abash'd to ask thy friendly aid?

I know

I know my need, I know thy giving hand,
I crave thy friendship at thy kind command;
But there are such who court the tuneful nine—
Heavens! should the branded character be mine!
Whose verse in manhood's pride sublimely flows,
Yet vilest reptiles in their begging prose.
Mark, how their lofty independent spirit
Soars on the spurning wing of injur'd merit!
Seek not the proofs in private life to find;
Pity the best of words should be but wind!
So, to heaven's gates the lark's shrill song ascends,
But groveling on the earth the carol ends.
In all the clam'rous cry of starving want,
They dun benevolence with shameless front;
Oblige them, patronize their tinsel lays,
They persecute you all your future days!
Ere my poor soul such deep damnation stain,
My horny fist assume the plough again;
The pie-ball'd jacket let me patch once more;
On eighteen pence a week I've liv'd before.
Though, thanks to Heaven, I dare even that last shift,
I trust meantime my boon is in thy gift;
That plac'd by thee upon the wish'd-for height,
Where, man and nature fairer in her sight,
My muse may imp her wing for some sublimer flight.*

No.

---

* This is our Poet's first epistle to Graham of Fintry. It is not equal to the second, printed vol. iii. p. 317; but it contains too much of the characteristic vigour of its author to be suppressed. A little more knowledge of natural history, or of chemistry, was wanted to enable him to execute the original conception correctly.   E.

No. LVII.

To Mr. PETER HILL.

―――

Mauchline, 1st October, 1788.

I HAVE been here in this country about three days, and all that time my chief reading has been the " Address to Lochlomond," you were so obliging as to send to me. Were I impannelled one of the author's jury to determine his criminality respecting the sin of poesy, my verdict should be " guilty! A poet of nature's making." It is an excellent method for improvement, and what I believe every poet does; to place some favourite classic author, in his own walks of study and composition, before him as a model. Though your author had not mentioned the name, I could have, at half a glance, guessed his model to be, Thomson. Will my brother-poet forgive me, if I venture to hint, that his imitation of that immortal bard is is, in two or three places, rather more servile than such a genius as his required.—*e. g.*

> To soothe the madding passions all to peace.
> ADDRESS.

> To soothe the throbbing passions into peace.
> THOMSON.

I think the *Address* is, in simplicity, harmony, and elegance of versification, fully equal to the *Seasons*. Like Thomson, too, he has looked into nature for himself: you meet with no copied description. One particular criticism I made at first reading; in no one instance has he said too much. He never flags in his progress, but, like a true poet of Nature's making, kindles in his course. His beginning is simple and modest, as if distrustful of the strength of his pinion; only, I do not altogether like—

> " Truth,
> The soul of every song that's nobly great."

Fiction is the soul of many a song that is nobly great. Perhaps I am wrong: this may be but a prose-criticism. Is not the phrase, in *line* 7, page 6, " Great lake," too much vulgarized by every-day language, for so sublime a poem?

"Great mass of waters, theme for nobler song,"

is perhaps no emendation. His enumeration of a comparison with other lakes is at once harmonious and poetic. Every reader's ideas must sweep the

"Winding margin of an hundred miles."

The perspective that follows mountains blue—the imprisoned billows beating in vain—the wooded isles—the digression on the yew-tree—"Ben-Lomond's lofty cloud-envelop'd head," &c. are beautiful. A thunder-storm is a subject which has been often tried; yet our poet, in his grand picture, has interjected a circumstance, so far as I know, entirely original:

"The gloom
Deep-seam'd with frequent streaks of moving fire."

In his preface to the Storm, "The glens, how dark between!" is noble highland landscape! The "rain ploughing the red mould," too, is beautifully fancied. Ben-Lomond's "lofty pathless top," is a good expression; and the surrounding view from it is truly great; the

"Silver mist
Beneath the beaming sun,"

is well described; and here he has contrived to enliven

enliven his poem with a little of that passion which bids fair, I think, to usurp the modern muses altogether. I know not how far this episode is a beauty upon the whole; but the swain's wish to carry " some faint idea of the vision bright," to entertain her, " partial listening ear," is a pretty thought. But, in my opinion, the most beautiful passages in the whole poem are the fowls crowding, in wintry frosts, to Loch-Lomond's " hospitable flood;" their wheeling round, their lighting, mixing, diving, &c.; and the glorious description of the sportsman. This last is equal to any thing in the *Seasons*. The idea of " the floating tribes distant seen, far glistering to the moon," provoking his eye as he is obliged to leave them, is a noble ray of poetic genius. " The howling winds," the " hideous roar" of " the white cascades," are all in the same style.

I forget that, while I am thus holding forth, with the heedless warmth of an enthusiast, I am perhaps tiring you with nonsense. I must, however mention, that the last verse of the sixteenth page is one of the most elegant compliments I have ever seen. I must likewise notice that beautiful paragraph, beginning, " The gleaming lake," &c. I dare not go into the particular beauties of the two last paragraphs, but they are admirably fine, and truly Ossianic.

I must beg your pardon for this lengthened scrawl. I had no idea of it when I began—I should like to know who the author is; but, whoever he be, please present him with my grateful thanks for the entertainment he has afforded me.*

A friend of mine desired me to commission for him two books, *Letters on the Religion essential to Man*, a book you sent me before; and, *The World unmasked, or the Philosopher the greatest Cheat*. Send me them by the first opportunity. The *Bible* you sent me is truly elegant: I only wish it had been in two volumes.

No.

---

* The poem, entitled *An Address to Loch-Lomond*, is said to be written by a gentleman, now one of the Masters of the High-school at Edinburgh, and the same who translated the beautiful story of the *Paria*, as published in the *Bee* of Dr. Anderson.   E.

No. LVIII.

To Mrs. DUNLOP, *at* MOREHAM MAINS.

Mauchline, 13th Nov. 1788.

MADAM,

I HAD the very great pleasure of dining at Dunlop yesterday. Men are said to flatter women because they are weak; if it is so, poets must be weaker still; for Misses R. and K., and Miss G. M'K., with their flattering attentions and artful compliments, absolutely turned my head. I own they did not lard me over as many a poet does his patron * * * * * * * * * * but they so intoxicated me with their sly insinuations and delicate innuendoes of compliment, that if it had not been for a lucky recollection, how much additional weight and lustre your good opinion and friendship must give me in that circle, I had certainly looked upon myself as a person of no small consequence. I dare not say one word how much

I was

I was charmed with the Major's friendly welcome, elegant manner, and acute remark, lest I should be thought to balance my orientalisms of applause over against the finest quey* in Ayrshire, which he made me a present of to help and adorn my farm-stock. As it was on Hallowday, I am determined annually, as that day returns, to decorate her horns with an ode of gratitude to the family of Dunlop.

* * * * * * *

So soon as I know of your arrival at Dunlop, I will take the first conveniency to dedicate a day, or perhaps two, to you and friendship, under the guarantee of the Major's hospitality. There will be soon three score and ten miles of permanent distance between us: and now that your friendship and friendly correspondence is entwisted with the heart-strings of my enjoyment of life, I must indulge myself in a happy day of "The feast of reason and the flow of soul."

---

* Heifer.

No. LIX.

To * * * * *.

Nov. 8, 1788.

SIR,

NOTWITHSTANDING the opprobrious epithets with which some of our philosophers and gloomy sectaries have branded our nature —the principle of universal selfishness, the proneness to all evil, they have given us; still the detestation in which inhumanity to the distressed, or insolence to the fallen, are held by all mankind, shews that they are not natives of the human heart. Even the unhappy partner of our kind, who is undone, the bitter consequence of his follies or his crimes;—who but sympathizes with the miseries of this ruined profligate brother? we forget the injuries, and feel for the man.

I went, last Wednesday, to my parish-church, most cordially to join in grateful acknowledgments to the AUTHOR OF ALL GOOD,

for

for the consequent blessings of the glorious Revolution. To that auspicious event we owe no less than our liberties, civil and religious; to it we are likewise indebted for the present Royal Family, the ruling features of whose administration have ever been, mildness to the subject, and tenderness of his rights.

Bred and educated in revolution principles, the principles of reason and common sense, it could not be any silly political prejudice which made my heart revolt at the harsh, abusive manner in which the reverend gentleman mentioned the house of Stewart, and which, I am afraid, was too much the language of the day. We may rejoice sufficiently in our deliverance from past evils, without cruelly raking up the ashes of those whose misfortune it was, perhaps as much as their crime, to be the authors of those evils; and we may bless GOD for all his goodness to us as a nation, without, at the same time, cursing a few ruined, powerless exiles, who only harboured ideas, and made attempts, that most of us would have done had we been in their situation.

" The bloody and tyrannical House of Stewart," may be said with propriety and justice, when compared with the present royal family,

mily, and the sentiments of our days; but is there no allowance to be made for the manners of the times? Were the royal contemporaries of the Stewarts more attentive to their subjects' rights? Might not the epithets of "bloody and tyrannical" be with at least equal justice, applied to the House of Tudor, of York, or any other of their predecessors?

The simple state of the case, Sir, seems to be this:—At that period, the science of government, the knowledge of the true relation between king and subject, was, like other sciences and other knowledge, just in its infancy, emerging from dark ages of ignorance and barbarity.

The Stewarts only contended for prerogatives which they knew their predecessors enjoyed, and which they saw their contemporaries enjoying; but these prerogatives were inimical to the happiness of a nation and the rights of subjects.

In this contest between prince and people, the consequence of that light of science which had lately dawned over Europe, the monarch of France, for example, was victorious over the struggling liberties of his people: with us, luckily, the monarch failed, and his unwarrantable

able pretensions fell a sacrifice to our rights and happiness. Whether it was owing to the wisdom of leading individuals, or to the justling of parties, I cannot pretend to determine; but likewise, happily for us, the kingly power was shifted into another branch of the family, who, as they owed the throne solely to the call of a free people, could claim nothing inconsistent with the covenanted terms which placed them there.

The Stewarts have been condemned and laughed at for the folly and impracticability of their attempts in 1715 and 1745. That they failed, I bless God; but cannot join in the ridicule against them. Who does not know that the abilities or defects of leaders and commanders are often hidden until put to the touchstone of exigency; and that there is a caprice of fortune, an omnipotence in particular accidents and conjunctures of circumstances, which exalt us as heroes, or brand us as madmen, just as they are for or against us?

Man, Mr. Publisher, is a strange, weak, inconsistent being: who would believe, Sir, that in this our Augustan age of liberality and refinement, while we seem so justly sensible and jealous of our rights and liberties, and animated

with

with such indignation against the very memory of those who would have subverted them—that a certain people under our national protection, should complain, not against our monarch and a few favourite advisers, but against our WHOLE LEGISLATIVE BODY, for similar oppression, and almost in the very same terms, as our forefathers did of the House of Stewart! I will not, I cannot enter into the merits of the cause, but I dare say the American Congress, in 1776, will be allowed to be as able and as enlightened as the English Convention was in 1688; and that their posterity will celebrate the centenary of their deliverance from us, as duly and sincerely as we do ours from the oppressive measures of the wrong-headed house of Stewart.

To conclude, Sir: let every man who has a tear for the many miseries incident to humanity, feel for a family illustrious as any in Europe, and unfortunate beyond historic precedent; and let every Briton, (and particularly every Scotsman) who ever looked with reverential pity on the dotage of a parent, cast a veil over the fatal mistakes of the kings of his forefathers.*

No.

---

* This letter was sent to the publisher of some newspaper, probably the publisher of the *Edinburgh Evening Courant*. E.

No. LX.

To Mrs. DUNLOP.

Ellisland, 17th Dec. 1788.

MY DEAR HONOURED FRIEND,

Yours, dated Edinburgh, which I have just read, makes me very unhappy. "Almost blind, and wholly deaf," are melancholy news of human nature; but when told of a much-loved and honoured friend, they carry misery in the sound. Goodness on your part, and gratitude on mine, began a tie, which has gradually and strongly entwisted itself among the dearest cords of my bosom; and I tremble at the omens of your late and present ailing habit and shattered health. You miscalculate matters widely, when you forbid my waiting on you, lest it should hurt my worldly concerns. My small scale of farming is exceedingly more simple and easy than what you have lately seen at Moreham Mains. But be that as it may, the heart of the man, and the fancy of the poet,

are

are the two grand considerations for which I live: if miry ridges and dirty dunghills are to engross the best part of the functions of my soul immortal, I had better been a rook or a magpie at once, and then I should not have been plagued with any idea superior to breaking of clods, and picking up grubs: not to mention barn-door cocks or mallards, creatures with which I could almost exchange lives at any time.—If you continue so deaf, I am afraid a visit will be of no great pleasure to either of us; but if I hear you are got so well again as to be able to relish conversation, look you to it, Madam, for I will make my threatenings good. I am to be at the new-year-day fair of Ayr, and, by all that is sacred in the word Friend! I *will* come and see you.

* * * * * * *

Your meeting, which you so well describe, with your old schoolfellow and friend, was truly interesting. Out upon the ways of the world!—They spoil these " social offsprings of the heart." Two veterans of the " men of the world" would have met with little more heart-workings than two old hacks worn out on the road. Apropos, is not the Scotch phrase; " Auld lang syne," exceedingly expressive.—There is an old song and tune which has often
thrilled

thrilled through my soul. You know I am an enthusiast in old Scotch songs: I shall give you the verses on the other sheet, as I suppose Mr. Kerr will save you the postage.*

Light be the turf on the breast of the Heaven-inspired poet who composed this glorious fragment! There is more of the fire of native genius in it than half a dozen of modern English Bacchanalians. Now I am on my hobby horse, I cannot help inserting two other old stanzas which please me mightily.

> Go fetch to me a pint o' wine,
>   An' fill it in a silver tassie;
> That I may drink before I go,
>   A service to my bonnie lassie;
> The boat rocks at the pier o' Leith;
>   Fu' loud the wind blaws frae the ferry;
> The ship rides by the Berwick-law,
>   And I maun lea'e my bonnie Mary.
>
> The trumpets sound, the banners fly,
>   The glittering spears are ranked ready;
> The shouts o' war are heard afar,
>   The battle closes thick and bloody;
> But it's not the roar o' sea or shore
>   Wad make me langer wish to tarry;
> Nor shouts o' war that's heard afar,
>   It's leaving thee, my bonnie Mary.

No.

---

* Here follows the song of *Auld lang Syne*, as printed vol. iv. p. 122.   E.

No. LXI.

To MISS DAVIES.

(A young Lady who had heard he had been making a Ballad on her, inclosing that Ballad.)

December, 1788.

MADAM,

I UNDERSTAND my very worthy neighbour, Mr. Riddel, has informed you that I have made you the subject of some verses. There is something so provoking in the idea of being the burden of a ballad, that I do not think Job or Moses, though such patterns of patience and meekness, could have resisted the curiosity to know what that ballad was: so my worthy friend has done me a mischief, which, I dare say, he never intended; and reduced me to the unfortunate alternative of leaving your curiosity ungratified, or else disgusting you with foolish

foolish verses, the unfinished production of a random moment, and never meant to have met your ear. I have heard or read somewhere of a gentleman, who had some genius, much eccentricity, and very considerable dexterity with his pencil. In the accidental group of life into which one is thrown, wherever this gentleman met with a character in a more than ordinary degree congenial to his heart, he used to steal a sketch of the face, merely, as he said, as a *nota bene* to point out the agreeable recollection to his memory. What this gentleman's pencil was to him, is my muse to me; and the verses I do myself the honour to send you are a *memento* exactly of the same kind that he indulged in.

It may be more owing to the fastidiousness of my caprice than the delicacy of my taste, but I am so often tired, disgusted, and hurt with the insipidity, affectation, and pride of mankind, that when I meet with a person " after my own heart," I positively feel what an orthodox protestant would call a species of idolatry, which acts on my fancy like inspiration; and I can no more desist rhyming on the impulse, than an Eolian harp can refuse its tones to the streaming air. A distich or two would be the consequence, though the object which hit my fancy were grey-bearded age:
but

but where my theme is youth and beauty, a young lady whose personal charms, wit, and sentiment, are equally striking and unaffected, by heavens! though I had lived threescore years a married man, and threescore years before I was a married man, my imagination would hallow the very idea; and I am truly sorry that the inclosed stanzas have done such poor justice to such a subject.

No. LXII.

From Mr. G. BURNS.

Mossgiel, 1st *Jan*. 1789.

DEAR BROTHER,

I HAVE just finished my new-year's-day breakfast in the usual form, which naturally makes me call to mind the days of former years, and the society in which we used to begin them; and when I look at our family vicissitudes, " thro' the dark postern of time long elapsed," I cannot help remarking to you, my dear brother, how good the GOD of SEASONS is to us, and that, however some clouds may seem to lour over the portion of time before us, we have great reason to hope that all will turn out well.

Your mother and sisters, with Robert the second, join me in the compliments of the season to you and Mrs. Burns, and beg you will remember us in the same manner to William, the first time you see him.

I am, dear brother, yours,
GILBERT BURNS.

No. LXIII.

To Mrs. DUNLOP.

Ellisland, New-Year-Day Morning, 1789.

This, dear Madam, is a morning of wishes; and would to God that I came under the apostle James's description!—*the prayer of a righteous man availeth much.* In that case, Madam, you should welcome in a year full of blessings: every thing that obstructs or disturbs tranquillity and self-enjoyment, should be removed, and every pleasure that frail humanity can taste should be yours. I own myself so little a presbyterian, that I approve of set times and seasons of more than ordinary acts of devotion, for breaking in on that habituated routine of life and thought which is so apt to reduce our existence to a kind of instinct, or even sometimes, and with some minds, to a state very little superior to mere machinery.

This day; the first Sunday of May; a breezy, blue-skyed noon some time about the beginning, and a hoary morning and calm sunny day about the end, of autumn;—these, time out of mind, have been with me a kind of holiday.

* * * * * * *

I believe I owe this to that glorious paper in the Spectator, " The Vision of Mirza;" a piece that struck my young fancy before I was capable of fixing an idea to a word of three syllables, " On the 5th day of the moon, which, according to the custom of my fore-fathers, I always *keep holy*, after having washed myself, and offered up my morning devotions, I ascended the high hill of Bagdat, in order to pass the rest of the day in meditation and prayer."

We know nothing, or next to nothing, of the substance or structure of our souls, so cannot account for those seeming caprices in them, that one should be particularly pleased with this thing, or struck with that, which, on minds of a different cast, makes no extraordinary impression. I have some favourite flowers in spring, among which are the mountain-daisy, the hare-bell, the fox-glove, the wild-brier rose, the

the budding birch, and the hoary hawthorn, that I view and hang over with particular delight. I never hear the loud, solitary whistle of the curlew in a summer noon, or the wild mixing cadence of a troop of grey plover in an autumnal morning, without feeling an elevation of soul like the enthusiasm of devotion or poetry. Tell me, my dear friend, to what can this be owing? Are we a piece of machinery, which, like the Eolian harp, passive, takes the impression of the passing accident? Or do these workings argue something within us above the trodden clod? I own myself partial to such proofs of those awful and important realities—a GOD that made all things—man's immaterial and immortal nature—and a world of weal or woe beyond death and the grave.

* * * * * * * *

No.

No. LXIV.

To Dr. MOORE.

Ellisland, near Dumfries, 4*th Jan.* 1789.

SIR,

As often as I think of writing to you, which has been three or four times every week these six months, it gives me something so like the idea of an ordinary-sized statue offering at a conversation with the Rhodian colossus, that my mind misgives me, and the affair always miscarries somewhere between purpose and resolve. I have, at last, got some business with you, and business-letters are written by the style-book. I say my business is with you, Sir, for you never had any with me, except the business that benevolence has in the mansion of poverty.

The character and employment of a poet were formerly my pleasure, but are now my pride.

pride. I know that a very great deal of my late eclat was owing to the singularity of my situation, and the honest prejudice of Scotsmen; but still, as I said in the preface to my first edition, I do look upon myself as having some pretensions from Nature to the poetic character. I have not a doubt but the knack, the aptitude, to learn the Muses' trade, is a gift bestowed by him, "who forms the secret bias of the soul;"—but I as firmly believe, that *excellence* in the profession is the fruit of industry, labour, attention, and pains. At least I am resolved to try my doctrine by the test of experience. Another appearance from the press I put off to a very distant day, a day that may never arrive—but poesy I am determined to prosecute with all my vigour. Nature has given very few, if any, of the profession, the talents of shining in every species of composition. I shall try (for until trial it is impossible to know) whether she has qualified me to shine in any one. The worst of it is, by the time one has finished a piece, it has been so often viewed and reviewed before the mental eye, that one loses, in a good measure, the powers of critical discrimination. Here the best criterion I know is a friend—not only of abilities to judge, but with good-nature enough, like a prudent teacher with a young learner, to

praise

praise perhaps a little more than is exactly just, lest the thin-skinned animal fall into that most deplorable of all poetic diseases—heart-breaking despondency of himself. Dare I, Sir, already immensely indebted to your goodness, ask the additional obligation of your being that friend to me? I inclose you an essay of mine in a walk of poesy to me entirely new; I mean the epistle addressed to R. G. Esq. or Robert Graham, of Fintry, Esq. a gentleman of uncommon worth, to whom I lie under very great obligations. The story of the poem, like most of my poems, is connected with my own story; and to give you the one I must give you something of the other. I cannot boast of———

* * * * * * * *

I believe I shall, in whole, 100l. copy-right included, clear about 400l. some little odds; and even part of this depends upon what the gentleman has yet to settle with me. I give you this information, because you did me the honour to interest yourself much in my welfare.

* * * * * * *

To give the rest of my story in brief, I have married " my Jean," and taken a farm: with the first step I have every day more and more reason

son to be satisfied; with the last, it is rather the reverse. I have a younger brother, who supports my aged mother; another still younger brother, and three sisters, in a farm. On my last return from Edinburgh, it cost me about 180l. to save them from ruin. Not that I have lost so much—I only interposed between my brother and his impending fate by the loan of so much. I give myself no airs on this, for it was mere selfishness on my part: I was conscious that the wrong scale of the balance was pretty heavily charged; and I thought that throwing a little filial piety, and fraternal affection, into the scale in my favour, might help to smooth matters at the *grand reckoning*. There is still one thing would make my circumstances quite easy: I have an excise-officer's commission, and I live in the midst of a country division. My request to Mr. Graham, who is one of the commissioners of excise, was, if in his power, to procure me that division. If I were very sanguine. I might hope that some of my great patrons might procure me a treasury warrant for supervisor, surveyor-general, &c.

* * * * * * *

Thus secure of a livelihood, " to thee, sweet poetry, delightful maid!" I would consecrate my future days.

No.

No. LXV.

To Professor D. STEWART.

Ellisland, near Dumfries, 20*th Jan.* 1789.

SIR,

The inclosed sealed packet I sent to Edinburgh a few days after I had the happiness of meeting you in Ayrshire, but you were gone for the Continent. I have now added a few more of my productions, those for which I am indebted to the Nithsdale Muses. The piece inscribed to R. G. Esq. is a copy of verses I sent Mr. Graham, of Fintry, accompanying a request for his assistance in a matter, to me, of very great moment. To that gentleman I am already doubly indebted, for deeds of kindness of serious import to my dearest interests, done in a manner grateful to the delicate feelings of sensibility. This poem is a species of composition new to me; but I do not intend it shall be my last

last essay of the kind, as you will see by the
" Poet's progress." These fragments, if my
design succeeds, are but a small part of the intended whole. I propose it shall be the work
of my utmost exertions ripened by years: of
course I do not wish it much known. The
fragment, beginning " A little, upright, pert,
tart," &c. I have not shewn to man living,
till now I send it you. It forms the postulata,
the axioms, the definition of a character, which,
if it appear at all, shall be placed in a variety
of lights. This particular part I send you
merely as a sample of my hand at portrait-sketching; but lest idle conjecture should pretend to point out the original, please let it be
for your single, sole inspection.

Need I make any apology for this trouble
to a gentleman who has treated me with such
marked benevolence and peculiar kindness;
who has entered into my interests with so
much zeal, and on whose critical decisions I
can so fully depend? A poet as I am by trade,
these decisions to me are of the last consequence. My late transient acquaintance among
some of the mere rank and file of greatness, I
resign with ease; but to the distinguished
champions of genius and learning, I shall be
ever ambitious of being known. The native
genius

genius and accurate discernment in Mr. Stewart's critical strictures; the justness (iron justice, for he has no bowels of compassion for a poor poetic sinner) of Dr. Gregory's remarks, and the delicacy of Professor Dalzel's taste, I shall ever revere. I shall be in Edinburgh some time next month.

I have the honour to be, Sir,

Your highly obliged,

and very humble servant,

ROBERT BURNS.

No.

No. LXVI.

To Bishop GEDDES.

Ellisland, near Dumfries, 3d Feb. 1789.

VENERABLE FATHER,

As I am conscious, that wherever I am, you do me the honour to interest yourself in my welfare, it gives me pleasure to inform you that I am here at last, stationary in the serious business of life, and have now not only the retired leisure, but the hearty inclination, to attend to those great and important questions—what I am? where I am? and for what I am destined?

In that first concern, the conduct of the man, there was ever but one side on which I was habitually blameable, and there I have secured myself in the way pointed out by Nature

and

and Nature's GOD. I was sensible that, to so helpless a creature as a poor poet, a wife and family were encumberances, which a species of prudence would bid him shun; but when the alternative was, being at eternal warfare with myself, on account of habitual follies, to give them no worse name, which no general example, no licentious wit, no sophistical infidelity, would to me, ever justify, I must have been a fool to have hesitated, and a madman to have made another choice.

* * * * * * * *

In the affair of a livelihood, I think myself tolerably secure: I have good hopes of my farm; but should they fail, I have an excise commission, which, on my simple petition, will, at any time procure me bread There is a certain stigma affixed to the character of an excise officer, but I do not intend to borrow honour from any profession; and though the salary be comparatively small, it is great to any thing that the first twenty-five years of my life taught me to expect.

* * * * * * *

Thus, with a rational aim and method in life, you may easily guess, my reverend and
much-

much-honoured friend, that my characteristical trade is not forgotten. I am, if possible, more than ever an enthusiast to the Muses. I am determined to study man and nature, and in that view incessantly; and to try if the ripening and corrections of years can enable me to produce something worth preserving.

You will see in your book, which I beg your pardon for detaining so long, that I have been tuning my lyre on the banks of Nith. Some large poetic plans that are floating in my imagination, or partly put in execution, I shall impart to you when I have the pleasure of meeting with you; which, if you are then in Edinburgh, I shall have about the beginning of March.

That acquaintance, worthy Sir, with which you were pleased to honour me, you must still allow me to challenge; for with whatever unconcern I give up my transient connexion with the merely great, I cannot lose the patronizing notice of the learned and good, without the bitterest regret.

No. LXVII.

From the Rev. P. CARFRAE.

2d Jan. 1789.

SIR,

If you have lately seen Mrs. Dunlop, of Dunlop, you have certainly heard of the author of the verses which accompany this letter. He was a man highly respectable for every accomplishment and virtue which adorns the character of a man or a christian. To a great degree of literature, of taste, and poetic genius, was added an invincible modesty of temper, which prevented, in a great degree, his figuring in life, and confined the perfect knowledge of his character and talents to the small circle of his chosen friends. He was untimely taken from us, a few weeks ago, by an inflammatory fever, in the prime of life—beloved by all who enjoyed his acquaintance, and lamented by all who

who have any regard for virtue or genius. There is a woe pronounced in Scripture against the person whom all men speak well of: if ever that woe fell upon the head of mortal man, it fell upon him. He has left behind him a considerable number of compositions, chiefly poetical, sufficient, I imagine, to make a large octavo volume. In particular, two complete and regular tragedies, a farce of three acts, and some smaller poems on different subjects. It falls to my share, who have lived in the most intimate and uninterrupted friendship with him from my youth upwards, to transmit to you the verses he wrote on the publication of your incomparable poems. It is probable they were his last, as they were found in his scrutoire, folded up with the form of a letter addressed to you, and, I imagine, were only prevented from being sent by himself, by that melancholy dispensation which we still bemoan. The verses themselves I will not pretend to criticise when writing to a gentleman whom I consider as entirely qualified to judge of their merit. They are the only verses he seems to have attempted in the Scottish style; and I hesitate not to say, in general, that they will bring no dishonour on the Scottish muse;—and allow me to add, that, if it is your opinion they are not unworthy of the author, and will be no discredit to you, it is the inclination of Mr. Mylne's friends that they should be immediately published in some periodical work, to give the world a specimen of what may be expected from his performances in the poetic line, which, perhaps, will be afterwards published for the advantage of his family.

* * * * * *

I must beg the favour of a letter from you, acknowledging the receipt of this; and to be allowed to subscribe myself, with great regard,

Sir, your most obedient servant,

P. CARFRAE.

No.

No. LXVIII.

To Mrs. DUNLOP.

Ellisland, 4th March, 1789.

HERE am I, my honoured friend, returned safe from the capital. To a man who has a home, however humble or remote—if that home is like mine, the scene of domestic comfort—the bustle of Edinburgh will soon be a business of sickening disgust.

" Vain pomp and glory of this world, I hate you."

When I must skulk into a corner, lest the rattling equipage of some gaping blockhead should mangle me in the mire, I am tempted to exclaim—" What merits has he had, or what demerit have I had, in some state of pre-existence, that he is ushered into this state of being with the sceptre of rule, and the key of riches in his puny fist, and I am kicked into the world, the sport of folly, o the victim of pride?" I have read some where of a monarch, (in Spain I think it was) who was so out of humour with the Ptolemean system of astronomy, that he said, had he been of the CREATOR's council, he could have saved him a great deal of labour and absurdity. I will not defend this blasphemous speech; but often, as I have glided with humble stealth through the pomp of Princes-street, it has suggested itself to me, as an improvement on the present human figure, that a man, in proportion to his own conceit of his consequence in the world, could have pushed out the longitude of his common size, as a snail pushes out his horns, or as we draw out a perspective. This trifling alteration, not to mention the prodigious saving it would be in the tear and wear of the neck and limb-sinews of many of his majesty's liege subjects, in the way of tossing the head and tiptoe-strutting, would evidently turn out a vast advantage, in enabling us at once to adjust the ceremonials in making a bow, or making way to a great man, and that too within a second of the precise spherical angle of reverence, or an inch of the particular point of respectful distance, which the important creature itself requires; as a measuring-glance

at

at its towering altitude would determine the affair like instinct.

You are right, Madam, in your idea of poor Mylne's poem, which he has addressed to me. The piece has a good deal of merit, but it has one great fault—it is, by far, too long. Besides, my success has encouraged such a shoal of ill-spawned monsters to crawl into public notice, under the title of Scottish Poets, that the very term Scottish Poetry borders on the burlesque. When I write to Mr. Carfrae, I shall advise him rather to try one of his deceased friend's English pieces. I am prodigiously hurried with my own matters, else I would have requested a perusal of all Mylne's poetic performances; and would have offered his friends my assistance in either selecting or correcting what would be proper for the press. What it is that occupies me so much, and perhaps a little oppresses my present spirits, shall fill up a paragraph in some future letter. In the mean time, allow me to close this epistle with a few lines done by a friend of mine * * * * *. I give you them, that, as you have seen the original, you may guess whether one or two alterations I have ventured to make in them, be any real improvement.

Like

Like the fair plant that from our touch withdraws,
Shrink, mildly fearful even from applause,
Be all a mother's fondest hope can dream,
And all you are, my charming ****, seem.
Straight as the fox-glove, ere her bells disclose,
Mild as the maiden-blushing hawthorn blows,
Fair as the fairest of each lovely kind,
Your form shall be the image of your mind;
Your manners shall so true your soul express,
That all shall long to know the worth they guess;
Congenial hearts shall greet with kindred love,
And even sick'ning envy must approve.*

---

* These beautiful lines, we have reason to believe, are the production of the lady to whom this letter is addressed.   E.

No. LXIX.

To the Rev. P. CARFRAE.

1789.

REV. SIR,

 I do not recollect that I have ever felt a severer pang of shame, than on looking at the date of your obliging letter which accompanied Mr. Mylne's poem.

* * * * * *

I am much to blame: the honour Mr. Mylne has done me, greatly enhanced in its value by the endearing, though melancholy circumstance of its being the last production of his muse, deserved a better return.

I have, as you hint, thought of sending a copy of the poem to some periodical publication; but, on second thoughts, I am afraid that, in the present case, it would be an improper

per step. My success, perhaps as much accidental as merited, has brought an inundation of nonsense under the name of Scottish poetry. Subscription-bills for Scottish poems have so dunned, and daily do dun, the public, that the very name is in danger of contempt. For these reasons, if publishing any of Mr. M.'s poems in a magazine, &c. be at all prudent, in my opinion, it certainly should not be a Scottish poem. The profits of the labours of a man of genius are, I hope, as honourable as any profits whatever; and Mr. Mylne's relations are most justly entitled to that honest harvest which fate has denied himself to reap. But let the friends of Mr. Mylne's fame (among whom I crave the honour of ranking myself) always keep in eye his respectability as a man and as a poet, and take no measure that, before the world knows any thing about him, would risk his name and character, being classed with the fools of the times.

I have, Sir, some experience of publishing; and the way in which I would proceed with Mr. Mylne's poems is this: I would publish, in two or three English and Scottish public papers, any one of his English poems which should, by private judges, be thought the most excellent, and mention it, at the same time, as one

one of the productions of a Lothian farmer, of respectable character, lately deceased, whose poems his friends had it in idea to publish soon, by subscription, for the sake of his numerous family:—not in pity to that family, but in justice to what his friends think the poetic merits of the deceased; and to secure, in the most effectual manner, to those tender connexions, whose right it is, the pecuniary reward of those merits.

No. LXX.

To Dr. MOORE.

Ellisland, 23d March, 1789.

SIR,

THE gentleman who will deliver you this is a Mr. Nielson, a worthy clergyman in my neighbourhood, and a very particular acquaintance of mine. As I have troubled him with this packet, I must turn him over to your goodness, to recompense him for it in a way in which he much needs your assistance, and where you can effectually serve him:—Mr. Nielson is on his way for France, to wait on his grace of Queensberry, on some little business of a good deal of importance to him, and he wishes for your instructions respecting the most eligible mode of travelling, &c. for him, when he has crossed the channel. I should not have dared to take this liberty with you, but that I am told, by those who have the

honour

honour of your personal acquaintance, that, to be a poor honest Scotchman, is a letter of recommendation to you, and that to have it in your power to serve such a character gives you much pleasure.

* * * * * * * * *

The inclosed ode is a compliment to the memory of the late Mrs. ******, of **********. You, probably, knew her personally, an honour of which I cannot boast; but I spent my early years in her neighbourhood, and among her servants and tenants, I know that she was detested with the most heartfelt cordiality. However, in the particular part of her conduct which roused my poetic wrath, she was much less blameable. In January last, on my road to Ayrshire, I had put up at Bailie Whigham's, in Sanquhar, the only tolerable inn in the place. The frost was keen, and the grim evening and howling wind were ushering in a night of snow and drift. My horse and I were both much fatigued with the labours of the day; and just as my friend the Bailie and I were bidding defiance to the storm, over a smoking bowl, in wheels the funeral pageantry of the late great Mrs. ******, and poor I am forced to brave all the horrors of the tempestuous night, and jade

my

my horse, my young favourite horse, whom I had just christened Pegasus, twelve miles farther on, through the wildest moors and hills of Ayrshire, to New Cumnock, the next inn. The powers of poesy and prose sink under me, when I would describe what I felt. Suffice it to say, that when a good fire, at New Cumnock, had so far recovered my frozen sinews, I sat down and wrote the inclosed ode.*

I was at Edinburgh lately, and settled finally with Mr. Creech; and I must own, that, at last, he has been amicable and fair with me.

---

* The Ode inclosed is that printed in vol. iii. *p.* 303.
E.

No. LXXI.

To Mr. HILL.

———

Ellisland, 2d April, 1789.

I will make no excuses, my dear Bibliopolus, (God forgive me for murdering language!) that I have sat down to write you on this vile paper.

* * * * * * * *

It is economy, Sir; it is that cardinal virtue, prudence; so I beg you will sit down, and either compose or borrow a panegyric. If you are going to borrow, apply to

* * * * * * * *

to compose, or rather to compound, something very clever on my remarkable frugality; that I write

write to one of my most esteemed friends on this wretched paper, which was originally intended for the venal fist of some drunken exciseman, to take dirty notes in a miserable vault of an ale-cellar.

O Frugality! thou mother of ten thousand blessings—thou cook of fat beef and dainty greens!—thou manufacturer of warm Shetland hose, and comfortable surtouts!—thou old housewife, darning thy decayed stockings with thy ancient spectacles on thy aged nose!—lead me, hand me, in thy clutching palsied fist, up those heights, and through those thickets, hitherto inaccessible, and impervious to my anxious, weary feet:—not those Parnassian crags, bleak and barren, where the hungry worshippers of fame are breathless, clambering, hanging between heaven and hell; but those glittering cliffs of Potosi, where the all-sufficient, all-powerful deity, Wealth, holds his immediate court of joys and pleasures; where the sunny exposure of plenty, and the hot walls of profusion, produce those blissful fruits of luxury, exotics in this world, and natives of Paradise!—Thou withered sybil, my sage conductress, usher me into the refulgent, adored presence!—The power, splendid and potent as he now is, was once the puling nursling of thy faithful

faithful care and tender arms! Call me thy son, thy cousin, thy kinsman, or favourite, and adjure the god, by the scenes of his infant years, no longer to repulse me as a stranger, or an alien, but to favour me with his peculiar countenance and protection! He daily bestows his greatest kindnesses on the undeserving and the worthless—assure him that I bring ample documents of meritorious demerits! Pledge yourself for me, that, for the glorious cause of LUCRE, I will do any thing, be any thing—but the horse-leech of private oppression, or the vulture of public robbery!

* * * * * * *

But, to descend from heroics,

* * * * * * *

I want a Shakespeare; I want likewise an English Dictionary—Johnson's, I suppose, is best. In these, and all my prose commissions, the cheapest is always the best for me. There is a small debt of honour that I owe Mr. Robert Cleghorn, in Saughton Mills, my worthy friend, and your well-wisher. Please give him, and urge him to take it, the first time you see him, ten shillings worth of any thing you have to sell, and place it to my account.

The

The library scheme that I mentioned to you is already begun, under the direction of Captain Riddel. There is another in emulation of it going on at Closeburn, under the auspices of Mr. Monteith of Closeburn, which will be on a greater scale than ours. Capt. R. gave his infant society a great many of his old books, else I had written you on that subject; but, one of these days, I shall trouble you with a commission for " The Monkland Friendly Society:"—a copy of *The Spectator, Mirror,* and *Lounger; Man of Feeling, Man of the World, Guthrie's Geographical Grammar,* with some religious pieces, will likewise be our first order.

When I grow richer I will write to you on gilt post, to make amends for this sheet. At present every guinea has a five-guinea errand with,

My dear Sir,

Your faithful, poor, but honest friend,

R. B.

No.

No. LXXII.

To Mrs. DUNLOP.

Ellisland, 4th April, 1789.

* * * * * * *

I no sooner hit on any poetic plan or fancy, but I wish to send it to you; and if knowing and reading these give half the pleasure to you, that communicating them to you gives to me, I am satisfied.

* * * * * * * *

I have a poetic whim in my head, which I at present dedicate, or rather inscribe, to the right hon. C. J. Fox: but how long that fancy may hold, I cannot say. A few of the first lines I have just rough-sketched, as follows:

SKETCH.

How wisdom and folly meet, mix, and unite;
How virtue and vice blend their black and their white;
How genius, th' illustrious father of fiction,
Confounds rule and law, reconciles contradiction—

I sing:

I sing: If these mortals, the critics, should bustle,
I care not, not I, let the critics go whistle.

But now for a patron, whose name and whose glory
At once may illustrate and honour my story.

Thou first of our orators, first of our wits;
Yet whose parts and acquirements seem mere lucky hits;
With knowledge so vast, and with judgment so strong,
No man with the half of 'em e'er went far wrong;
With passions so potent, and fancies so bright,
No man with the half of 'em e'er went quite right;
A sorry, poor misbegot son of the muses,
For using thy name offers fifty excuses.

Good L—d, what is man! for as simple he looks,
Do but try to develope his hooks and his crooks;
With his depths and his shallows, his good and his evil,
All in all he's a problem must puzzle the devil.

On his one ruling passion Sir Pope hugely labours,
That, like the old Hebrew-walking switch, eats up its neighbours:
Mankind are his show box—a friend, would you know him?
Pull the string, ruling passion the picture will shew him.
What pity, in rearing so beauteous a system,
One trifling particular, truth, should have miss'd him;
For, in spite of his fine theoretic positions,
Mankind is a science defies definitions.

Some sort all our qualities each to its tribe,
And think human nature they truly describe;

Have

Have you found this, or t'other? there's more in the wind,
As by one drunken fellow his comrades you'll find.
But such is the flaw, or the depth of the plan,
In the make of that wonderful creature, call'd Man,
No two virtues, whatever relation they claim,
Nor even two different shades of the same,
Though like as was ever twin brother to brother,
Possessing the one shall imply you've the other.

* * * * * * * *

On the 20th current I hope to have the honour of assuring you, in person, how sincerely I am—

* * * * * * * *

No. LXXIII.

To Mr. CUNNINGHAM.

Ellisland, 4th May, 1789.

MY DEAR SIR,

Your *duty-free* favour of the 26th April I received two days ago: I will not say I perused it with pleasure; that is the cold compliment of ceremony: I perused it, Sir, with delicious satisfaction—In short, it is such a letter, that not you, nor your friend, but the legislature, by express proviso in their postage-laws, should frank. A letter informed with the soul of friendship is such an honour to human nature, that they should order it free ingress and egress to and from their bags and mails, as an encouragement and mark of distinction to super-eminent virtue.

I have just put the last hand to a little poem which I think will be something to your taste.
One

One morning lately, as I was out pretty early in the fields sowing some grass-seeds, I heard the burst of a shot from a neighbouring plantation, and presently a poor little wounded hare came crippling by me. You will guess my indignation at the inhuman fellow who could shoot a hare at this season, when they all of them have young ones. Indeed there is something in that business of destroying, for our sport, individuals in the animal creation that do not injure us materially, which I could never reconcile to my ideas of virtue.

. . . .

On seeing a Fellow wound a Hare with a Shot, April, 1789.

INHUMAN man! curse on thy barb'rous art,
  And blasted be thy murder-aiming eye,
  May never pity soothe thee with a sigh,
Nor ever pleasure glad thy cruel heart.

Go live, poor wanderer of the wood and field,
  The bitter little that of life remains;
  No more the thickening brakes or verdant plains,
To thee a home, or food, or pastime yield.

Seek, mangled innocent, some wonted form,
  That wonted form, alas! thy dying bed,
  The sheltering rushes whistling o'er thy head,
The cold earth with thy blood-stain'd bosom warm.

Perhaps a mother's anguish adds its woe;
  The playful pair croud fondly by thy side;
  Ah! helpless nurslings, who will now provide
That life a mother only can bestow?

Oft as by winding Nith, I musing, wait
  The sober eve, or hail the cheerful dawn,
  I'll miss thee sporting o'er the dewy lawn,
And curse the ruthless wretch, and mourn thy hapless
  fate.

. . . .

Let me know how you like my poem. I am doubtful whether it would not be an improvement to keep out the last stanza but one altogether.

C—— is a glorious production of the author of man. You, he, and the noble Colonel of the C—— F—— are to me

" Dear as the ruddy drops which warm my breast."

I have a good mind to make verses on you all, to the tune of " *Three guid fellows ayont the glen.*"

No.

No. LXXIV.

The poem in the preceding letter had also been sent by our Bard to Dr. Gregory for his criticism. The following is that gentleman's reply.

From Dr. GREGORY.

Edinburgh, 2d June, 1789.

DEAR SIR,

I TAKE the first leisure hour I could command, to thank you for your letter, and the copy of verses inclosed in it. As there is real poetic merit, I mean both fancy and tenderness, and some happy expressions in them, I think they well deserve that you should revise them carefully, and polish them to the utmost. This I am sure you can do if you please, for you

you have great command both of expression and of rhymes: and you may judge from the two last pieces of Mrs. Hunter's poetry, that I gave you, how much correctness and high polish enhance the value of such compositions. As you desire it, I shall, with great freedom, give you my *most rigorous* criticisms on your verses. I wish you would give me another edition of them, much amended, and I will send it to Mrs. Hunter, who I am sure will have much pleasure in reading it. Pray give me likewise for myself, and her too, a copy (as much amended as you please) of the *Water Fowl on Loch Turit*.

The *Wounded Hare* is a pretty good subject; but the measure or stanza you have chosen for it, is not a good one; it does not *flow* well; and the rhyme of the fourth line is almost lost by its distance from the first, and the two interposed, close rhymes. If I were you, I would put it into a different stanza yet.

Stanza 1. The execrations in the first two lines are too strong or coarse; but they may pass. " Murder-aiming" is a bad compound epithet, and not very intelligible. " Bloodstained," in stanza iii. line 4, has the same fault: *Bleeding* bosom is infinitely better. You have
accustomed

accustomed yourself to such epithets, and have no notion how stiff and quaint they appear to others, and how incongruous with poetic fancy and tender sentiments. Suppose Pope had written, " Why that blood-stained bosom gored," how would you have liked it? *Form* is neither a poetic, nor a dignified, nor a plain common word: it is a mere sportsman's word; unsuitable to pathetic or serious poetry.

" Mangled" is a coarse word. " Innocent," in this sense, is a nursery word, but both may pass.

Stanza 4. " Who will now provide that life a mother only can bestow?" will not do at all: it is not grammar—it is not intelligible. Do you mean, " provide for that life which the mother had bestowed and used to provide for?"

There was a ridiculous slip of the pen, " Feeling" (I suppose) for " Fellow," in the title of your copy of verses; but even fellow would be wrong; it is but a colloquial and vulgar word, unsuitable to your sentiments. " Shot" is improper too.—On seeing a *person* (or a sportsman) wound a hare; it is needless to add with what weapon; but if you think otherwise,

otherwise, you should say, *with a fowling-piece.*

Let me see you when you come to town, and I will shew you some more of Mrs. Hunter's poems.*

---

* It must be admitted, that this criticism is not more distinguished by its good sense, than by its freedom from ceremony. It is impossible not to smile at the manner in which the poet may be supposed to have received it. In fact it appears, as the sailors say, to have thrown him *quite aback.* In a letter which he wrote soon after, he says, " Dr. G—— is a good man, but he crucifies me."— And again, " I believe in the iron justice of Dr. G—— ; but, like the devils, " I believe and tremble." However, he profited by these criticisms, as the reader will find by comparing this first edition of the poem with that published, vol. iii. p. 335.   E.

No. LXXV.

To Mr. M'AULEY, of Dumbarton.

4th June, 1789.

DEAR SIR,

Though I am not without my fears respecting my fate, at that grand, universal inquest of right and wrong, commonly called *The Last Day*, yet I trust there is one sin, which that arch-vagabond, Satan, who I understand is to be king's evidence, cannot throw in my teeth, I mean ingratitude. There is a certain pretty large quantum of kindness for which I remain, and from inability, I fear must still remain, your debtor; but, though unable to repay the debt, I assure you, Sir, I shall ever warmly remember the obligation. It gives me the sincerest pleasure to hear, by my old acquaintance, Mr. Kennedy, that you are, in immortal Allan's language, " Hale and weel, and living;" and that your charming family are well, and promising to be an amiable and respectable addition to the company of performers, whom the great Manager of the drama of Man is bringing into action for the succeeding age.

With

With respect to my welfare, a subject in which you once warmly and effectively interested yourself, I am here in my old way, holding my plough, marking the growth of my corn, or the health of my dairy; and at times sauntering by the delightful windings of the Nith, on the margin of which I have built my humble domicile, praying for seasonable weather, or holding an intrigue with the muses, the only gipseys with whom I have now any intercourse. As I am entered into the holy state of matrimony, I trust my face is turned completely Zion-ward; and as it is a rule with all honest fellows to repeat no grievances, I hope that the little poetic licences of former days will of course fall under the oblivious influence of some good-natured statute of celestial proscription. In my family devotion, which, like a good presbyterian, I occasionally give to my household folks, I am extremely fond of the psalm, " Let not the errors of my youth," &c. and that other, " Lo, children are God's heri-" tage," &c. in which last Mrs. Burns, who, by the bye, has a glorious " wood-note wild" at either old song or psalmody, joins me with the pathos of Handel's Messiah.

* * * * * * *

No. LXXVI.

To Mrs. DUNLOP.

Ellisland, 21st June, 1789.

DEAR MADAM,

WILL you take the effusions, the miserable effusions, of low spirits, just as they flow from their bitter spring? I know not of any particular cause for this worst of all my foes besetting me, but for some time my soul has been beclouded with a thickening atmosphere of evil imaginations and gloomy presages.

* * * * * * * *

Monday Evening.

I have just heard * * * * * give a sermon. He is a man famous for his benevolence, and I revere him; but from such ideas of my Creator, good Lord deliver me! Religion, my honoured friend, is surely a simple business,

business, as it equally concerns the ignorant and the learned, the poor and the rich. That there is an incomprehensibly Great Being, to whom I owe my existence, and that he must be intimately acquainted with the operations and progress of the internal machinery, and consequent outward deportment of this creature which he has made; these are, I think, self-evident propositions. That there is a real and eternal distinction between virtue and vice, and consequently, that I am an accountable creature; that from the seeming nature of the human mind, as well as from the evident imperfection, nay, positive injustice, in the administration of affairs, both in the natural and moral worlds, there must be a retributive scene of existence beyond the grave—must, I think, be allowed by every one who will give himself a moment's reflection. I will go farther, and affirm, that from the sublimity, excellence, and purity of his doctrine and precepts, unparalleled by all the aggregated wisdom and learning of many preceding ages, though, *to appearance*, he himself was the obscurest and most illiterate of our species; therefore Jesus Christ was from God.

* * * * * * * *

Whatever mitigates the woes, or increases the

the happiness of others, this is my criterion of goodness; and whatever injuries society at large, or any individual in it, this is my measure of iniquity.

What think you, Madam, of my creed? I trust that I have said nothing that will lessen me in the eye of one whose good opinion I value almost next to the approbation of my own mind.

No.

No. LXXVII.

From Dr. MOORE.

Clifford-street, 10th June, 1789.

DEAR SIR,

I THANK you for the different communications you have made me of your occasional productions in manuscript, all of which have merit, and some of them merit of a different kind from what appears in the poems you have published. You ought carefully to preserve all your occasional productions, to correct and improve them at your leisure; and when you can select as many of these as will make a volume, publish it either at Edinburgh or London, by subscription: on such an occasion, it may be in my power, as it is very much in my inclination, to be of service to you.

If I were to offer an opinion, it would be, that, in your future productions, you should abandon

abandon the Scottish stanza and dialect, and adopt the measure and language of modern English poetry.

The stanza which you use in imitation of *Christ Kirk on the Green*, with the tiresome repetition of "that day," is fatiguing to English ears, and I should think not very agreeable to Scottish.

All the fine satire and humour of your *Holy Fair* is lost on the English; yet, without more trouble to yourself, you could have conveyed the whole to them. The same is true of some of your other poems. In your *Epistle to J. S*——, the stanzas, from that beginning with this line, "This life, so far's I understand," to that which ends with—"Short while it grieves," are easy, flowing, gaily philosophical, and of Horatian elegance—the language is English, with a *few* Scottish words, and some of those so harmonious as to add to the beauty; for what poet would not prefer gloaming to *twilight?*

I imagine, that by carefully keeping, and occasionally polishing and correcting those verses, which the Muse dictates, you will, within a year or two, have another volume as large

large as the first, ready for the press; and this, without diverting you from every proper attention to the study and practice of husbandry, in which I understand you are very learned, and which I fancy you will choose to adhere to as a wife, while poetry amuses you from time to time as a mistress. The former, like a prudent wife, must not show ill-humour, although you retain a sneaking kindness to this agreeable gipsey, and pay her occasional visits, which in no manner alienates your heart from your lawful spouse, but tends, on the contrary, to promote her interest.

I desired Mr. Cadell to write to Mr. Creech to send you a copy of *Zeluco*. This performance has had great success here; but I shall be glad to have your opinion of it, because I value your opinion, and because I know you are above saying what you do not think.

I beg you will offer my best wishes to my very good friend, Mrs. Hamilton, who I understand is your neighbour. If she is as happy as I wish her, she is happy enough. Make my compliments also to Mrs. Burns; and believe me to be, with sincere esteem,

Dear Sir, yours, &c.

No.

No. LXXVIII.

From Miss J. LITTLE.

Loudon House, 12*th July*, 1789.

SIR,

Though I have not the happiness of being personally acquainted with you, yet, amongst the number of those who have read and admired your publications, may I be permitted to trouble you with this. You must know, Sir, I am somewhat in love with the Muses, though I cannot boast of any favours they have deigned to confer upon me as yet; my situation in life has been very much against me as to that. I have spent some years in and about Ecclefechan, (where my parents reside) in the station of a servant, and am now come to Loudon House, at present possessed by Mrs. H——: she is daughter to Mrs. Dunlop of Dunlop,

Dunlop, whom I understand you are particularly acquainted with. As I had the pleasure of perusing your poems, I felt a partiality for the author, which I should not have experienced had you been in a more dignified station. I wrote a few verses of address to you which I did not then think of ever presenting; but as fortune seems to have favoured me in this, by bringing me into a family, by whom you are well known and much esteemed, and where perhaps I may have an opportunity of seeing you, I shall, in hopes of your future friendship, take the liberty to transcribe them.

. . . .

   FAIR fa' the honest rustic swain,
   The pride o' a' our Scottish plain;
   Thou gi'es us joy to hear thy strain,
      And notes sae sweet:
   Old Ramsay's shade reviv'd again
      In thee we greet.

   Lov'd Thalia, that delightfu' muse,
   Seem'd lang shut up as a recluse;
   To all she did her aid refuse,
      Since Allan's day:
   Till Burns arose, then did she chuse
      To grace his lay.

To hear thy sang all ranks desire,
Sae weel you strike the dormant lyre;
Apollo with poetic fire
    Thy breast does warm;
And critics silently admire
    Thy art to charm.

Cæsar and Luath weel can speak,
'Tis pity e'er their gabs should steek,
But into human nature keek,
    And knots unravel:
To hear their lectures once a week,
    Nine miles I'd travel.

Thy dedication to G. H.
An unco bonnie hamespun speech,
Wi' winsome glee the heart can teach
    A better lesson,
Than servile bards, who fawn and fleech
    Like beggar's messon.

When slighted love becomes your theme,
And women's faithless vows you blame;
With so much pathos you exclaim,
    In your Lament;
But glanc'd by the most frigid dame,
    She would relent.

The daisy, too, ye sing wi' skill;
And weel ye praise the whisky gill;
In vain I blunt my feckless quill
    Your fame to raise;
While echo sounds from ilka hill,
    To Burns's praise.

Did Addison or Pope but hear,
Or Sam, that critic most severe,
A ploughboy sing with throat sae clear,
  They, in a rage,
Their works would a' in pieces tear,
    And curse your page.

Sure Milton's eloquence were faint,
The beauties of your verse to paint;
My rude unpolish'd strokes but taint
  Their brilliancy;
Th' attempt would doubtless vex a saint,
    And weel may thee.

The task I'll drop, with heart sincere
To heaven present my humble pray'r,
That all the blessings mortals share,
  May be by turns
Dispens'd by an indulgent care,
    To Robert Burns!

. . . .

Sir, I hope you will pardon my boldness in this; my hand trembles while I write to you, conscious of my unworthiness of what I would most earnestly solicit, viz. your favour and friendship; yet hoping you will shew yourself possessed of as much generosity and good nature as will prevent your exposing what may
         justly

justly be found liable to censure in this measure, I shall take the liberty to subscribe myself,
Sir,
Your most obedient humble servant,
JANET LITTLE.

P. S. If you would condescend to honour me with a few lines from your hand, I would take it as a particular favour: and direct to me at Loudon House, near *Galston*.

No. LXXIX.

From Mr. ******.

London, 5th August, 1789.

MY DEAR SIR,

Excuse me when I say, that the uncommon abilities which you possess must render your correspondence very acceptable to any one. I can assure you I am particularly proud of your partiality, and shall endeavour, by every method in my power, to merit a continuance of your politeness.

* * * * * * * *

When you can spare a few moments, I should be proud of a letter from you, directed for me, Gerrard-street, Soho.

* * * * * *

I cannot express my happiness sufficiently

at the instance of your attachment to my late inestimable friend, Bob Fergusson, who was particularly intimate with myself and relations.* While I recollect with pleasure his extraordinary talents, and many amiable qualities, it affords me the greatest consolation that I am honoured with the correspondence of his successor in national simplicity and genius.— That Mr. Burns has refined in the art of poetry, must readily be admitted; but notwithstanding many favourable representations, I am yet to learn that he inherits his convivial powers.

There was such a richness of conversation, such a plenitude of fancy and attraction in him, that when I call the happy period of our intercourse to my memory, I feel myself in a state of delirium. I was then younger than him by eight or ten years, but his manner was so felicitous, that he enraptured every person around him, and infused into the hearts of the young and old the spirit and animation which operated on his own mind.

I am, Dear Sir, yours, &c.

No.

---

* The erection of a monument to him.

E.

No. LXXX.

To Mr. ******,

In answer to the foregoing.

MY DEAR SIR,

The hurry of a farmer in this particular season, and the indolence of a poet at all times and seasons, will, I hope, plead my excuse for neglecting so long to answer your obliging letter of the fifth of August.

That you have done well in quitting your laborious concern in * * * * I do not doubt; the weighty reasons you mention, were, I hope, very, and deservedly indeed, weighty ones, and your health is a matter of the last importance: but whether the remaining proprietors of the paper have also done well, is what I much doubt. The * * * *, so far as I was a reader, exhibited such

such a brilliancy of point, such an elegance of paragraph, and such a variety of intelligence, that I can hardly conceive it possible to continue a daily paper in the same degree of excellence; but if there was a man who had abilities equal to the task, that man's assistance the proprietors have lost.

* * * * * *

When I received your letter, I was transcribing for * * * *, my letter to the magistrates of the Canongate, Edinburgh, begging their permission to place a tomb-stone over poor Fergusson, and their edict in consequence of my petition, but now I shall send them to * * * * * * *. Poor Fergusson! If there be a life beyond the grave, which I trust there is; and if there be a good God presiding over all nature, which I am sure there is; thou art now enjoying existence in a glorious world, where worth of the heart alone is distinction in the man; where riches, deprived of all their pleasure-purchasing powers, return to their native sordid matter; where titles and honours are the disregarded reveries of an idle dream; and where that heavy virtue, which is the negative consequence of steady dulness, and those thoughtless, though often destructive follies,

which

which are the unavoidable aberrations of frail human nature, will be thrown into equal oblivion as if they had never been!

Adieu, my dear Sir! So soon as your present views and schemes are concentred in an aim, I shall be glad to hear from you; as your welfare and happiness is by no means a subject indifferent to

Yours, &c.

No.

No. LXXXI.

To Miss WILLIAMS.

1789.

MADAM,

Of the many problems in the nature of that wonderful creature Man, this is one of the most extraordinary, that he shall go on from day to day, from week to week, from month to month, or perhaps from year to year, suffering a hundred times more in an hour from the impotent consciousness of neglecting what he ought to do, than the very doing of it would cost him. I am deeply indebted to you, first for a most elegant poetic compliment;* then for a polite, obliging letter; and, lastly, for your excellent poem on the Slave-Trade; and yet, wretch that I am! though the debts were debts of honour, and the creditor a lady, I have put off and put off even the very acknowledgment of the obligation, until you must indeed be the very angel I take you for, if you can forgive me.

Your

---

* See page 46.

Your poem I have read with the highest pleasure. I have a way, whenever I read a book, I mean a book in our own trade, Madam, a poetic one, and when it is my own property, that I take a pencil and mark at the ends of verses, or note on margins and odd paper, little criticisms of approbation or disapprobation as I peruse along. I will make no apology for presenting you with a few unconnected thoughts that occurred to me in my repeated perusals of your poem. I want to shew you that I have honesty enough to tell you what I take to be truths, even when they are not quite on the side of approbation; and I do it in the firm faith that you have equal greatness of mind to hear them with pleasure.

I had lately the honour of a letter from Dr. Moore, where he tells me that he has sent me some books. They are not yet come to hand, but I hear they are on the way.

Wishing you all success in your progress in the path of fame; and that you may equally escape the danger of stumbling through incautious speed, or losing ground through loitering neglect,

I have the honour to be, &c.

No.

No. LXXXII.

From Miss WILLIAMS.

7th August, 1789.

DEAR SIR,

I DO not lose a moment in returning you my sincere acknowledgments for your letter, and your criticism on my poem, which is a very flattering proof that you have read it with attention. I think your objections are perfectly just, except in one instance———

* * * * * * * *

You have indeed been very profuse of panegyric on my little performance. A much less portion of applause from *you* would have been gratifying to me; since I think its value depends entirely upon the source from whence it proceeds—the incense of praise, like other incense, is more grateful from the quality, than the quantity of the odour.

I hope

I hope you still cultivate the pleasures of poetry, which are precious, even independent of the rewards of fame. Perhaps the most valuable property of poetry is its power of disengaging the mind from worldly cares, and leading the imagination to the richest springs of intellectual enjoyment; since, however frequently life may be chequered with gloomy scenes, those who truly love the Muse can always find one little path adorned with flowers and cheered by sunshine.

* * * * * * * *

No.

No. LXXXIII.

To Mrs. DUNLOP.

Ellisland, 6th Sept. 1789.

DEAR MADAM,

I HAVE mentioned, in my last, my appointment to the Excise, and the birth of little Frank, who, by the bye, I trust, will be no discredit to the honourable name of Wallace, as he has a fine manly countenance, and a figure that might do credit to a little fellow two months older; and likewise an excellent good temper, though, when he pleases, he has a pipe, only not quite so loud as the horn that his immortal namesake blew as a signal to take out the pin of Stirling bridge.

I had some time ago an epistle, part poetic, and part prosaic, from your poetess, Mrs. J. Little, a very ingenious but modest composition.

position. I should have written her, as she requested, but for the hurry of this new business. I have heard of her and her compositions in this country; and I am happy to add, always to the honour of her character. The fact is, I know not well how to write to her: I should sit down to a sheet of paper that I knew not how to stain. I am no dab at fine-drawn letter-writing; and except when prompted by friendship or gratitude, or, which happens extremely rarely, inspired by the Muse (I know not her name) that presides over epistolary writing, I sit down, when necessitated to write, as I would sit down to beat hemp.

Some parts of your letter of the 20th August struck me with the most melancholy concern for the state of your mind at present.

* * * * * * *

Would I could write you a letter of comfort! I would sit down to it with as much pleasure as I would to write an epic poem of my own composition that should equal the *Iliad.* Religion, my dear friend, is the true comfort! A strong persuasion in a future state of existence; a proposition so obviously probable, that, setting revelation aside, every nation and people, so far

as

as investigation has reached, for at least near four thousand years, have in some mode or other firmly believed it. In vain would we reason and pretend to doubt. I have myself done so to a very daring pitch; but when I reflected that I was opposing the most ardent wishes, and the most darling hopes of good men, and flying in the face of all human belief, in all ages, I was shocked at my own conduct.

I know not whether I have ever sent you the following lines, or if you have ever seen them; but it is one of my favourite quotations, which I keep constantly by me in my progress through life, in the language of the Book of Job.

" Against the day of battle and of war"—

spoken of religion.

" 'Tis *this*, my friend, that streaks our morning bright,
'Tis *this* that gilds the horror of our night.
When wealth forsakes us, and when friends are few;
When friends are faithless, or when foes pursue;
'Tis this that wards the blow, or stills the smart,
Disarms affliction, or repels his dart;
Within the breast bids purest raptures rise,
Bids smiling conscience spread her cloudless skies."

I have been very busy with *Zeluco*. The Doctor is so obliging as to request my opinion of it; and I have been revolving in my mind some kind of criticisms on novel-writing, but it is a depth beyond my research. I shall, however, digest my thoughts on the subject as well as I can. *Zeluco* is a most sterling performance.

Farewel! *A Dieu, le bon Dieu, je vous commende!*

No.

No. LXXXIV.

From Dr. BLACKLOCK.

Edinburgh, 24th August, 1789.

Dear Burns, thou brother of my heart,
Both for thy virtues and thy art;
If art it may be call'd in thee,
Which Nature's bounty, large and free,
With pleasure on thy breast diffuses,
And warms thy soul with all the Muses.
Whether to laugh with easy grace,
Thy numbers move the sage's face,
Or bid the softer passions rise,
And ruthless souls with grief surprise,
'Tis Nature's voice distinctly felt,
Thro' thee her organ, thus to melt.

   Most anxiously I wish to know,
With thee of late how matters go;
How keeps thy much-lov'd Jean her health?
What promises thy farm of wealth?

Whether the Muse persists to smile,
And all thy anxious cares beguile?
Whether bright fancy keeps alive?
And how thy darling infants thrive?

   For me, with grief and sickness spent,
Since I my journey homeward bent,
Spirits depress'd no more I mourn,
But vigour, life, and health return.
No more to gloomy thoughts a prey,
I sleep all night, and live all day;
By turns my book and friend enjoy,
And thus my circling hours employ:
Happy while yet these hours remain,
If Burns could join the cheerful train,
With wonted zeal, sincere and fervent,
Salute once more his humble servant,

                THO. BLACKLOCK.

No. LXXXV.

To Dr. BLACKLOCK.

―――

Ellisland, 21st October, 1789.

Wow, but your letter made me vauntie!
And are ye hale, and weel, and cantie?
I kenn'd it still your wee bit jauntie
    Wad bring ye to:
Lord send you ay as weel's I want ye,
    And then ye'll do.

The ill-thief blaw the Heron south!
And never drink be near his drouth!
He tald mysel by word o' mouth,
    He'd tak my letter;
I lippen'd to the chiel in trouth,
    And bade nae better.

But aiblins honest Master Heron
Had at the time some dainty fair one,
To ware his theologic care on,
      And holy study;
And tir'd o' sauls to waste his lear on,
      E'en tried the body.*

But what d'ye think, my trusty fier,
I'm turn'd a gauger—Peace be here!
Parnassian queens, I fear, I fear
      Ye'll now disdain me,
And then my fifty pounds a year,
      Will little gain me.

Ye glaiket, gleesome, dainty damies,
Wha by Castalia's wimplin streamies,
Lowp, sing, and lave your pretty limbies,
      Ye ken, ye ken,
That strang necessity supreme is
      'Mang sons o' men.

      I hae

---

* Mr. Heron, author of the History of Scotland, lately published; (1800) and, among various other works, of a respectable life of our Poet himself.   E.

I hae a wife and twa wee laddies,
They maun hae brose and brats o' duddies;
Ye ken yoursels my heart right proud is,
    I need na vaunt,
But I'll sned besoms—thraw saugh woodies,
    Before they want.

Lord help me thro' this warld o' care!
I'm weary sick o't late and air!
Not but I hae a richer share
    Than mony ithers;
But why should ae man better fare,
    And a' men brithers?

Come FIRM RESOLVE take thou the van,
Thou stalk o' carl-hemp in man!
And let us mind, faint heart ne'er wan
    A lady fair;
Wha does the utmost that he can,
    Will whyles do mair.

But to conclude my silly rhyme,
(I'm scant o' verse, and scant o' time)
To make a happy fire-side clime
    To weans and wife,
That's the true pathos and sublime
    Of human life.

My compliments to sister Beckie;
And eke the same to honest Lucky,
I wat she is a dainty chuckie,
        As e'er tread clay!
And gratefully, my guid auld cockie,
        I'm yours for ay.

                ROBERT BURNS.

No.

No. LXXXVI.

To R. GRAHAM, Esq. of FINTRY.

9th December, 1789.

SIR,

I HAVE a good while had a wish to trouble you with a letter, and had certainly done it long ere now—but for a humiliating something that throws cold water on the resolution, as if one should say, "You have found Mr. Graham a very powerful and kind friend indeed; and that interest he is so kindly taking in your concerns, you ought, by every thing in your power to keep alive and cherish." Now though since God has thought proper to make one powerful and another helpless, the connexion of obliger and obliged is all fair; and though my being under your patronage is to me highly honourable, yet, Sir, allow me to flatter myself, that as a poet and an honest man, you first interested yourself in my welfare, and principally as such still, you permit me to approach you.

I have

I have found the excise-business go on a great deal smoother with me than I expected; owing a good deal to the generous friendship of Mr. Mitchell, my collector, and the kind assistance of Mr. Findlater, my supervisor. I dare to be honest, and I fear no labour. Nor do I find my hurried life greatly inimical to my correspondence with the Muses. Their visits to me, indeed, and I believe to most of their acquaintance, like the visits of good angels, are short and far between: but I meet them now and then as I jog through the hills of Nithsdale, just as I used to do on the banks of Ayr. I take the liberty to inclose you a few bagatelles, all of them the productions of my leisure thoughts in my excise rides.

If you know or have ever seen Captain Grose the antiquarian, you will enter into any humour that is in the verses on him. Perhaps you have seen them before, as I sent them to a London newspaper. Though I dare say you have none of the solemn-league-and-covenant fire, which shone so conspicuous in Lord George Gordon and the Kilmarnock weavers, yet I think you must have heard of Dr. M'Gill, one of the clergymen of Ayr, and his heretical book. God help him, poor man! Though he is one of the worthiest, as well as one of the ablest of the whole priesthood of the Kirk of Scotland, in
every

every sense of that ambiguous term, yet the poor Doctor and his numerous family are in imminent danger of being thrown out to the mercy of the winter-winds. The inclosed ballad on that business is, I confess, too local, but I laughed myself at some conceits in it, though I am convinced in my conscience that there are a good many heavy stanzas in it too.

The election ballad, as you will see, alludes to the present canvass in our string of boroughs. I do not believe there will be such a hard-run match in the whole general election.*

* * * * * *

I am too little a man to have any political attachments; I am deeply indebted to, and have the warmest veneration for, individuals of both parties; but a man who has it in his power to be the father of a country, and who * * * * * * is a character that one cannot speak of with patience.

Sir J. J. does " what man can do ;" but yet I doubt his fate.

* * * * * * *

No.

---

* This alludes to the contest for the borough of Dumfries, between the Duke of Queensberry's interest and that of Sir James Johnstone.   E.

No. LXXXVII.

To Mrs. DUNLOP.

Ellisland, 13th December, 1789.

Many thanks, dear Madam, for your sheet-full of rhymes. Though at present I am below the veriest prose, yet from you every thing pleases. I am groaning under the miseries of a diseased nervous system; a system the state of which is most conducive to our happiness—or the most productive of our misery. For now near three weeks I have been so ill with a nervous head-ache, that I have been obliged to give up for a time my excise-books, being scarcely able to lift my head, much less to ride once a-week over ten muir parishes. What is man? To-day in the luxuriance of health, exulting in the enjoyment of existence; in a few days, perhaps in a few hours, loaded with conscious painful being, counting the tardy pace of the lingering moments by the repercussions of anguish, and refusing or denied a comforter. Day follows night, and night comes after

after day, only to curse him with life which gives him no pleasure; and yet the awful, dark termination of that life, is a something at which he recoils.

> " Tell us, ye dead; will none of you in pity
> Disclose the secret———
> *What 'tis you are, and we must shortly be!*
> ————————————'tis no matter :
> A little time will make us learn'd as you are."

Can it be possible, that when I resign this frail, feverish being, I shall still find myself in conscious existence! When the last gasp of agony has announced that I am no more to those that knew me, and the few who loved me; when the cold, stiffened, unconscious, ghastly corse is resigned into the earth, to be the prey of unsightly reptiles, and to become in time a trodden clod, shall I yet be warm in life, seeing and seen, enjoying and enjoyed? Ye venerable sages, and holy flamens, is there probability in your conjectures, truth in your stories, of another world beyond death; or are they all alike, baseless visions, and fabricated fables? If there is another life, it must be only for the just, the benevolent, the amiable, and the humane: what a flattering idea, then, is a world to come! Would to God I as firmly believed it, as I ardently wish it! There I should meet an
aged

aged parent, now at rest from the many buffetings of an evil world, against which he so long and so bravely struggled. There should I meet the friend, the disinterested friend of my early life; the man who rejoiced to see me, because he loved me and could serve me.——Muir! thy weaknesses were the aberrations of human nature, but thy heart glowed with every thing generous, manly, and noble; and if ever emanation from the All-good Being animated a human form, it was thine!—There should I, with speechless agony of rapture, again recognise my lost, my ever dear Mary! whose bosom was fraught with truth, honour, constancy, and love

> My Mary, dear departed shade!
>   Where is thy place of heavenly rest?
> Seest thou thy lover lowly laid?
>   Hear'st thou the groans that rend his breast?

. . . .

Jesus Christ, thou amiablest of characters! I trust thou art no impostor, and that thy revelation of blissful scenes of existence beyond death and the grave, is not one of the many impositions which, time after time, have been palmed on credulous mankind. I trust that in thee " shall all the families of the earth be blessed," by being yet connected together in a better world, where every tie that bound heart to heart in this state of existence, shall be, far beyond our present conceptions, more endearing.

I am a good deal inclined to think with those who maintain, that what are called nervous affections are in fact diseases of the mind. I cannot reason, I cannot think; and but to you I would not venture to write any thing above an order to a cobler. You have felt too much of the ills of life not to sympathize with a diseased wretch, who is impaired more than half of any faculties he possessed. Your goodness will excuse this distracted scrawl, which the writer dare scarcely read, and which he would throw into the fire were he able to write any thing better, or indeed any thing at all.

Rumour told me something of a son of yours who was returned from the East or West Indies. If you have gotten news of James or Anthony, it was cruel in you not to let me know; as I promise you on the sincerity of a man who is weary of one world and anxious about another, that scarce any thing could give me so much pleasure as to hear of any good thing bafalling my honoured friend.

If you have a minute's leisure, take up your pen in pity to *le pauvre miserable*.   R. B.

No. LXXXVIII.

To Sir JOHN SINCLAIR.

SIR,

The following circumstance has, I believe, been omitted in the statistical account, transmitted to you, of the parish of Dunscore, in Nithsdale. I beg leave to send it to you, because it is new, and may be useful. How far it is deserving of a place in your patriotic publication, you are the best judge.

To store the minds of the lower classes with useful knowledge is certainly of very great importance, both to them as individuals, and to society at large. Giving them a turn for reading and reflection, is giving them a source of innocent and laudable amusement; and, besides, raises them to a more dignified degree in the scale of rationality. Impressed with this idea, a gentleman in this parish, Robert Riddel,

del, Esq. of Glenriddel, set on foot a species of circulating library, on a plan so simple as to be practicable in any corner of the country; and so useful as to deserve the notice of every country gentleman, who thinks the improvement of that part of his own species, whom chance has thrown into the humble walks of the peasant and the artisan, a matter worthy of his attention.

Mr. Riddel got a number of his own tenants, and farming neighbours, to form themselves into a society for the purpose of having a library among themselves. They entered into a legal engagement to abide by it for three years; with a saving clause or two, in case of removal to a distance, or of death. Each member, at his entry, paid five shillings; and at each of their meetings, which were held every fourth Saturday, six-pence more. With their entry-money, and the credit which they took on the faith of their future funds, they laid in a tolerable stock of books at the commencement. What authors they were to purchase, was always decided by the majority. At every meeting, all the books, under certain fines and forfeitures, by way of penalty, were to be produced; and the members had their choice of the volumes in rotation. He whose name stood for that night first on the list, had his choice of what volume he pleased in the whole collection; the second had his choice after the first; the third after the second; and so on to the last. At next meeting, he who had been first on the list at the preceding meeting was last at this; he who had been second was first; and so on through the whole three years. At the expiration of the engagement, the books were sold by auction, but only among the members themselves; and each man had his share of the common stock, in money or in books, as he chose to be a purchaser or not.

At the breaking up of this little society, which was formed under Mr. Riddel's patronage, what with benefactions of books from him, and what with their own purchases, they had collected together upwards of one hundred and fifty volumes. It will easily be guessed, that a good deal of trash would be bought. Among the books, however, of this little library, were, *Blair's Sermons, Robertson's History of Scotland, Hume's History of the Stuarts, The Spectator, Idler, Adventurer, Mirror, Lounger, Observer, Man of Feeling, Man of the World, Chrysal, Don Quixote, Joseph Andrews, &c.* A peasant who can read and enjoy such books, is certainly a much superior being to his neighbour, who perhaps stalks beside his team, very little

little removed, except in shape, from the brutes he drives.

Wishing your patriotic exertions their so much-merited success.

I am,

Sir,

Your humble servant,

*A PEASANT.**

---

* The above is extracted from the third volume of Sir John Sinclair's Statistics, p. 598.—It was inclosed to Sir John by Mr. Riddel himself in the following letter, also printed there:

" Sir John,

" I inclose you a letter, written by Mr. Burns, as an
" addition to the account of Dunscore parish. It con-
" tains an account of a small library which he was so good
" (at my desire) as to set on foot, in the barony of Monk-
" land, or Friar's Carse, in this parish. As its utility has
" been felt, particularly among the younger class of peo-
" ple, I think, that if a similar plan were established in
" the different parishes of Scotland, it would tend greatly
" to the speedy improvement of the tenantry, trades
" people,

" people, and work people. Mr. Burns was so good as
" to take the whole charge of this small concern. He was
" treasurer, librarian, and censor, to this little society, who
" will long have a grateful sense of his public spirit and
" exertions for their improvement and information.

" I have the honour to be, Sir John,

" Yours most sincerely,

" ROBERT RIDDEL."

To Sir John Sinclair,
of Ulbster, Bart.

No. LXXXIX.

To CHARLES SHARPE, Esq.

OF HODDAM,

Under a fictitious Signature, inclosing a Ballad, 1790 or 1791.

It is true, Sir, you are a gentleman of rank and fortune, and I am a poor devil: you are a feather in the cap of society, and I am a very hobnail in his shoes; yet I have the honour to belong to the same family with you, and on that score I now address you. You will perhaps suspect that I am going to claim affinity with the ancient and honourable house of Kilpatrick: No, no, Sir: I cannot indeed be properly said to belong to any house, or even any province or kingdom; as my mother, who for many years was spouse to a marching regiment, gave me into this bad world, aboard the packet-boat, somewhere between Donaghadee and Portpatrick. By our common family, I mean, Sir,

the family of the Muses. I am a fiddler and a poet; and you, I am told, play an exquisite violin, and have a standard taste in the Belles Lettres. The other day, a brother catgut gave me a charming Scots air of your composition. If I was pleased with the tune, I was in raptures with the title you have given it; and, taking up the idea, I have spun it into the three stanzas inclosed. Will you allow me, Sir, to present you them, as the dearest offering that a misbegotten son of poverty and rhyme has to give! I have a longing to take you by the hand and unburthen my heart, by saying—" Sir, I
" honour you as a man who supports the dig-
" nity of human nature, amid an age when
" frivolity and avarice have, between them,
" debased us below the brutes that perish!"
But alas, Sir! to me you are unapproachable. It is true, the Muses baptized me in Castalian streams, but the thoughtless gipseys forgot to give me a Name. As the sex have served many a good fellow, the Nine have given me a great deal of pleasure, but, bewitching jades! they have beggared me. Would they but spare me a little of their cast-linen! were it only to put it in my power to say that I have a shirt on my back! But the idle wenches, like Solomon's lilies, " they toil not, neither do they spin;" so I must e'en continue to tie my remnant of a

cravat,

cravat, like the hangman's rope, round my naked throat, and coax my galligaskins to keep together their many-coloured fragments. As to the affair of shoes, I have given that up.—My pilgrimages in my ballad-trade from town to town, and on your stony-hearted turnpikes too, are what not even the hide of Job's Behemoth could bear. The coat on my back is no more: I shall not speak evil of the dead. It would be equally unhandsome and ungrateful to find fault with my old surtout, which so kindly supplies and conceals the want of that coat. My hat indeed is a great favourite; and though I got it literally for an old song, I would not exchange it for the best beaver in Britain. I was, during several years, a kind of fac-totum servant to a country clergyman, where I pickt up a good many scraps of learning, particularly in some branches of the mathematics. Whenever I feel inclined to rest myself on my way, I take my seat under a hedge, laying my poetic wallet on the one side, and my fiddle-case on the other, and placing my hat between my legs, I can by means of its brim, or rather brims, go through the whole doctrine of the Conic Sections.

However, Sir, don't let me mislead you, as if I would interest your pity. Fortune has so
much

much forsaken me, that she has taught me to live without her; and, amid all my rags and poverty, I am as independent, and much more happy than a monarch of the world. According to the hackneyed metaphor, I value the several actors in the great drama of life, simply as they act their parts. I can look on a worthless fellow of a duke with unqualified contempt; and can regard an honest scavenger with sincere respect. As you, Sir, go through your rôle with such distinguished merit, permit me to make one in the chorus of universal applause, and assure you that, with the highest respect,

I have the honour to be, &c.

No.

No. XC.

To Mr. GILBERT BURNS.

Ellisland, 11th January, 1790.

DEAR BROTHER,

I MEAN to take advantage of the frank, though I have not, in my present frame of mind, much appetite for exertion in writing. My nerves are in a **** state. I feel that horrid hypochondria pervading every atom of both body and soul. This farm has undone my enjoyment of myself. It is a ruinous affair on all hands. But let it go to ****! I'll fight it out and be off with it.

We have gotten a set of very decent players here just now. I have seen them an evening or two. David Campbell, in Ayre, wrote to me by the manager of the company, a Mr. Sutherland, who is a man of apparent worth. On New-

New-year-day evening I gave him the following prologue, which he spouted to his audience with applause:

No Song nor dance I bring from yon great city
That queens it o'er our taste—the more's the pity:
Tho' by the bye, abroad why will you roam?
Good sense and taste are natives here at home:
But not for panegyric I appear,
I come to wish you all a good new year!
Old Father Time deputes me here before ye,
Not for to preach, but tell his simple story:
The sage grave ancient cough'd, and bade me say,
" You're one year older this important day,"
If *wiser too*—he hinted some suggestion,
But 'twould be rude, you know, to ask the question;
And with a would-be roguish leer and wink,
He bade me on you press this one word—" THINK!"

Ye sprightly youths, quite flush with hope and spirit,
Who think to storm the world by dint of merit,
To you the dotard has a deal to say,
In his sly, dry, sententious, proverb way!
He bids you mind, amid your thoughtless rattle,
That the first blow is ever half the battle;
That tho' some by the skirt may try to snatch him,
Yet by the forelock is the hold to catch him,
That whether doing, suffering, or forbearing,
You may do miracles by persevering.

Last, tho' not least in love, ye youthful fair,
Angelic forms, high Heaven's peculiar care!

To you old Bald-pate smooths his wrinkled brow,
And humbly begs you'll mind the important—N o w !
To crown your happiness he asks your leave,
And offers, bliss to give and to receive.

For our sincere, tho' haply weak endeavours,
With grateful pride we own your many favours;
And howsoe'er our tongues may ill reveal it,
Believe our glowing bosoms truly feel it.

. . . .

I can no more.—If once I was clear of this
**** farm, I should respire more at ease.

No.

No. XCI.

To Mrs. DUNLOP.

Ellisland, 25th January, 1790.

It has been owing to unremitting hurry of business that I have not written to you, Madam, long ere now. My health is greatly better, and I now begin once more to share in satisfaction and enjoyment with the rest of my fellow-creatures.

Many thanks, my much esteemed friend, for your kind letters; but why will you make me run the risk of being contemptible and mercenary in my own eyes? When I pique myself on my independent spirit, I hope it is neither poetic license, nor poetic rant; and I am so flattered with the honour you have done me, in making me your compeer in friendship and friendly correspondence, that I cannot without pain, and a degree of mortification, be reminded of the real inequality between our situations.

Most

Most sincerely do I rejoice with you, dear Madam, in the good news of Anthony. Not only your anxiety about his fate, but my own esteem for such a noble, warm-hearted, manly young fellow, in the little I had of his acquaintance, has interested me deeply in his fortunes.

Falconer, the unfortunate author of the *Shipwreck*, which you so much admire, is no more. After witnessing the dreadful catastrophe he so feelingly describes in his poem, and after weathering many hard gales of fortune, he went to the bottom with the Aurora frigate! I forget what part of Scotland had the honour of giving him birth, but he was the son of obscurity and misfortune.* He was one of those daring adventurous

---

* Falconer was in early life a sea-boy, to use a word of Shakespear, on board a man of war, in which capacity he attracted the notice of Campbell, the author of the satire on Dr. Johnson, entitled *Lexiphanes*, then purser of the ship. Campbell took him as his servant, and delighted in giving him instruction; and, when Falconer afterwards acquired celebrity, boasted of him as his scholar. The Editor had this information from a surgeon of a man of war, in 1777, who knew both Campbell and Falconer, and who himself perished soon after by shipwreck on the coast of America.

Though

venturous spirits which Scotland, beyond any other country, is remarkable for producing. Little does the fond mother think, as she hangs delighted over the sweet little leech at her bosom, where the poor fellow may hereafter wander, and what may be his fate. I remember a stanza in an old Scottish ballad, which, notwithstanding its rude simplicity, speaks feelingly to the heart:

> " Little did my mother think,
>   That day she cradled me,
> What land I was to travel in,
>   Or what death I should die!"

Old Scottish songs are, you know, a favourite

Though the death of Falconer happened so lately as 1770 or 1771, yet in the biography prefixed by Dr. Anderson to his works, in the complete edition of the *Poets of Great Britain*, it is said—" Of the family, birth-" place, and education of William Falconer, there are no " memorials." On the authority already given, it may be mentioned, that he was a native of one of the towns on the coast of Fife; and that his parents, who had suffered some misfortunes, removed to one of the sea-ports of England, where they both died soon after of an epidemic fever, leaving poor Falconer, then a boy, forlorn and destitute. In consequence of which he entered on board a man of war. These last circumstances are, however, less certain. E.

ite study and pursuit of mine; and, now I am on that subject, allow me to give you two stanzas of another old simple ballad, which I am sure will please you. The catastrophe of the piece is a poor ruined female lamenting her fate. She concludes with this pathetic wish:

" O that my father had ne'er on me smil'd;
   O that my mother had ne'er to me sung!
O that my cradle had never been rock'd;
   But that I had died when I was young!

O that the grave it were my bed;
   My blankets were my winding sheet;
The clocks and the worms my bedfellows a';
   And O sae sound as I should sleep!"

I do not remember in all my reading to have met with any thing more truly the language of misery than the exclamation in the last line. Misery is like love; to speak its language truly, the author must have felt it.

I am every day expecting the doctor to give your little godson* the small pox. They are *rife* in the country, and I tremble for his fate. By the way, I cannot help congratulating you

---

* The Bard's second son, Francis.   E.

on his looks and spirit. Every person who sees him acknowledges him to be the finest, handsomest child he has ever seen. I am myself delighted with the manly swell of his little chest, and a certain miniature dignity in the carriage of his head, and the glance of his fine black eye, which promise the undaunted gallantry of an independent mind.

I thought to have sent you some rhymes, but time forbids. I promise you poetry until you are tired of it, next time I have the honour of assuring you how truly I am, &c.

No.

No. XCII.

From Mr. CUNNINGHAM.

28th January, 1790.

In some instances it is reckoned unpardonable to quote any one's own words; but the value I have for your friendship nothing can more truly or more elegantly express than

> " Time but the impression stronger makes,
> As streams their channels deeper wear."

Having written to you twice without having heard from you, I am apt to think my letters have miscarried. My conjecture is only framed upon the chapter of accidents turning up against me, as it too often does, in the trivial, and, I may with truth add, the more important affairs of life; but I shall continue occasionally to inform you what is going on among the circle of your friends in these parts. In these days of merriment, I have frequently heard your name *proclaimed* at the jovial board—under the roof of our hospitable friend at Stenhouse-mills; there were no

" Lingering moments number'd with care."

I saw your *Address to the New-year*, in the Dumfries Journal. Of your productions I shall say nothing; but my acquaintances allege that when your name is mentioned, which every man of celebrity must know often happens, I am the champion, the Mendoza, against all snarling critics and narrow-minded reptiles, of whom *a few* on this planet do *crawl*.

With best compliments to your wife, and her black-eyed sister, I remain yours, &c.

No.

No. XCIII.

To Mr. CUNNINGHAM.

Ellisland, 13th February, 1790.

I BEG your pardon, my dear and much-valued friend, for writing to you on this very unfashionable, unsightly sheet—

" My poverty but not my will consents."

But to make amends, since of modish post I have none, except one poor widowed half-sheet of gilt which lies in my drawer among my plebeian fools-cap pages, like the widow of a man of fashion, whom that unpolite scoundrel, Necessity, has driven from Burgundy and Pineapple to a dish of Bohea, with the scandal-bearing help-mate of a village-priest; or a glass of whisky-toddy, with the ruby-nosed yoke-fellow of a foot-padding exciseman—I make a vow to inclose this sheet-full of epistolary fragments in that my only scrap of gilt paper.

I am

I am indeed your unworthy debtor for three friendly letters. I ought to have written to you long ere now, but it is a literal fact, I have scarcely a spare moment. It is not that I *will not* write to you; Miss Burnet is not more dear to her guardian angel, nor his grace the Duke of ********* to the powers of ******* than my friend Cunningham to me. It is not that I *cannot* write to you: should you doubt it, take the following fragment which was intended for you some time ago, and be convinced that I can *antithesize* sentiment, and *circumvolute* periods, as well as any coiner of phrase in the regions of philology.

. . . .

December, 1789.

MY DEAR CUNNINGHAM,

Where are you? And what are you doing? Can you be that son of levity, who takes up a friendship as he takes up a fashion; or are you, like some other of the worthiest fellows in the world, the victim of indolence, laden with fetters of ever-increasing weight?

What strange beings we are! Since we have a portion of conscious existence, equally capable of of enjoying pleasure, happiness, and rapture, or of suffering pain, wretchedness and misery, it is surely worthy of an inquiry, whether there be not such a thing as a science of life; whether method, economy, and fertility of expedients, be not applicable to enjoyment; and whether there be not a want of dexterity in pleasure, which renders our little scantling of happiness still less; and a profuseness, and intoxication in bliss, which leads to satiety, disgust, and self-abhorrence. There is not a doubt but that health, talents, character, decent competency, respectable friends, are real substantial blessings; and yet do we not daily see those who enjoy many or all of these good things, contrive, notwithstanding, to be as unhappy as others to whose lot few of them have fallen? I believe one great source of this mistake or misconduct is owing to a certain stimulus, with us called ambition, which goads us up the hill of life, not as we ascend other eminences, for the laudable curiosity of viewing an extended landscape, but rather for the dishonest pride of looking down on others of our fellow-creatures, seemingly diminutive in humbler stations, &c. &c.

. . . .

Sunday

Sunday, 14th February, 1790.

God help me! I am now obliged to join

" Night to day, and Sunday to the week."

If there be any truth in the orthodox faith of these churches, I am ****** past redemption, and what is worse, ****** to all eternity. I am deeply read in *Boston's Four-fold State, Marshal on Sanctification, Guthrie's Trial of a Saving Interest*, &c. but " there is no balm in Gi-" lead, there is no physician there," for me; so I shall e'en turn Arminian, and trust to " sincere though imperfect obedience."

? . . . .

Tuesday, 16*th.*

Luckily for me I was prevented from the discussion of the knotty point at which I had just made a full stop. All my fears and cares are of this world: if there is another, an honest man has nothing to fear from it. I hate a man that wishes to be a Deist; but, I fear every fair unprejudiced inquirer must in some degree be a Sceptic. It is not that there are any very staggering arguments against the immortality of man; but, like electricity, phlogiston, &c. the

the subject is so involved in darkness, that we want data to go upon. One thing frightens me much: that we are to live for ever, seems *too good news to be true.* That we are to enter into a new scene of existence, where, exempt from want and pain, we shall enjoy ourselves and our friends without satiety or separation— how much should I be indebted to any one who could fully assure me that this was certain!

* * * * * *

My time is once more expired. I will write to Mr. Cleghorn soon. God bless him and all his concerns! And may all the powers that preside over conviviality and friendship be present with all their kindest influence, when the bearer of this, Mr. Syme, and you meet! I wish I could also make one.—I think we should be * * * *.

Finally, brethren, farewel! Whatsoever things are lovely, whatsoever things are gentle, whatsoever things are charitable, whatsoever things are kind, think on these things, and think on

ROBERT BURNS.

No.

No. XCIV.

To Mr. HILL.

Ellisland, 2d March, 1790.

At a late meeting of the Monkland Friendly Society, it was resolved to augment their library by the following books, which you are to send us as soon as possible:—*The Mirror, The Lounger, Man of Feeling, Man of the World,* (these for my own sake, I wish to have by the first carrier) *Knox's History of the Reformation; Rae's History of the Rebellion in* 1715; any good *History of the Rebellion in* 1745; *A Display of the Secession Act and Testimony,* by Mr. Gibb; *Hervey's Meditations; Beveridge's Thoughts;* and another copy of *Watson's Body of Divinity.*

I wrote to Mr. A. Masterton three or four months ago, to pay some money he owed me into

into your hands, and lately I wrote to you to the same purpose, but I have heard from neither one nor other of you.

In addition to the books I commissioned in my last, I want very much, *An Index to the Excise Laws, or an Abridgment of all the Statutes now in force relative to the Excise*, by Jellinger Symons; I want three copies of this book: if it is now to be had, cheap or dear, get it for me. An honest country neighbour of mine wants, too, *A Family Bible*, the larger the better, but second-handed, for he does not choose to give above ten shillings for the book. I want likewise for myself, as you can pick them up, second-handed or cheap, copies of *Otway's Dramatic Works, Ben Jonson's, Dryden's, Congreve's, Wycherley's, Vanbrugh's, Cibber's*, or any *Dramatic Works* of the more modern, *Macklin, Garrick, Foote, Colman*, or *Sheridan*. A good copy too, of *Moliere*, in French, I much want. Any other good dramatic authors in that language I want also; but comic authors chiefly, though I should wish to have *Racine, Corneille*, and *Voltaire* too. I am in no hurry for all, or any of these; but if you accidentally meet with them very cheap, get them for me.

And

And now to quit the dry walk of business, how do you do, my dear friend? and how is Mrs. Hill? I trust, if now and then not so *elegantly* handsome, at least as amiable, and sings as divinely as ever. My good wife, too, has a charming " wood-note wild;" now could we four———

* * * * * * * *

I am out of all patience with this vile world for one thing. Mankind are by nature benevolent creatures: except in a few scoundrelly instances, I do not think that avarice of the good things we chance to have, is born with us: but we are placed here amid so much nakedness, and hunger, and poverty, and want, that we are under a cursed necessity of studying selfishness, in order that we may EXIST! Still there are, in every age, a few souls, that all the wants and woes of life cannot debase to selfishness, or even to the necessary alloy of caution and prudence. If ever I am in danger of vanity, it is when I contemplate myself on this side of my disposition and character. God knows I am no saint; I have a whole host of follies and sins to answer for; but if I could, and I believe I do it as far as I can, I would wipe away all tears from all eyes. Adieu!

No.

No. XCV.

To Mrs. DUNLOP.

Ellisland, 10*th April,* 1790.

I HAVE just now, my ever-honoured friend, enjoyed a very high luxury, in reading a paper of the *Lounger*. You know my national prejudices. I had often read and admired the *Spectator, Adventurer, Rambler,* and *World;* but still with a certain regret, that they were so thoroughly and entirely English. Alas! have I often said to myself, what are all the boasted advantages which my country reaps from the union, that can counterbalance the annihilation of her independence, and even her very name! I often repeat that couplet of my favourite poet, Goldsmith—

" ———States of native liberty possest,
  Tho' very poor, may yet be very blest."

Nothing

Nothing can reconcile me to the common terms, "English embassador, English court," &c. And I am out of all patience to see that equivocal character, Hastings, impeached by "the Commons of England." Tell me, my friend, is this weak prejudice? I believe in my conscience such ideas as, "my country; her independence; her honour; the illustrious names that mark the history of my native land;" &c. I believe these, among your *men of the world*, men who in fact guide for the most part and govern our world, are looked on as so many modifications of wrongheadedness. They know the use of bawling out such terms, to rouse or lead THE RABBLE; but for their own private use, with almost all the *able statesmen* that ever existed, or now exist, when they talk of right and wrong, they only mean proper and improper, and their measure of conduct is, not what they OUGHT, but what they DARE. For the truth of this I shall not ransack the history of nations, but appeal to one of the ablest judges of men, and himself one of the ablest men that ever lived—the celebrated Earl of Chesterfield. In fact, a man who could thoroughly control his vices whenever they interfered with his interests, and who could completely put on the appearance of every virtue as often as it suited his purposes, is, on the Stanhopian

hopian plan, the *perfect man;* a man to lead nations. But are great abilities, complete without a flaw, and polished without a blemish, the standard of human excellence? This is certainly the staunch opinion of *men of the world;* but I call on honour, virtue, and worth, to give the stygian doctrine a loud negative! However, this must be allowed, that, if you abstract from man the idea of an existence beyond the grave, *then* the true measure of human conduct is, *proper* and *improper:* Virtue and vice, as dispositions of the heart, are, in that case, of scarcely the same import and value to the world at large, as harmony and discord in the modifications of sound; and a delicate sense of honour, like a nice ear for music, though it may sometimes give the possessor an ecstasy unknown to the coarser organs of the herd, yet, considering the harsh gratings and inharmonic jars, in this illtuned state of being, it is odds but the individual would be as happy, and certainly would be as much respected by the true judges of society, as it would then stand, without either a good ear or a good heart.

You must know I have just met with the *Mirror* and *Lounger* for the first time, and I am quite in raptures with them; I should be glad to have your opinion of some of the papers. The

The one I have just read, *Lounger*, No. 61, has cost me more honest tears than any thing I have read of a long time. M'Kenzie has been called the Addison of the Scots; and, in my opinion, Addison would not be hurt at the comparison. If he has not Addison's exquisite humour, he as certainly outdoes him in the tender and the pathetic. His *Man of Feeling* (but I am not counsel learned in the laws of criticism) I estimate as the first performance in its kind I ever saw. From what book moral or even pious, will the susceptible young mind receive impressions more congenial to humanity and kindness, generosity and benevolence; in short, more of all that ennobles the soul to herself, or endears her to others—than from the simple affecting tale of poor Harley?

Still, with all my admiration of M'Kenzie's writings, I do not know if they are the fittest reading for a young man who is about to set out, as the phrase is, to make his way into life. Do not you think, Madam, that among the few favoured of Heaven in the structure of their minds, (for such there certainly are) there may be a purity, a tenderness, a dignity, an elegance of soul, which are of no use, nay, in some degree, absolutely disqualifying for the truly important business of making a man's way

way into life. If I am not much mistaken, my gallant young friend, A******, is very much under these disqualifications; and for the young females of a family I could mention, well may they excite parental solicitude; for I, a common acquaintance, or, as my vanity will have it, an humble friend, have often trembled for a turn of mind which may render them eminently happy—or peculiarly miserable!

I have been manufacturing some verses lately; but as I have got the most hurried season of excise-business over, I hope to have more leisure to transcribe any thing that may shew how much I have the honour to be, Madam, yours, &c.

No. XCVI.

From Mr. CUNNINGHAM.

Edinburgh, 25th May, 1789.

MY DEAR BURNS,

I AM much indebted to you for your last friendly, elegant epistle, and it shall make a part of the vanity of *my composition*, to retain your correspondence through life. It was remarkable your introducing the name of Miss Burnet, at a time when she was in such ill health: and I am sure it will grieve your gentle heart, to hear of her being in the last stage of a consumption. Alas! that so much beauty, innocence, and virtue, should be nipt in the bud. Hers was the smile of cheerfulness—of sensibility, not of allurement; and her elegance of manners corresponded with the purity and elevation of her mind.

How

How does your friendly Muse? I am sure she still retains her affection for you, and that you have many of her favours in your possession, which I have not seen. I weary much to hear from you.

* * * * * * * *

I beseech you do not forget me.

* * * * * * * *

I most sincerely hope all your concerns in life prosper, and that your roof-tree enjoys the blessing of good health. All your friends here are well, among whom, and *not the least*, is your acquaintance, Cleghorn. As for myself, I am well, as far as * * * * * * * will let a man be, but with these I am happy.

* * * * * * * *

When you meet with my very agreeable friend J. Syme, give him for me a hearty squeeze, and bid God bless him.

Is there any probability of your being soon in Edinburgh?

No. XCVII.

To Dr. MOORE.

Dumfries, Excise-office, 14*th July,* 1790.

SIR,

COMING into town this morning, to attend my duty in this office, it being collection-day, I met with a gentleman who tells me he is on his way to London; so I take the opportunity of writing to you, as franking is at present under a temporary death. I shall have some snatches of leisure through the day, amid our horrid business and bustle, and I shall improve them as well as I can; but let my letter be as stupid as * * * * * * * *, as miscellaneous as a newspaper, as short as a hungry grace-before-meat, or as long as a law-paper in the Douglas cause; as ill-spelt as country John's billet-doux, or as unsightly a scrawl as Betty Byre-Mucker's answer to it—I hope, considering

sidering circumstances, you will forgive it; and, as it will put you to no expense of postage, I shall have the less reflection about it.

I am sadly ungrateful in not returning you my thanks for your most valuable present, *Zeluco*. In fact, you are in some degree blameable for my neglect. You were pleased to express a wish for my opinion of the work, which so flattered me, that nothing less would serve my overweening fancy, than a formal criticism on the book. In fact, I have gravely planned a comparative view of you, Fielding, Richardson, and Smollet, in your different qualities and merits as novel-writers. This, I own, betrays my ridiculous vanity, and I may probably never bring the business to bear; but I am fond of the spirit young Elihu shews in the Book of Job—" And I said, I will also declare my opinion." I have quite disfigured my copy of the book with my annotations. I never take it up without at the same time taking my pencil, and marking with asterisms, parentheses, &c. wherever I meet with an original thought, a nervous remark on life and manners, a remarkably well-turned period, or a character sketched with uncommon precision.

Though I shall hardly think of fairly writing

ing out my " Comparative View," I shall certainly trouble you with my remarks, such as they are.

I have just received from my gentleman, that horrid summons in the book of Revelations—" That time shall be no more!"

The little collection of sonnets have some charming poetry in them. If *indeed* I am indebted to the fair author for the book, and not, as I rather suspect, to a celebrated author of the other sex, I should certainly have written to the lady, with my grateful acknowledgments, and my own ideas of the comparative excellence of her pieces. I would do this last, not from any vanity of thinking that my remarks could be of much consequence to Mrs. Smith, but merely from my own feelings as an author, doing as I would be done by.

No.

No. XCVIII.

To Mrs. DUNLOP.

8th Aug. 1790.

DEAR MADAM,

After a long day's toil, plague, and care, I sit down to write to you. Ask me not why I have delayed it so long? It was owing to hurry, indolence, and fifty other things; in short, to any thing—but forgetfulness of *la plus aimable de son sexe.* By the bye, you are indebted your best courtesy to me for this last compliment, as I pay it from my sincere conviction of its truth—a quality rather rare in compliments of these grinning, bowing, scraping times.

Well, I hope writing to *you* will ease a little my troubled soul. Sorely has it been bruised to-day!

to day! A ci-devant friend of mine, and an intimate acquaintance of yours, has given my feelings a wound that I perceive will gangrene dangerously ere it cure. He has wounded my pride!

* * * * * * * * *

No.

No. XCIX.

To Mr. CUNNINGHAM.

Ellisland, 8*th August,* 1790.

Forgive me, my once dear, and ever dear friend, my seeming negligence. You cannot sit down and fancy the busy life I lead.

I laid down my goose feather to beat my brains for an apt simile, and had some thoughts of a country grannum at a family christening; a bride on the market-day before her marriage;
* * * * * * * * * * * * * *
* * * * * * * * * * *; a tavern-keeper at an election-dinner; &c. &c.—but the resemblance that hits my fancy best, is that blackguard miscreant, Satan, who roams about like a roaring lion, seeking, *searching* whom he may devour. However, tossed about as I am, if I choose (and who would not choose) to bind down with the crampets of attention the brazen foundation of integrity, I may rear up the superstructure

perstructure of Independence, and, from its daring turrets, bid defiance to the storms of fate. And is not this a " consummation devoutly to be wished?"

" Thy spirit, Independence, let me share;
    Lord of the lion-heart, and eagle-eye!
Thy steps I follow with my bosom bare,
    Nor heed the storm that howls along the sky!"

Are not these noble verses? They are the introduction of *Smollet's Ode to Independence:* If you have not seen the poem, I will send it to you.—How wretched is the man that hangs on by the favours of the great! To shrink from every dignity of man, at the approach of a lordly piece of self-consequence, who, amid all his tinsel glitter and stately hauteur, is but a creature, formed as thou art—and perhaps not so well formed as thou art—came into the world a puling infant as thou didst, and must go out of it as all men must, a naked corse.*

* * * * * * *

No.

---

* The preceding letter explains the feelings under which this was written. The strain of indignant invective goes on some time longer in the style which our Bard was too apt to indulge, and of which the reader has already seen so much.   E.

C.

From Dr. BLACKLOCK.

Edinburgh, 1st September, 1790.

How does my dear friend, much I languish to hear,
His fortune, relations, and all that are dear?
With love of the Muses so strongly still smitten,
I meant this epistle in verse to have written;
But from age and infirmity indolence flows,
And this, much I fear, will restore me to prose.
Anon to my business I wish to proceed,
Dr. Anderson guides and provokes me to speed,
A man of integrity, genius, and worth,
Who soon a performance intends to set forth;
A work miscellaneous, extensive, and free,
Which will weekly appear, by the name of the *Bee.*
Of this from himself I inclose you a plan,
And hope you will give what assistance you can.
Entangled with business, and haunted with care,
In which more or less human nature must share,

Some moments of leisure the Muses will claim,
A sacrifice due to amusement and fame.
The Bee, which sucks honey from ev'ry gay bloom,
With some rays of your genius her work may illume,
Whilst the flow'r whence her honey spontaneously flows,
As fragrantly smells, and as vig'rously grows.

Now with kind gratulations 'tis time to conclude,
And add, your promotion is here understood;
Thus free from the servile employ of excise, Sir,
We hope soon to hear you commence Supervisor;
You then more at leisure, and free from control,
May indulge the strong passion that reigns in your soul,
But I, feeble I, must to nature give way;
Devoted cold death's, and longevity's prey.
From verses tho' languid my thoughts must unbend,
Tho' still I remain your affectionate friend,

THO. BLACKLOCK.

No.

No. CI.

EXTRACT OF A LETTER

From Mr. CUNNINGHAM.

Edinburgh, 14th October, 1790.

I LATELY received a letter from our friend B**********,—what a charming fellow lost to society—born to great expectations—with superior abilities, a pure heart, and untainted morals, his fate in life has been hard indeed—still I am persuaded he is happy; not like the gallant, the gay Lothario, but in the simplicity of rural enjoyment, unmixed with regret at the remembrance of "the days of other years."*

I saw

---

* The person here alluded to is Mr. S. who engaged the Editor in this undertaking. See the Dedication.   E.

I saw Mr. Dunbar put under the cover of your newspaper Mr. Wood's poem on Thomson. This poem has suggested an idea to me which you alone are capable to execute—a song adapted to *each* season of the year. The task is difficult, but the theme is charming: should you succeed, I will undertake to get new music worthy of the subject. What a fine field for your imagination! and who is there alive can draw so many beauties from Nature and pastoral imagery as yourself? It is, by the way, surprising, that there does not exist, so far as I know, *a proper song* for each season. We have songs on hunting, fishing, skaiting, and one autumnal song, *Harvest Home*. As your Muse is neither spavined nor rusty, you may mount the hill of Parnassus, and return with a sonnet in your pocket for every season. For my suggestions, if I be rude, correct me; if impertinent, chastise me; if presuming, despise me. But if you blend all my weaknesses, and pound out one grain of insincerity, then am I not thy

Faithful Friend, &c.

No.

No. CII.

To Mrs. DUNLOP.

November, 1790.

"As cold waters to a thirsty soul, so is good news from a far country."

Fate has long owed me a letter of good news from you, in return for the many tidings of sorrow which I have received. In this instance I most cordially obey the apostle—"Rejoice with them that do rejoice,"—for me, *to sing* for joy, is no new thing; but *to preach* for joy, as I have done in the commencement of this epistle, is a pitch of extravagant rapture to which I never rose before.

I read your letter—I literally jumped for joy—How could such a mercurial creature as a poet lumpishly keep his seat on the receipt of the best news from his best friend? I seized my my gilt headed Wangee rod, an instrument indispensably necessary in my left hand, in the moment of inspiration and rapture; and stride, stride—quick and quicker—out skipt I among the broomy banks of Nith, to muse over my joy by retail. To keep within the bounds of prose was impossible. Mrs. Little's is a more elegant, but not a more sincere compliment, to the sweet little fellow, than I, extempore almost, poured out to him in the following verses. *See the poem, vol. iii. p.* 365.—*On the Birth of a Posthumous Child.*

. . . .

I am much flattered by your approbation of my *Tam o' Shanter*, which you express in your former letter; though, by the bye, you load me in that said letter with accusations heavy and many; to all which I plead, *not guilty!* Your book is, I hear, on the road to reach me. As to printing of poetry, when you prepare it for the press, you have only to spell it right, and place the capital letters properly: as to the punctuation, the printers do that themselves.

I have a copy of *Tam o' Shanter* ready to send you by the first opportunity: it is too heavy to send by post.

I heard

I heard of Mr. Corbet lately. He, in consequence of your recommendation, is most zealous to serve me. Please favour me soon with an account of your good folks; if Mrs. H. is recovering, and the young gentleman doing well.

No. CIII.

To Mr. CUNNINGHAM.

Ellisland, 23d January, 1791.

Many happy returns of the season to you, my dear friend! As many of the good things of this life as is consistent with the usual mixture of good and evil in the cup of Being!

I have just finished a poem, which you will receive inclosed. It is my first essay in the way of tales.

I have these several months been hammering at an elegy on the amiable and accomplished Miss Burnet. I have got, and can get no farther than the following fragment, on which please give me your strictures. In all kinds of poetic composition I set great store by your opinion; but in sentimental verses, in the

poetry

poetry of the heart, no Roman Catholic ever set more value on the infallibility of the Holy Father than I do on yours.

I mean the introductory couplets as text verses.

. . . .

ELEGY

On the late Miss BURNET *of* MONBODDO.

LIFE ne'er exulted in so rich a prize
As Burnet, lovely from her native skies;
Nor envious death so triumph'd in a blow,
As that which laid th' accomplished Burnet low.

Thy form and mind, sweet maid, can I forget?
In richest ore the brightest jewel set!
In thee, high Heaven above was truest shown,
As by his noblest work the Godhead best is known.

In vain ye flaunt in summer's pride, ye groves;
   Thou crystal streamlet with thy flowery shore,
Ye woodland choir that chant your idle loves,
   Ye cease to charm—Eliza is no more!

Ye heathy wastes immix'd with reedy fens;
   Ye mossy streams, with sedge and rushes stor'd;
Ye rugged cliffs o'erhanging dreary glens,
   To you I fly, ye with my soul accord.

Princes, whose cumb'rous pride was all their worth,
    Shall venal lays their pompous exit hail?
And thou, sweet excellence! forsake our earth,
    And not a muse in honest grief bewail?

We saw thee shine in youth and beauty's pride,
    And virtue's light that beams beyond the spheres;
But like the sun eclips'd at morning tide,
    Thou left'st us darkling in a world of tears.

. . . .

Let me hear from you soon.   Adieu!

No.

No. CIV.

To Mr. PETER HILL.

17th January, 1791.

Take these two guineas, and place them over against that ⁎ ⁎ ⁎ ⁎ ⁎ ⁎ account of yours! which has gagged my mouth these five or six months! I can as little write good things as apologies to the man I owe money to. O the supreme curse of making three guineas do the business of five! Not all the labours of Hercules; not all the Hebrews' three centuries of Egyptian bondage, were such an insuperable business, such an ⁎ ⁎ ⁎ ⁎ ⁎ ⁎ ⁎ ⁎ task!! Poverty! thou half-sister of death, thou cousin-german of hell! where shall I find force of execration equal to the amplitude of thy demerits? Oppressed by thee, the venerable ancient, grown hoary in the practice of every virtue, laden with years and wretchedness, implores a little—little aid to support his existence, from a stony-hearted

hearted son of Mammon, whose sun of prosperity never knew a cloud; and is by him denied and insulted. Oppressed by thee, the man of sentiment, whose heart glows with independence, and melts with sensibility, inly pines under the neglect, or writhes in bitterness of soul under the contumely of arrogant, unfeeling wealth. Oppressed by thee, the son of genius, whose ill-starred ambition plants him at the tables of the fashionable and polite, must see in suffering silence his remark neglected, and his person despised, while shallow greatness, in his idiot attempts at wit, shall meet with countenance and applause. Nor is it only the family of worth that have reason to complain of thee: the children of folly and vice, though in common with thee the offspring of evil, smart equally under thy rod. Owing to thee, the man of unfortunate disposition and neglected education, is condemned as a fool for his dissipation, despised and shunned as a needy wretch, when his follies as usual bring him to want; and when his unprincipled necessities drive him to dishonest practices, he is abhorred as a miscreant, and perishes by the justice of his country. But far otherwise is the lot of the man of family and fortune. *His* early follies and extravagance are spirit and fire; *his* consequent wants are the embarrassments of an honest fellow;

low; and when, to remedy the matter, he has gained a legal commission to plunder distant provinces, or massacre peaceful nations, he returns, perhaps, laden with the spoils of rapine and murder; lives wicked and respected, and dies a ******* and a lord.—Nay, worst of all, alas for helpless woman! the needy prostitute, who has shivered at the corner of the street, waiting to earn the wages of casual prostitution, is left neglected and insulted, ridden down by the chariot-wheels of the coroneted RIP, hurrying on to the guilty assignation; she who without the same necessities to plead, riots nightly in the same guilty trade.

Well! Divines may say of it what they please, but execration is to the mind what phlebotomy is to the body: the vital sluices of both are wonderfully relieved by their respective evacuations,

No.

No. CV.

From A. F. TYTLER, Esq.

Edinburgh, 12th March, 1791.

DEAR SIR,

Mr. Hill yesterday put into my hands a sheet of *Grose's Antiquities*, containing a poem of yours, entitled, *Tam o' Shanter*, a tale. The very high pleasure I have received from the perusal of this admirable piece, I feel, demands the warmest acknowledgments. Hill tells me he is to send off a packet for you this day; I cannot resist, therefore, putting on paper what I must have told you in person, had I met with you after the recent perusal of your tale, which is, that I feel I owe you a debt, which, if undischarged, would reproach me with ingratitude. I have seldom in my life tasted of higher enjoyment from any work of genius, than I have received from this composition; and I am much mistaken, if this poem alone, had you never

written

written another syllable, would not have been sufficient to have transmitted your name down to posterity with high reputation. In the introductory part, where you paint the character of your hero, and exhibit him at the alehouse *ingle*, with his tippling cronies, you have delineated nature with a humour and *naïveté* that would do honour to Matthew Prior; but when you describe the infernal orgies of the witches' sabbath, and the hellish scenery in which they are exhibited, you display a power of imagination that Shakespeare himself could not have exceeded. I know not that I have ever met with a picture of more horrible fancy than the following:

" Coffins stood round like open presses,
  That shaw'd the dead in their last dresses;
  And by some devilish cantrip slight,
  Each in his cauld hand held a light."

But when I came to the succeeding lines, my blood ran cold within me:

" A knife, a father's throat had mangled,
  Whom his ain son of life bereft;
  The grey hairs yet stack to the heft."

And here, after the two following lines, " Wi' mair o' horrible and awfu'," &c. the descriptive part might perhaps have been better closed,

closed, than the four lines which succeed, which, though good in themselves, yet as they derive all their merit from the satire they contain, are here rather misplaced among the circumstances of pure horror.* The initiation of the young witch is most happily described—the effect of her charms exhibited in the dance on Satan himself—the apostrophe—" Ah, little thought thy reverend graunie !"—the transport of Tam, who forgets his situation, and enters completely into the spirit of the scene, are all features of high merit in this excellent composition. The only fault it possesses, is, that the winding up, or conclusion of the story, is not commensurate to the interest which is excited by the descriptive and characteristic painting of the preceding parts.—The preparation is fine, but the result is not adequate. But for this, perhaps you have a good apology—you stick to the popular tale.

And now that I have got out my mind, and feel a little relieved of the weight of that debt I owed you, let me end this desultory scroll by an advice: you have proved your talent for a species

---

* Our Bard profited by Mr. Tytler's criticism, and expunged the four lines accordingly. *See* vol. iii. *Appendix, p.* 21.   E.

species of composition in which but a very few of our own poets have succeeded—Go on—write more tales in the same style—you will eclipse Prior and La Fontaine; for, with equal wit, equal power of numbers, and equal *naïveté* of expression, you have a bolder, and more vigorous imagination.

I am, dear Sir, with much esteem,

Yours, &c.

No.

No. CVI.

To A. F. TYTLER, Esq.

SIR,

Nothing less than the unfortunate accident I have met with could have prevented my grateful acknowledgments for your letter. His own favourite poem, and that an essay in a walk of the muses entirely new to him, where consequently his hopes and fears were on the most anxious alarm for his success in the attempt; to have that poem so much applauded by one of the first judges, was the most delicious vibration that ever trilled along the heart-strings of a poor poet. However, Providence, to keep up the proper proportion of evil with the good, which it seems is necessary in this sublunary state, thought proper to check my exultation by a very serious misfortune. A day or two after I received your letter, my horse came down with me and broke my right arm. As

As this is the first service my arm has done me since its disaster, I find myself unable to do more than just in general terms to thank you for this additional instance of your patronage and friendship. As to the faults you detected in the piece, they are truly there: one of them, the hit at the lawyer and priest, I shall cut out: as to the falling off in the catastrophe, for the reason you justly adduce, it cannot easily be remedied. Your approbation, Sir, has given me such additional spirits to persevere in this species of poetic composition, that I am already revolving two or three stories in my fancy. If I can bring these floating ideas to bear any kind of embodied form, it will give me an additional opportunity of assuring you how much I have the honour to be, &c.

No. CVII.

To Mrs. DUNLOP.

Ellisland, 7th Feb. 1791.

WHEN I tell you, Madam, that by a fall, not from my horse, but with my horse, I have been a cripple some time, and that this is the first day my arm and hand have been able to serve me in writing, you will allow that it is too good an apology for my seemingly ungrateful silence. I am now getting better, and am able to rhyme a little, which implies some tolerable ease; as I cannot think that the most poetic genius is able to compose on the rack.

I do not remember if ever I mentioned to you my having an idea of composing an elegy on the late Miss Burnet of Monboddo. I had the honour of being pretty well acquainted with her, and have seldom felt so much at the loss of an acquaintance, as when I heard that so amiable and accomplished a piece of God's works was no more. I have as yet gone no farther than the following fragment, of which please let me have your opinion. You know that elegy is a subject so much exhausted, that any new idea on the business is not to be expected; 'tis well if we can place an old idea in a new light. How far I have succeeded as to this last, you will judge from what follows—

(*Here follows the Elegy, &c. as in page* 323, *adding this verse*)

>The parent's heart that nestled fond in thee,
>   That heart how sunk, a prey to grief and care:
>So deckt the woodbine sweet yon aged tree,
>   So from it ravish'd, leaves it bleak and bare.

* * * * * *

I have proceeded no further.

Your kind letter, with your kind *remembrance* of your godson, came safe. This last, Madam, is scarcely what my pride can bear. As to the little fellow, he is, partiality apart, the finest boy I have of a long time seen. He is now seventeen months old, has the small-pox and measles over, has cut several teeth, and yet never

never had a grain of doctor's drugs in his bowels.

I am truly happy to hear that the " little floweret" is blooming so fresh and fair, and that the " mother-plant" is rather recovering her drooping head. Soon and well may her " cruel wounds" be healed! I have written thus far with a good deal of difficulty. When I get a little abler, you shall hear farther from,

Madam, yours, &c.

No.

No. CVIII.

To Lady W. M. CONSTABLE.

Acknowledging a present of a valuable Snuff-box, with a fine picture of MARY *Queen of* SCOTS *on the Lid.*

MY LADY,

NOTHING less than the unlucky accident of having lately broken my right arm, could have prevented me, the moment I received your ladyship's elegant present by Mrs. Miller, from returning you my warmest and most grateful acknowledgments. I assure your ladyship I shall set it apart: the symbols of religion shall only be more sacred. In the moment of poetic composition, the box shall be my inspiring genius. When I would breathe the comprehensive wish of benevolence for the happiness of others, I shall recollect your ladyship; when I would interest my fancy in the distresses incident to humanity, I shall remember the unfortunate Mary.

No. CIX.

To Mrs. GRAHAM, of FINTRY.

MADAM,

WHETHER it is that the story of our Mary, Queen of Scots, has a peculiar effect on the feelings of a poet, or whether I have in the inclosed ballad succeeded beyond my usual poetic success, I know not; but it has pleased me beyond any effort of my muse for a good while past; on that account I inclose it particularly to you. It is true, the purity of my motives may be suspected. I am already deeply indebted to Mr. G——'s goodness; and what, *in the usual ways of men*, is of infinitely greater importance, Mr. G. can do me service of the utmost importance in time to come. I was born a poor dog; and however I may occasionally pick a better bone than I used to do, I know I must live and die poor; but I will indulge the flattering faith that my poetry will
considerably

considerably outlive my poverty; and, without any fustian affectation of spirit, I can promise and affirm, that it must be no ordinary craving of the latter shall ever make me do any thing injurious to the honest fame of the former. Whatever may be my failings, for failings are a part of human nature, may they ever be those of a generous heart and an independent mind! It is no fault of mine that I was born to dependence; nor is it Mr. G———'s chiefest praise that he can command influence; but it is his merit to bestow, not only with the kindness of a brother, but with the politeness of a gentleman; and I trust it shall be mine to receive with thankfulness, and remember with undiminished gratitude.

No. CX.

From the Rev. G. BAIRD.

London, 8*th February,* 1791.

SIR,

I TROUBLE you with this letter to inform you that I am in hopes of being able very soon to bring to the press, a new edition (long since talked of) of *Michael Bruce's Poems.* The profits of the edition are to go to his mother—a woman of eighty years of age—poor and helpless. The poems are to be published by subscription; and it may be possible, I think, to make out a 2s. 6d. or 3s. volume, with the assistance of a few hitherto unpublished verses, which I have got from the mother of the poet.

But the design I have in view in writing to you, is not merely to inform you of these facts, it is to solicit the aid of your name and pen in support of the scheme. The reputation of Bruce is already high with every reader of classical taste,

taste, and I shall be anxious to guard against tarnishing his character, by allowing any new poems to appear that may lower it. For this purpose, the MSS I am in possession of have been submitted to the revision of some whose critical talents I can trust to, and I mean still to submit them to others.

May I beg to know, therefore, if you will take the trouble of perusing the MSS—of giving your opinion, and suggesting what curtailments, alterations, or amendments, occur to you as advisable? And will you allow us to let it be known, that a few lines by you will be added to the volume?

I know the extent of this request. It is bold to make it. But I have this consolation, that though you see it proper to refuse it, you will not blame me for having made it; you will see my apology in the *motive*.

May I just add, that Michael Bruce is one in whose company, from his past appearance, you would not, I am convinced, blush to be found; and as I would submit every line of his that should now be published, to your own criticisms, you would be assured that nothing derogatory, either to him or you, would be admitted in that appearance he may make in future.

You

You have already paid an honourable tribute to kindred genius, in Fergusson—I fondly hope that the mother of Bruce will experience your patronage.

I wish to have the subscription-papers circulated by the 14th of March, Bruce's birthday, which I understand some friends in Scotland talk this year of observing—at that time it will be resolved, I imagine, to place a plain, humble stone over his grave. This at least I trust you will agree to do—to furnish, in a few couplets, an *inscription* for it.

On these points may I solicit an answer as early as possible? a short delay might disappoint us in procuring that relief to the mother, which is the object of the whole.

You will be pleased to address for me under cover to the Duke of Athole, London.

. . . .

P. S. Have you ever seen an engraving published here some time ago, from one of your poems, " *O thou pale Orb!* " If you have not, I shall have the pleasure of sending it to you.

No.

No. CXI.

To the Rev. G. BAIRD.

In Answer to the foregoing.

WHY did you, my dear Sir, write to me in such a hesitating style, on the business of poor Bruce? Don't I know, and have I not felt the many ills, the peculiar ills, that poetic flesh is heir to? You shall have your choice of all the unpublished poems I have; and had your letter had my direction so as to have reached me sooner (it only came to my hand this moment) I should have directly put you out of suspense on the subject. I only ask that some prefatory advertisement in the book, as well as the subscription-bills, may bear, that the publication is solely for the benefit of Bruce's mother. I would not put it in the power of ignorance to surmise, or malice to insinuate, that I clubbed a share in the work from mercenary motives. Nor need you give me credit for

for any remarkable generosity in my part of the business. I have such a host of peccadilloes, failings, follies, and backslidings, (any body but myself might perhaps give some of them a worse appellation) that by way of some balance, however trifling, in the account, I am fain to do any good that occurs in my very limited power to a fellow-creature, just for the selfish purpose of clearing a little the vista of retrospection.

* * * * * * * *

No. CXII.

To Dr. MOORE.

Ellisland, 28th February, 1791.

I do not know, Sir, whether you are a subscriber to *Grose's Antiquities of Scotland.* If you are, the inclosed poem will not be altogether new to you. Captain Grose did me the favour to send me a dozen copies of the proof-sheet, of which this is one. Should you have read the piece before, still this will answer the principal end I have in view: it will give me another opportunity of thanking you for all your goodness to the rustic bard; and also of shewing you, that the abilities you have been pleased to commend and patronize, are still employed in the way you wish.

The *Elegy on Captain Henderson* is a tribute to the memory of a man I loved much. Poets have in this the same advantage as Roman Catholics; they can be of service to their friends after

after they have past that bourne where all other kindness ceases to be of any avail. Whether, after all, either the one or the other be of any real service to the dead, is, I fear, very problematical; but I am sure they are highly gratifying to the living: and, as a very orthodox text, I forget where in Scripture, says, " whatsoever is not of faith, is sin;" so say I, whatsoever is not detrimental to society, and is of positive enjoyment, is of God, the giver of all good things, and ought to be received and enjoyed by his creatures with thankful delight. As almost all my religious tenets originate from my heart, I am wonderfully pleased with the idea, that I can still keep up a tender intercourse with the dearly beloved friend, or still more dearly beloved mistress, who is gone to the world of spirits.

The ballad on Queen Mary was begun while I was busy with *Percy's Reliques of English Poetry*. By the way, how much is every honest heart, which has a tincture of Caledonian prejudice, obliged to you for your glorious story of Buchanan and Targe! 'Twas an unequivocal proof of your loyal gallantry of soul, giving Targe the victory. I should have been mortified to the ground if you had not.

* * * * * * * *

I have

I have just read over once more of many times, your *Zeluco*. I marked with my pencil, as I went along, every passage that pleased me particularly above the rest; and one, or two I think, which with humble deference, I am disposed to think unequal to the merits of the book. I have sometimes thought to transcribe these marked passages, or at least so much of them as to point where they are, and send them to you. Original strokes that strongly depict the human heart, is your and Fielding's province, beyond any other novelist I have ever perused. Richardson indeed might perhaps be excepted; but, unhappily, his *dramatis personæ* are beings of some other world; and however they may captivate the unexperienced romantic fancy of a boy or a girl, they will ever, in proportion as we have made human nature our study, dissatisfy our riper minds.

As to my private concerns, I am going on, a mighty tax-gatherer before the Lord, and have lately had the interest to get myself ranked on the list of Excise as a supervisor. I am not yet employed as such, but in a few years I shall fall into the file of supervisorship by seniority. I have had an immense loss in the death of the Earl of Glencairn, the patron from whom all my fame and good fortune took its rise. Independent of my grateful attachment to him,
which

which was indeed so strong that it pervaded my very soul, and was entwined with the thread of my existence: so soon as the prince's friends had got in, (and every dog, you know, has his day) my getting forward in the Excise would have been an easier business than otherwise it will be. Though this was a consummation devoutly to be wished, yet, thank Heaven, I can live and rhyme as I am; and as to my boys, poor little fellows! if I cannot place them on as high an elevation in life as I could wish, I shall, if I am favoured so much of the Disposer of events as to see that period, fix them on as broad and independent a basis as possible. Among the many wise adages which have been treasured up by our Scottish ancestors, this is one of the best, *Better be the head o' the commonalty, as the tail o' the gentry.*

But I am got on a subject, which, however interesting to me, is of no manner of consequence to you; so I shall give you a short poem on the other page, and close this with assuring you how sincerely I have the honour to be yours, &c.

. . . .

Written on the blank leaf of a book which I presented to a very young lady whom I had formerly characterised under the denomination of *The Rose-bud. See vol.* iii. 348.

No.

No. CXIII.

From Dr. MOORE.

London, 29th March, 1791.

DEAR SIR,

Your letter of the 28th of February I received only two days ago, and this day I had the pleasure of waiting on the Rev. Mr. Baird, at the Duke of Athole's, who had been so obliging as to transmit it to me, with the printed verses on *Aloa Church*, the *Elegy on Capt. Henderson*, and the *Epitaph*. There are many poetical beauties in the former: what I particularly admire, are the three striking similies from—

" Or like the snow-falls in the river,"

and the eight lines which begin with

" By this time he was cross the ford,"*

---

* *See vol.* iii. *p.* 329.

so exquisitely expressive of the superstitious impressions of the country. And the twenty-two lines from

" Coffins stood round like open presses,"

which, in my opinion, are equal to the ingredients of Shakespear's cauldron in *Macbeth*.

As for the *Elegy*, the chief merit of it consists in the very graphical description of the objects belonging to the country in which the poet writes, and which none but a Scottish poet could have described, and none but a real poet, and a close observer of Nature, could have *so* described.

* * * * * * * *

There is something original, and to me wonderfully pleasing, in the *Epitaph*.

I remember you once hinted before, what you repeat in your last, that you had made some remarks on *Zeluco*, on the margin. I should be very glad to see them, and regret you did not send them before the last edition, which is just published. Pray transcribe them for me; I sincerely value your opinion very highly, and pray do not suppress one of those in which you
censure

censure the sentiment or expression. Trust me it will break no squares between us—I am not akin to the Bishop of Grenada.

I must now mention what has been on my mind for some time: I cannot help thinking you imprudent, in scattering abroad so many copies of your verses. It is most natural to give a few to confidential friends, particularly to those who are connected with the subject, or who are perhaps themselves the subject, but this ought to be done under promise not to give other copies. Of the poem you sent me on Queen Mary, I refused every solicitation for copies, but I lately saw it in a newspaper. My motive for cautioning you on this subject, is, that I wish to engage you to collect all your fugitive pieces, not already printed, and after they have been re-considered, and polished to the utmost of your power, I would have you publish them by another subscription: in promoting of which I will exert myself with pleasure.

In your future compositions, I wish you would use the modern English. You have shewn your powers in Scottish sufficiently. Although in certain subjects it gives additional zest to the humour, yet it is lost to the English; and

and why should you write only for a part of the island, when you can command the admiration of the whole?

If you chance to write to my friend Mrs. Dunlop, of Dunlop, I beg to be affectionately remembered to her. She must not judge of the warmth of my sentiments respecting her by the number of my letters: I hardly ever write a line but on business; and I do not know that I should have scribbled all this to you, but for the business part, that is, to instigate you to a new publication; and to tell you, that when you think you have a sufficient number to make a volume, you should set your friends on getting subscriptions. I wish I could have a few hours' conversation with you—I have many things to say, which I cannot write. If I ever go to Scotland, I will let you know, that you may meet me at your own house, or my friend Mrs. Hamilton's, or both.

Adieu, my dear Sir, &c.

No.

No. CXIV.

To the Rev. ARCH. ALISON.

Ellisland, near Dumfries, 14*th Feb.* 1791.

SIR,

You must, by this time, have set me down as one of the most ungrateful of men. You did me the honour to present me with a book which does honour to science and the intellectual powers of man, and I have not even so much as acknowledged the receipt of it. The fact is, you yourself are to blame for it. Flattered as I was by your telling me that you wished to have my opinion of the work, the old spiritual enemy of mankind, who knows well that vanity is one of the sins that most easily beset me, put it into my head to ponder over the performance with the look-out of a critic, and to draw up, forsooth, a deep-learned digest of strictures, on a composition, of which, in fact, until I read the book, I did not even know the first principles. I own, Sir, that, at first glance, several of your propositions startled me as paradoxical. That the martial clangor of a trumpet had something in it vastly more grand, heroic, and sublime, than the twingle twangle of a jew's-harp; that the delicate flexure of a rose-twig, when the half-blown flower is heavy with the tears of the dawn, was infinitely more beautiful and elegant than the upright stub of a burdock; and that from something innate and independent of all association of ideas;—these I had set down as irrefragable, orthodox truths, until perusing your book shook my faith.—In short, Sir, except *Euclid's Elements of Geometry*, which I made a shift to unravel by my father's fire-side, in the winter evening of the first season I held the plough, I never read a book which gave me such a quantum of information, and added so much to my stock of ideas as your " *Essays on the Principles of Taste.*" One thing, Sir, you must forgive my mentioning as an uncommon merit in the work, I mean the language. To clothe abstract philosophy in elegance of style, sounds something like a contradiction in terms; but you have convinced me that they are quite compatible.

I inclose you some poetic bagatelles of my late composition. The one in print is my first essay in the way of telling a tale.

I am, Sir, &c.

No.

No. CXV.

EXTRACT OF A LETTER

To Mr. CUNNINGHAM.

12*th March,* 1791.

If the foregoing piece be worth your strictures, let me have them. For my own part, a thing that I have just composed always appears through a double portion of that partial medium in which an author will ever view his own works. I believe, in general, novelty has something in it that inebriates the fancy, and not unfrequently dissipates and fumes away like other intoxication, and leaves the poor patient, as usual, with an aching heart. A striking instance of this might be adduced in the revolution of many a hymeneal honeymoon. But, lest I sink into stupid prose, and so sacrilegiously intrude on the office of my parish priest, I shall fill up the page in my own way, and give you another song of my late composition, which will appear perhaps in Johnson's work, as well as the former.

You must know a beautiful Jacobite air, *There'll never be peace till Jamie comes hame.* When political combustion ceases to be the object of princes and patriots, it then, you know, becomes the lawful prey of historians and poets.

. . . .

By yon castle wa' at the close of the day,
I heard a man sing, tho' his head it was grey;
And as he was singing, the tears fast down came—
There'll never be peace till Jamie comes hame.

The church is in ruins, the state is in jars,
Delusions, oppressions, and murderous wars:
We dare na' weel say't, but we ken wha's to blame—
There'll never be peace till Jamie comes hame.

My seven braw sons for Jamie drew sword,
And now I greet round their green beds in the yerd:
It brak the sweet heart o' my faithfu' auld dame—
There'll never be peace till Jamie comes hame.

Now life is a burden that bows me down,
Sin' I tint my bairns, and he tint his crown;
But till my last moment my words are the same—
There'll never be peace till Jamie comes hame.

. . . .

If

If you like the air, and if the stanzas hit your fancy, you cannot imagine, my dear friend, how much you would oblige me, if, by the charms of your delightful voice, you would give my honest effusion to " the memory of joys that are past!" to the few friends whom you indulge in that pleasure. But I have scribbled on 'till I hear the clock has intimated the near approach of

" That hour, o' night's black arch the key-stane."

So, good night to you! Sound be your sleep, and delectable your dreams!—Apropos, how do you like this thought in a ballad I have just now on the tapis?

   I look to the west when I gae to rest,
      That happy my dreams and my slumbers may be;
   For far in the west is he I lo'e best,
      The lad that is dear to my babie and me!

. . . .

Good night, once more, and God bless you!

No.

No. CXVI.

To Mrs. DUNLOP.

Ellisland, 11th April, 1791.

I am once more able, my honoured friend, to return you, with my own hand, thanks for the many instances of your friendship, and particularly for your kind anxiety in this last disaster that my evil genius had in store for me. However, life is chequered—joy and sorrow—for on Saturday morning last, Mrs. Burns made me a present of a fine boy, rather stouter, but not so handsome as your godson was at his time of life. Indeed I look on your little namesake to be my *chef d'œuvre* in that species of manufacture, as I look on *Tam o' Shanter* to be my standard performance in the poetical line. 'Tis true, both the one and the other discover a spice of roguish waggery that might perhaps be as well spared; but then they also

also shew, in my opinion, a force of genius, and a finishing polish, that I despair of ever excelling. Mrs. Burns is getting stout again, and laid as lustily about her to-day at breakfast, as a reaper from the corn-ridge. That is the peculiar privilege and blessing of our hale sprightly damsels, that are bred among the *hay and heather*. We cannot hope for that highly polished mind, that charming delicacy of soul, which is found among the female world in the more elevated stations of life, and which is certainly by far the most bewitching charm in the famous cestus of Venus. It is indeed such an inestimable treasure, that where it can be had in its native heavenly purity, unstained by some one or other of the many shades of affectation, and unalloyed by some one or other of the many species of caprice, I declare to Heaven, I should think it cheaply purchased at the expense of every other earthly good! But as this angelic creature is, I am afraid, extremely rare in any station and rank of life, and totally denied to such a humble one as mine; we meaner mortals must put up with the next rank of female excellence—as fine a figure and face we can produce as any rank of life whatever; rustic, native grace; unaffected modesty, and unsullied purity; nature's mother-wit, and the rudiments of taste; a simplicity of soul, unsuspicious of,

because

because unacquainted with, the crooked ways of a selfish, interested, disingenuous world; and the dearest charm of all the rest, a yielding sweetness of disposition, and a generous warmth of heart, grateful for love on our part, and ardently glowing with a more than equal return; these, with a healthy frame, a sound, vigorous constitution, which your higher ranks can scarcely ever hope to enjoy, are the charms of lovely woman in my humble walk of life.

This is the greatest effort my broken arm has yet made. Do let me hear, by first post, how *cher petit Monsieur* comes on with his small-pox. May Almighty Goodness preserve and restore him!

No.

No. CXVII.

To ——————.

DEAR SIR,

I AM exceedingly to blame in not writing you long ago; but the truth is, that I am the most indolent of all human beings; and when I matriculate in the Herald's office, I intend that my supporters shall be two sloths, my crest a slow-worm, and the motto, " Deil tak the foremost!" So much by way of apology for not thanking you sooner for your kind execution of my commission.

I would have sent you the poem: but somehow or other it found its way into the public papers, where you must have seen it.

* * * * * *

I am ever, dear Sir, yours sincerely,

ROBERT BURNS.

No.

No. CXVIII.

To Mr. CUNNINGHAM.

11th June, 1791.

LET me interest you, my dear Cunningham, in behalf of the gentleman who waits on you with this. He is a Mr. Clarke, of Moffat, principal schoolmaster there, and is at present suffering severely under the ****** of one or two powerful individuals of his employers. He is accused of harshness to **** that were placed under his care. God help the teacher, if a man of sensibility and genius, and such is my friend Clarke, when a booby father presents him with his booby son, and insists on lighting up the rays of science in a fellow's head whose skull is impervious and inaccessible by any other way than a positive fracture with a cudgel: a fellow whom, in fact, it savours of impiety to attempt making a scholar of, as he has been marked a blockhead in the book of fate, at the almighty fiat of his Creator.

The

The patrons of Moffat-school are the ministers, magistrates, and town-council of Edinburgh; and as the business comes now before them, let me beg my dearest friend to do every thing in his power to serve the interests of a man of genius and worth, and a man whom I particularly respect and esteem. You know some good fellows among the magistracy and council, * * * * * * * * * * * * but particularly you have much to say with a reverend gentleman, to whom you have the honour of being very nearly related, and whom this country and age have had the honour to produce. I need not name the historian of Charles V.* I tell him through the medium of his nephew's influence, that Mr. Clarke is a gentleman who will not disgrace even his patronage. I know the merits of the cause thoroughly, and say it, that my friend is falling a sacrifice to prejudiced ignorance, and ******. God help the children of dependence! Hated and persecuted by their enemies, and too often, alas! almost unexceptionably, received by their friends with disrespect and reproach, under the thin disguise of cold civility and humiliating advice. O to be a sturdy savage, stalking in the

---

* Dr. Robertson was uncle to Mr. Cunningham.

E.

the pride of his independence, amid the solitary wilds of his desarts; rather than in civilized life, helplessly to tremble for a subsistence, precarious as the caprice of a fellow-creature! Every man has his virtues, and no man is without his failings; and curse on that privileged plain-dealing of friendship, which, in the hour of my calamity, cannot reach forth the helping hand, without at the same time pointing out those failings, and apportioning them their share in procuring my present distress. My friends, for such the world calls ye, and such ye think yourselves to be, pass by my virtues if you please, but do, also, spare my follies: the first will witness in my breast for themselves, and the last will give pain enough to the ingenuous mind without you. And since deviating more or less from the paths of propriety and rectitude must be incident to human nature, do thou, Fortune, put it in my power, always from myself, and of myself, to bear the consequences of those errors! I do not want to be independent that I may sin, but I want to be independent in my sinning.

To return, in this rambling letter, to the subject I set out with, let me recommend my friend, Mr. Clarke, to your acquaintance and good offices; his worth entitles him to the one, and his gratitude will merit the other. I long much to hear from you. Adieu!

No.

No. CXIX.

From the EARL *of* BUCHAN.

Dryburgh Abbey, 17*th June,* 1791.

LORD BUCHAN has the pleasure to invite Mr. Burns to make one at the coronation of the bust of Thomson, on Ednam Hill, on the 22d of September; for which day perhaps his muse may inspire an ode suited to the occasion. Suppose Mr. Burns should, leaving the Nith, go across the country, and meet the Tweed at the nearest point from his farm—and, wandering along the pastoral banks of Thomson's pure parent stream, catch inspiration on the devious walk, till he finds Lord Buchan sitting on the ruins of Dryburgh. There the commendator will give him a hearty welcome, and try to light his lamp at the pure flame of native genius, upon the altar of Caledonian virtue. This poetical perambulation of the Tweed, is a
thought

thought of the late Sir Gilbert Elliot's, and of Lord Minto's, followed out by his accomplished grandson, the present Sir Gilbert, who having been with Lord Buchan lately, the project was renewed, and will, they hope, be executed in the manner proposed.

No.

No. CXX.

To the Earl *of* BUCHAN.

MY LORD,

Language sinks under the ardour of my feelings when I would thank your lordship for the honour you have done me in inviting me to make one at the coronation of the bust of Thomson. In my first enthusiasm in reading the card you did me the honour to write me, I overlooked every obstacle, and determined to go; but I fear it will not be in my power. A week or two's absence, in the very middle of my harvest, is what I much doubt I dare not venture on.

Your lordship hints at an ode for the occasion: but who would write after Collins? I read over his verses to the memory of Thomson, and despaired.—I got indeed, to the length of three or four stanzas, in the way of address to the shade of the bard, on crowning his bust. I shall trouble your lordship with the subjoined copy of them, which, I am afraid, will be but too convincing a proof how unequal I am to the task. However, it affords me an opportunity of approaching your lordship, and declaring how sincerely and gratefully I have the honour to be, &c.

* * * * * * * *

No.

No. CXXI.

FROM THE SAME.

Dryburgh Abbey, 16th Sept. 1791.

SIR,

Your address to the shade of Thomson has been well received by the public; and though I should disapprove of your allowing Pegasus to ride with you off the field of your honourable and useful profession, yet I cannot resist an impulse which I feel at this moment to suggest to your Muse, *Harvest Home,* as an excellent subject for her grateful song, in which the peculiar aspect and manners of our country might furnish an excellent portrait and landscape of Scotland, for the employment of happy moments of leisure and recess from your more important occupations.

Your *Halloween*, and *Saturday Night*, will remain to distant posterity as interesting pictures of rural innocence and happiness in your native country, and were happily written in the dialect of the people; but *Harvest Home*, being suited to descriptive poetry, except where colloquial, may escape the disguise of a dialect which admits of no elegance or dignity of expression. Without the assistance of any god or goddess, and without the invocation of any foreign Muse, you may convey in epistolary form the description of a scene so gladdening and picturesque, with all the concomitant local position, landscape, and costume, contrasting the peace, improvement, and happiness of the borders of the once hostile nations of Britain, with their former oppression and misery, and shewing, in lively and beautiful colours, the beauties and joys of a rural life. And as the unvitiated heart is naturally disposed to overflow with gratitude in the moment of prosperity, such a subject would furnish you with an amiable opportunity of perpetuating the names of Glencairn, Miller, and your other eminent benefactors; which from what I know of your spirit, and have seen of your poems and letters, will not deviate from the chastity of praise that is so uniformly united to true taste and genius.

I am, Sir, &c.

No.

No. CXXII.

To Lady E. CUNNINGHAM.

MY LADY,

I WOULD, as usual, have availed myself of the privilege your goodness has allowed me, of sending you any thing I compose in my poetical way; but as I had resolved, so soon as the shock of my irreparable loss would allow me, to pay a tribute to my late benefactor, I determined to make that the first piece I should do myself the honour of sending you. Had the wing of my fancy been equal to the ardour of my heart, the inclosed had been much more worthy your perusal: as it is, I beg leave to lay it at your ladyship's feet. As all the world knows my obligations to the late Earl of Glencairn, I would wish to shew as openly that my heart glows, and shall ever glow, with the most grateful sense and remembrance of his lordship's goodness. The sables I did myself the honour to wear to his lordship's memory, were not the " mockery of woe." Nor shall my gratitude perish with me!—If, among my children, I shall have a son that has a heart, he shall hand it down to his child as a family honour, and a family debt, that my dearest existence I owe to the noble house of Glencairn!

I was about to say, my lady, that if you think the poem may venture to see the light, I would, in some way or other, give it to the world.*

* * * * * * *

No.

---

* The poem inclosed is published, *vol.* iii. *p.* 320. *The Lament for James, Earl of Glencairn.*   E.

No. CXXIII.

To Mr. AINSLIE.

MY DEAR AINSLIE,

Can you minister to a mind diseased? Can you, amid the horrors of penitence, regret, remorse, head-ache, nausea, and all the rest of the d——d hounds of hell, that beset a poor wretch who has been guilty of the sin of drunkenness—can you speak peace to a troubled soul?

Miserable perdu that I am! I have tried every thing that used to amuse me, but in vain: here must I sit, a monument of the vengeance laid up in store for the wicked, slowly counting every chick of the clock as it slowly—slowly, numbers over these lazy scoundrels of hours, who, d—n them, are ranked up before me, every one at his neighbour's backside, and every one with a burden of anguish on his back, to pour on my devoted head—and there is none to pity me. My wife scolds me! my business torments me, and my sins come staring me in the face, every one telling a more bitter tale than his fellow.—When I tell you even * * * has lost its power to please, you will guess something of my hell within, and all around me.—I began *Elibanks and Elibraes*, but the stanzas fell unenjoyed and unfinished from my listless tongue; at last I luckily thought of reading over an old letter of yours that lay by me in my book-case, and I felt something, for the first time since I opened my eyes, of pleasurable existence.——— Well—I begin to breathe a little, since I began to write you. How are you? and what are you doing? How goes Law? Apropos, for connexion's sake, do not address to me supervisor, for that is an honour I cannot pretend to—I am on the list, as we call it, for a supervisor, and will be called out by-and-by to act as one; but at present I am a simple gauger, tho' t'other day I got an appointment to an excise division of 25*l. per ann.* better than the rest. My present income, down money, is 70*l. per ann.*

* * * * * * *

I have one or two good fellows here whom you would be glad to know.

* * * * * * *

No.

No. CXXIV.

From Sir JOHN WHITEFOORD.

Near Maybole, 16th October, 1791.

SIR,

Accept of my thanks for your favour, with the *Lament* on the death of my much-esteemed friend, and your worthy patron, the perusal of which pleased and affected me much. The lines addressed to me are very flattering.

I have always thought it most natural to suppose, (and a strong argument in favour of a future existence) that when we see an honourable and virtuous man labouring under bodily infirmities, and oppressed by the frowns of fortune in this world, that there was a happier state beyond the grave; where that worth and honour, which were neglected here, would meet with their just reward; and where temporal misfortunes

fortunes would receive an eternal recompense. Let us cherish this hope for our departed friend, and moderate our grief for that loss we have sustained, knowing that he cannot return to us, but we may go to him.

Remember me to your wife; and with every good wish for the prosperity of you and your family, believe me at all times,

Your most sincere friend,

JOHN WHITEFOORD.

No.

No. CXXV.

From A. F. TYTLER, Esq.

Edinburgh, 27th November, 1791.

DEAR SIR,

You have much reason to blame me for neglecting till now to acknowledge the receipt of a most agreeable packet, containing *The Whistle*, a ballad; and *The Lament;* which reached me about six weeks ago in London, from whence I am just returned. Your letter was forwarded to me there from Edinburgh, where, as I observed by the date, it had lain for some days. This was an additional reason for me to have answered it immediately on receiving it; but the truth was, the bustle of business, engagements, and confusion of one kind or another, in which I found myself immersed all the time I was in London, absolutely put it out of my power. But to have done with apologies,

apologies, let me now endeavour to prove myself in some degree deserving of the very flattering compliment you pay me, by giving you at least a frank and a candid, if it should not be a judicious, criticism on the poems you sent me.

The ballad of *The Whistle* is, in my opinion, truly excellent. The old tradition which you have taken up is the best adapted for a Bacchanalian composition of any I ever met with, and you have done it full justice. In the first place, the strokes of wit arise naturally from the subject, and are uncommonly happy. For example,

" The bands grew the tighter the more they were wet."

" Cynthia hinted he'd find them next morn."

" Tho' Fate said a hero should perish in light;
So up rose bright Phœbus, and down fell the knight."

In the next place, you are singularly happy in the discrimination of your heroes, and in giving each the sentiments and language suitable to his character. And, lastly, you have much merit in the delicacy of the panegyric which you have contrived to throw on each of the *dramatis personæ*, perfectly appropriate to his character.

character. The compliment to Sir Robert, the blunt soldier, is peculiarly fine. In short, this composition, in my opinion, does you great honour, and I see not a line or a word in it which I could wish to be altered.

As to *The Lament*, I suspect, from some expressions in your letter to me, that you are more doubtful with respect to the merits of this piece than of the other; and I own I think you have reason; for although it contains some beautiful stanzas, as the first, " The wind blew hollow," &c. the fifth, " Ye scatter'd birds;" the thirteenth, " Awake thy last sad voice," &c. yet it appears to me faulty as a whole, and inferior to several of those you have already published in the same strain. My principal objection lies against the plan of the piece. I think it was unnecessary and improper to put the lamentation in the mouth of a fictitious character, an *aged bard.*—It had been much better to have lamented your patron in your own person, to have expressed your genuine feelings for the loss, and to have spoken the language of nature, rather than that of fiction, on the subject. Compare this with your poem of the same title in your printed volume, which begins, *O thou pale Orb!* and observe what it is that forms the charm of that composition. It is, that it speaks the

the language of *truth* and of *nature*. The change is, in my opinion, injudicious too in this respect, that an *aged* bard has much less need of a patron and a protector than a *young* one. I have thus given you, with much freedom, my opinion of both the pieces. I should have made a very ill return to the compliment you paid me, if I had given you any other than my genuine sentiments.

It will give me great pleasure to hear from you when you find leisure; and I beg you will believe me ever, dear Sir, yours, &c.

No. CXXVI.

To Miss DAVIES.

It is impossible, Madam, that the generous warmth and angelic purity of your youthful mind can have any idea of that moral disease under which I unhappily must rank as the chief of sinners; I mean a torpitude of the moral powers, that may be called a lethargy of conscience.—In vain remorse rears her horrent crest, and rouses all her snakes: beneath the deadly-fixed eye and leaden hand of Indolence, their wildest ire is charmed into the torpor of the bat, slumbering out the rigours of winter in the chink of a ruined wall. Nothing less, Madam, could have made me so long neglect your obliging commands. Indeed I had one apology—the bagatelle was not worth presenting. Besides, so strongly am I interested in Miss D——'s fate and welfare in the serious business of life, amid its chances and changes; that to make her the subject of a silly ballad, is downright mockery of these ardent feelings; 'tis like an impertinent jest to a dying friend.

Gracious

Gracious Heaven! why this disparity between our wishes and our powers? Why is the most generous wish to make others blest, impotent and ineffectual—as the idle breeze that crosses the pathless desert? In my walks of life I have met with a few people to whom how gladly would I have said—" Go, be happy! I
" know that your hearts have been wounded by
" the scorn of the proud, whom accident has
" placed above you—or worse still, in whose
" hands are, perhaps, placed many of the com-
" forts of your life. But there! ascend that
" rock, Independence, and look justly down on
" their littleness of soul. Make the worthless
" tremble under your indignation, and the fool-
" ish sink before your contempt; and largely
" impart that happiness to others, which, I am
" certain, will give yourselves so much pleasure
" to bestow!"

Why, dear Madam, must I wake from this delightful reverie, and find it all a dream? Why, amid my generous enthusiasm, must I find myself poor and powerless, incapable of wiping one tear from the eye of pity, or of adding one comfort to the friend I love!—Out upon the world! say I, that its affairs are administered so ill! They talk of reform;—good Heaven! what a reform would I make among the sons, and even

the

the daughters of men!—Down, immediately, should go fools from the high places where misbegotten chance has perked them up, and through life should they skulk, ever haunted by their native insignificance, as the body marches accompanied by its shadow.—As for a much more formidable class, the knaves, I am at a loss what to do with them: had I a world, there should not be a knave in it.

* * * * * * *

But the hand that could give, I would liberally fill; and I would pour delight on the heart that could kindly forgive and generously love.

Still, the inequalities of life are, among men, comparatively tolerable—but there is a delicacy, a tenderness, accompanying every view in which we can place lovely Woman, that are grated and shocked at the rude, capricious distinctions of fortune. Woman is the blood-royal of life: let there be slight degrees of precedency among them—but let them be ALL sacred.—Whether this last sentiment be right or wrong, I am not accountable; it is an original component feature of my mind.

No.

No. CXXVII.

To Mrs. DUNLOP.

Ellisland, 17th December, 1791.

MANY thanks to you, Madam, for your good news respecting the little floweret and the mother-plant. I hope my poetic prayers have been heard, and will be answered up to the warmest sincerity of their fullest extent; and then Mrs. Henri will find her little darling the representative of his late parent, in every thing but his abridged existence.

I have just finished the following song, which, to a lady the descendant of Wallace, and many heroes of his truly illustrious line, and herself the mother of several soldiers, needs neither preface nor apology.

. . . .

Scene—A Field of Battle—Time of the Day, Evening— the wounded and dying of the victorious Army are supposed to join in the following

SONG OF DEATH.

Farewel thou fair day, thou green earth, and ye skies,
    Now gay with the broad setting sun;
Farewel, loves and friendships; ye dear, tender ties,
    Our race of existence is run!

Thou grim king of terrors, thou life's gloomy foe,
    Go, frighten the coward and slave;
Go, teach them to tremble, fell tyrant! but know,
    No terrors hast thou to the brave!

Thou strik'st the poor peasant—he sinks in the dark,
    Nor saves e'en the wreck of a name:
Thou strik'st the young hero—a glorious mark!
    He falls in the blaze of his fame!

In the field of proud honour—our swords in our hands,
    Our king and our country to save—
While victory shines on life's last ebbing sands—
    O, who would not die with the brave!

. . . .

    The circumstance that gave rise to the foregoing verses, was looking over, with a musical friend, M'Donald's collection of Highland airs, I was struck with one, an Isle of Skye tune, entitled

entitled *Oran an Aoig*, or, *The Song of Death*, to the measure of which I have adapted my stanzas. I have of late composed two or three other little pieces, which, ere yon full-orbed moon, whose broad impudent face now stares at old mother earth all night, shall have shrunk into a modest crescent, just peeping forth at dewy dawn, I shall find an hour to transcribe for you. *A Dieu je vous commende!*

No. CXXVIII.

To Mrs. DUNLOP.

5th January, 1792.

You see my hurried life, Madam; I can only command starts of time: however, I am glad of one thing; since I finished the other sheet, the political blast that threatened my welfare is overblown. I have corresponded with Commissioner Graham, for the Board had made me the subject of their animadversions; and now I have the pleasure of informing you, that all is set to rights in that quarter. Now as to these informers, may the devil be let loose to —— but hold! I was preying most fervently in my last sheet, and I must not so soon fall a swearing in this.

Alas! how little do the wantonly or idly officious think what mischief they do by their malicious insinuations, indirect impertinence, or thoughtless blabbings! What a difference there is in intrinsic worth, candour, benevolence, generosity, kindness—in all the charities and all the virtues, between one class of human beings and another! For instance, the amiable circle I so lately mixed with in the hospitable hall of D——, their generous hearts—their uncontaminated dignified minds—their informed and polished understandings—what a contrast, when compared—if such comparing were not downright sacrilege—with the soul of the miscreant who can deliberately plot the destruction of an honest man that never offended him, and with a grin of satisfaction see the unfortunate being, his faithful wife and prattling innocents, turned over to beggary and ruin!

Your cup, my dear Madam, arrived safe. I had two worthy fellows dining with me the other day, when I, with great formality, produced my whigmeleerie cup, and told them that it had been a family-piece among the descendants of Sir William Wallace. This roused such an enthusiasm, that they insisted on bumpering the punch round in it; and, by and by, never did your great ancestor lay a *Suthron* more completely to rest, than for a time did your cup my two friends. Apropos! this is the season of wishing. May God bless you, my dear friend! and bless me, the humblest and sincerest of your friends, by granting you yet many returns of the season! May all good things attend you and yours wherever they are scattered over the earth!

No.

No. CXXIX.

To Mr. WILLIAM SMELLIE, *Printer*.

Dumfries, 22d January, 1792.

I sit down, my dear Sir, to introduce a young lady to you, and a lady in the first rank of fashion, too. What a task! to you—who care no more for the herd of animals called young ladies, than you do for the herd of animals called young gentlemen. To you—who despise and detest the groupings and combinations of fashion, as an idiot painter that seems industrious to place staring fools and unprincipled knaves in the foreground of his picture, while men of sense and honesty are too often thrown in the dimmest shades. Mrs. Riddel, who will take this letter to town with her, and send it to you, is a character that, even in your own way as a naturalist and a philosopher, would be an acquisition to your acquaintance.

The

The lady too is a votary of the muses; and as I think myself somewhat of a judge in my own trade, I assure you that her verses, always correct, and often elegant, are much beyond the common run of the *lady-poetesses* of the day. She is a great admirer of your book; and, hearing me say that I was acquainted with you, she begged to be known to you, as she is just going to pay her first visit to our Caledonian capital. I told her that her best way was, to desire her near relation, and your intimate friend, Craigdarroch, to have you at his house while she was there; and lest you might think of a lively West Indian girl of eighteen, as girls of eighteen too often deserve to be thought of, I should take care to remove that prejudice. To be impartial, however, in appreciating the lady's merits, she has one unlucky failing: a failing which you will easily discover, as she seems rather pleased with indulging in it; and a failing that you will as easily pardon, as it is a sin which very much besets yourself;—where she dislikes or despises, she is apt to make no more a secret of it, than where she esteems and respects.

I will not present you with the unmeaning *compliments of the season*, but I will send you my warmest wishes and most ardent prayers,
that

that FORTUNE may never throw your SUBSISTENCE to the mercy of a knave, or set your CHARACTER on the judgment of a FOOL; but that, upright and erect, you may walk to an honest grave, where men of letters shall say, Here lies a man who did honour to science! and men of worth shall say, Here lies a man who did honour to human nature.

No.

No. CXXX.

To Mr. W. NICOL.

20th February, 1792.

O THOU, wisest among the wise, meridian blaze of prudence, full moon of discretion, and chief of many counsellors! How infinitely is thy puddle-headed, rattle-headed, wrong-headed, round-headed slave indebted to thy super-eminent goodness, that from the luminous path of thy own right-lined rectitude, thou lookest benignly down on an erring wretch, of whom the zig-zag wanderings defy all the powers of calculation, from the simple copulation of units up to the hidden mysteries of fluxions: May one feeble ray of that light of wisdom which darts from thy sensorium, straight as the arrow of heaven, and bright as the meteor of inspiration, may it be my portion, so that I may be less unworthy of the face and favour of that father of proverbs and master of
maxims,

maxims, that antipode of folly, and magnet among the sages, the wise and witty Willie Nicol! Amen! Amen! Yea, so be it!

For me! I am a beast, a reptile, and know nothing! From the cave of my ignorance, amid the fogs of my dulness, and pestilential fumes of my political heresies, I look up to thee, as doth a toad through the iron-barred lucerne of a pestiferous dungeon, to the cloudless glory of a summer sun! Sorely sighing in bitterness of soul, I say, when shall my name be the quotation of the wise, and my countenance be the delight of the godly, like the illustrious lord of Laggan's many hills?* As for him, his works are perfect: never did the pen of calumny blur the fair page of his reputation, nor the bolt of hatred fly at his dwelling.

* * * * * * *

Thou mirror of purity, when shall the elfine lamp of my glimmerous understanding, purged from sensual appetites and gross desires, shine like the constellation of thy intellectual powers? —As for thee, thy thoughts are pure, and thy lips are holy. Never did the unhallowed breath
of

---

* Mr. Nicol.

of the powers of darkness, and the pleasures of darkness, pollute the sacred flame of thy sky-descended and heaven-bound desires: never did the vapours of impurity stain the unclouded serene of thy cerulean imagination. O that like thine were the tenor of my life, like thine the tenor of my conversation! then should no friend fear for my strength, no enemy rejoice in my weakness! then should I lie down and rise up, and none to make me afraid.—May thy pity and thy prayer be exercised for, O thou lamp of wisdom and mirror of morality! thy devoted slave.*

---

* This strain of irony was excited by a letter of Mr. Nicol, containing good advice.

E.

No. CXXXI.

To Mr. CUNNINGHAM.

3d March, 1792.

Since I wrote to you the last lugubrious sheet, I have not had time to write you farther. When I say that I had not time, that, as usual, means, that the three demons, indolence, business, and ennui, have so completely shared my hours among them, as not to leave me a five-minutes fragment to take up a pen in.

Thank heaven, I feel my spirits buoying upwards with the renovating year. Now I shall in good earnest take up Thomson's songs. I dare say he thinks I have used him unkindly, and I must own with too much appearance of truth. Apropos! Do you know the much-admired old Highland air called *The Suior's Dochter?* It is a first-rate favourite of mine, and I have written what I reckon one of my best songs to it. I will send it to you as it was sung

sung with great applause in some fashionable circles by Major Robertson of Lude, who was here with his corps.

* * * * * *

There is one commission that I must trouble you with. I lately lost a valuable seal, a present from a departed friend, which vexes me much. I have gotten one of your Highland pebbles, which I fancy would make a very decent one; and I want to cut my armorial bearing on it; will you be so obliging as inquire what will be the expence of such a business? I do not know that my name is matriculated, as the heralds call it, at all; but I have invented arms for myself, so you know I shall be chief of the name; and, by courtesy of Scotland, will likewise be entitled to supporters. These, however, I do not intend having on my seal. I am a bit of a herald, and shall give you, *secundum artem*, my arms. On a field, azure, a holly bush, seeded, proper, in base; a shepherd's pipe and crook, saltier-wise, also proper, in chief. On a wreath of the colours, a wood-lark perching on a sprig of bay-tree, proper, for crest. Two mottoes; round the top of the crest, *Wood notes wild;* at the bottom of the shield, in the usual place, *Better a wee bush than nae bield.* By the shepherd's pipe and crook I do

not

not mean the nonsense of painters of Arcadia, but a *Stock and Horn*, and a *Club*, such as you see at the head of Allan Ramsay, in Allan's quarto edition of the *Gentle Shepherd*. By the by, do you know Allan? He must be a man of very great genius—Why is he not more known? —Has he no patrons? or do " Poverty's cold " wind and crushing rain beat keen and heavy" on him? I once, and but once, got a glance of that noble edition of that noblest pastoral in the world; and dear as it was, I mean, dear as to my pocket, I would have bought it; but I was told that it was printed and engraved for subscribers only. He is the *only* artist who has hit *genuine* pastoral *costume*. What, my dear Cunningham, is there in riches, that they narrow and harden the heart so? I think, that were I as rich as the sun, I should be as generous as the day; but as I have no reason to imagine my soul a nobler one than any other man's, I must conclude that wealth imparts a bird-lime quality to the possessor, at which the man, in his native poverty, would have revolted. What has led me to this, is the idea of such merit as Mr. Allan possesses, and such riches as a nabob or government contractor possesses, and why they do not form a mutual league. Let wealth shelter and cherish unprotected merit, and the gratitude and celebrity of that merit will richly repay it.

* * * * * * *

No.

No. CXXXII.

To Mrs. DUNLOP.

Annan Water Foot, 22d *August*, 1792.

Do not blame me for it, Madam—my own conscience, hackneyed and weather-beaten as it is, in watching and reproving my vagaries, follies, indolence, &c. has continued to blame and punish me sufficiently.

* * * * * * * *

Do you think it possible, my dear and honoured friend, that I could be so lost to gratitude for many favours; to esteem for much worth, and to the honest, kind, pleasurable tie of, now old acquaintance, and I hope and am sure of progressive increasing friendship—as, for a single day, not to think of you—to ask the Fates what they are doing and about to do with my much-loved friend and her wide-scatteréd connexions, and to beg of them to be as kind to you and yours as they possibly can?

Apropos!

Apropos! (though how it is apropos, I have not leisure to explain) Do you know that I am almost in love with an acquaintance of yours?—Almost! said I—I am in love, souse! over head and ears, deep as the most unfathomable abyss of the boundless ocean; but the word Love, owing to the *intermingledoms* of the good and the bad, the pure and the impure, in this world, being rather an equivocal term for expressing one's sentiments and sensations, I must do justice to the sacred purity of my attachment. Know, then, that the heart-struck awe; the distant humble approach; the delight we should have in gazing upon and listening to a Messenger of Heaven, appearing in all the unspotted purity of his celestial home, among the coarse, polluted, far inferior sons of men, to deliver to them tidings that make their hearts swim in joy, and their imaginations soar in transport—such, so delighting and so pure, were the emotions of my soul on meeting the other day with Miss L— B—, your neighbour, at M———. Mr. B. with his two daughters, accompanied by Mr. H. of G. passing through Dumfries a few days ago, on their way to England, did me the honour of calling on me; on which I took my horse, (though God knows I could ill spare the time) and accompanied them fourteen or fifteen miles, and dined and spent the day

day with them. 'Twas about nine, I think, when left them, and, riding home, I composed the following ballad, of which you will probably think you have a dear bargain, as it will cost you another groat of postage. You must know that there is an old ballad beginning with—

" My bonnie Lizie Bailie
I'll rowe thee in my plaidie," &c.

So I parodied it as follows, which is literally the first copy, " unanointed, unanneal'd;" as Hamlet says.—*See vol.* iv. *p.* 15.

So much for ballads. I regret that you are gone to the east country, as I am to be in Ayrshire in about a fortnight. This world of ours, notwithstanding it has many good things in it, yet it has ever had this curse, that two or three people, who would be the happier the oftener they meet together, are almost without exception, always so placed as never to meet but once or twice a-year, which, considering the few years of a man's life, is a very great " evil under the sun," which I do not recollect that Solomon has mentioned in his catalogue of the miseries of man. I hope and believe that there is a state of existence beyond the grave, where the worthy of this life will renew their former intimacies,

intimacies, with this endearing addition, that, "we meet to part no more!"

* * * * * * * * * *

"Tell us, ye dead!
Will none of you in pity disclose the secret
What 'tis you are, and we must shortly be?"

A thousand times have I made this apostrophe to the departed sons of men, but not one of them has ever thought fit to answer the question. "O that some courteous ghost would blab it out!" but it cannot be; you and I, my friend, must make the experiment by ourselves, and for ourselves. However, I am so convinced that an unshaken faith in the doctrines of religion is not only necessary, by making us better men, but also by making us happier men, that I shall take every care that your little godson, and every little creature that shall call me father, shall be taught them.

So ends this heterogeneous letter, written at this wild place of the world, in the intervals of my labour of discharging a vessel of rum from Antigua.

No. CXXXIII.

To Mr. CUNNINGHAM.

Dumfries, 10*th September*, 1792.

No! I will not attempt an apology.—Amid all my hurry of business, grinding the faces of the publican and the sinner on the merciless wheels of the Excise; making ballads, and then drinking, and singing them; and, over and above all, the correcting the press-work of two different publications, still, still I might have stolen five minutes to dedicate to one of the first of my friends and fellow-creatures. I might have done, as I do at present, snatched an hour near " witching time of night," and scrawled a page or two. I might have congratulated my friend on his marriage; or I might have thanked the Caledonian archers for the honour they have done me, (though to do myself justice, I intended to have done both in rhyme, else I had done both long ere now.)

now.) Well, then, here is to your good health! for you must know, I have set a nipperkin of toddy by me, just by way of spell, to keep away the meikle-horned Deil, or any of his subaltern imps who may be on their nightly rounds.

But what shall I write to you? " The voice said, Cry!" and I said, " What shall I cry?"— O, thou spirit! whatever thou art, or wherever thou makest thyself visible! be thou a bogle by the eerie side of an auld thorn, in the dreary glen through which the herd-callan maun bicker in his gloamin route frae the faulde! Be thou a brownie, set, at dead of night, to thy task by the blazing ingle, or in the solitary barn, where the repercussions of thy iron flail half affright thyself as thou performest the work of twenty of the sons of men, ere the cock-crowing summon thee to thy ample cog of substantial brose. —Be thou a kelpie, haunting the ford or ferry, in the starless night, mixing thy laughing yell with the howling of the storm and the roaring of the flood, as thou viewest the perils and miseries of man on the foundering horse, or in the tumbling boat!—Or, lastly, be thou a ghost, paying thy nocturnal visits to the hoary ruins of decayed grandeur; or performing thy mystic rites in the shadow of the time-worn church, while the moon looks, without a cloud, on the

silent,

silent, ghastly dwellings of the dead around thee; or taking thy stand by the bedside of the villain, or the murderer, pourtraying on his dreaming fancy, pictures, dreadful as the horrors of unveiled hell, and terrible as the wrath of incensed Deity!—Come, thou spirit! but not in these horrid forms; come with the milder, gentle, easy inspirations which thou breathest round the wig of a prating advocate, or the tête of a tea-sipping gossip, while their tongues run at the light-horse gallop of clishmaclaver for ever and ever—come and assist a poor devil who is quite jaded in the attempt to share half an idea among half a hundred words; to fill up four quarto pages, while he has not got one single sentence of recollection, information, or remark, worth putting pen to paper for.

I feel, I feel the presence of supernatural assistance! circled in the embrace of my elbow-chair, my breast labours like the bloated Sybil on her three-footed stool, and like her too, labours with Nonsense. Nonsense, auspicious name! Tutor, friend, and finger-post in the mystic mazes of law; the cadaverous paths of physic; and particularly in the sightless soarings of SCHOOL DIVINITY, who, leaving Common Sense confounded at his strength of pinion, Reason, delirious with eyeing his giddy flight;

flight; and Truth creeping back into the bottom of her well, cursing the hour that ever she offered her scorned alliance to the wizard power of Theologic Vision—raves abroad on all the winds. "On earth Discord! a gloomy Heaven "above, opening her jealous gates to the nine- "teen thousandth part of the tithe of mankind! "and below, an inescapable and inexorable "hell, expanding its leviathan jaws for the "vast residue of mortals!!!"—O doctrine! comfortable and healing to the weary, wounded soul of man! Ye sons and daughters of affliction, ye *pauvres misérables*, to whom day brings no pleasure, and night yields no rest, be comforted! " 'Tis but *one* to nineteen hundred "thousand that your situation will mend in "this world;" so, alas! the experience of the poor and the needy too often affirms; and 'tis nineteen hundred thousand to *one*, but the dogmas of ********, that you will be damned eternally in the world to come!

But of all Nonsense, Religious Nonsense is the most nonsensical; so enough, and more than enough, of it. Only, by the bye, will you, or can you tell me, my dear Cunningham, why a sectarian turn of mind has always a tendency to narrow and illiberalize the heart? They are orderly; they may be just; nay, I have known them

them merciful; but still your children of sanctity move among their fellow-creatures, with a nostril-snuffing putrescence, and a foot-spurning filth, in short, with a conceited dignity that your titled * * * * * * * * * * or any other of your Scottish lordlings of seven centuries standing, display when they accidentally mix among the many-aproned sons of mechanical life. I remember, in my ploughboy days, I could not conceive it possible that a noble lord could be a fool, or a godly man could be a knave.—How ignorant are ploughboys!—Nay, I have since discovered that a *godly woman* may be a *****!—But hold—Here's t'ye again—this rum is generous Antigua, so a very unfit menstruum for scandal.

Apropos! How do you like, I mean *really* like, the married life? Ah, my friend! matrimony is quite a different thing from what your love-sick youths and sighing girls take it to be! But marriage, we are told, is appointed by God, and I shall never quarrel with any of his institutions. I am a husband of older standing than you, and shall give you *my* ideas of the conjugal state, *(en passant,* you know I am no Latinist: is not *conjugal* derived from *jugum,* a yoke?) -Well, then, the scale of good wifeship I divide into ten parts.—Good-nature, four;
Good

Good Sense, two; Wit, one; Personal Charms, viz. a sweet face, eloquent eyes, fine limbs, graceful carriage, (I would add a fine waist too, but that is so soon spoilt you know) all these, one; as for the other qualities belonging to, or attending on, a wife, such as Fortune, Connexions, Education, (I mean education extraordinary) Family blood, &c. divide the two remaining degrees among them as you please; only remember that all these minor properties must be expressed by *fractions*, for there is not any one of them, in the aforesaid scale, entitled to the dignity of an *integer*.

As for the rest of my fancies and reveries—how I lately met with Miss L—— B————, the most beautiful, elegant woman in the world—how I accompanied her and her father's family fifteen miles on their journey out of pure devotion, to admire the loveliness of the works of God, in such an unequalled display of them—how, in galloping home at night, I made a ballad on her, of which these two stanzas make a part—

> Thou, bonnie L——, art a queen,
>   Thy subjects we before thee;
> Thou, bonnie L——, art divine,
>   The hearts o' men adore thee.

>   The very Deil he could na scathe
>   Whatever wad belang thee!
>   He'd look into thy bonnie face,
>   And say, 'I canna wrang thee!'

—Behold all these things are written in the chronicles of my imaginations, and shall be read by thee, my dear friend, and by thy beloved spouse, my other dear friend, at a more convenient season.

Now, to thee, and to thy before-designed *bosom*-companion, be given the precious things brought forth by the sun, and the precious things brought forth by the moon, and the benignest influences of the stars, and the living streams which flow from the fountains of life, and by the tree of life, for ever and ever! Amen!

No.

No. CXXXIV.

To Mrs. DUNLOP.

Dumfries, 24th September, 1792.

I HAVE this moment, my dear Madam, yours of the twenty-third. All your other kind reproaches, your news, &c. are out of my head when I read and think on Mrs. H——'s situation. Good God! a heart-wounded, helpless young woman—in a strange foreign land, and that land convulsed with every horror that can harrow the human feelings—sick—looking, longing for a comforter, but finding none—a mother's feelings, too—but it is too much: he who wounded (he only can) may He heal!*

. . . .

I wish

---

* This much-lamented lady was gone to the south of France with her infant son, where she died soon after.

E.

I wish the farmer great joy of his new acquisition to his family. * * * * * * * *
I cannot say that I give him joy of his life as a farmer. 'Tis, as a farmer paying a dear, unconscionable rent, a *cursed life!* As to a laird farming his own property; sowing his own corn in hope; and reaping it, in spite of brittle weather, in gladness; knowing that none can say unto him, ' what dost thou?'—fattening his herds; shearing his flocks; rejoicing at Christmas; and begetting sons and daughters, until he be the venerated, gray-haired leader of a little tribe—'tis a heavenly life!—But devil take the life of reaping the fruits that another must eat!

Well, your kind wishes will be gratified, as to seeing me, when I make my Ayrshire visit. I cannot leave Mrs. B— until her nine months' race is run, which may perhaps be in three or four weeks. She, too, seems determined to make me the patriarchal leader of a band. However, if Heaven will be so obliging as to let me have them in the proportion of three boys to one girl, I shall be so much the more pleased. I hope, if I am spared with them, to shew a set of boys that will do honour to my cares and name; but I am not equal to the task of rearing girls. Besides, I am too poor; a girl should always

always have a fortune.—Apropos! your little godson is thriving charmingly, but is a very devil. He, though two years younger, has completely mastered his brother. Robert is indeed the mildest, gentlest creature I ever saw. He has a most surprising memory, and is quite the pride of his schoolmaster.

You know how readily we get into prattle upon a subject dear to our heart: you can excuse it. God bless you and yours!

No.

No. CXXXV.

To Mrs. DUNLOP.

Supposed to have been written on the Death of Mrs. H——, her Daughter.

I HAD been from home, and did not receive your letter until my return the other day. What shall I say to comfort you, my much-valued, much-afflicted friend! I can but grieve with you; consolation I have none to offer, except that which religion holds out to the children of affliction—*Children of affliction!* —how just the expression! and, like every other family, they have matters among them which they hear, see, and feel in a serious, all-important manner, of which the world has not, nor cares to have, any idea. The world looks indifferently on, makes the passing remark, and proceeds to the next novel occurrence.

Alas,

Alas, Madam! who would wish for many years? What is it but to drag existence until our joys gradually expire, and leave us in a night of misery; like the gloom which blots out the stars one by one, from the face of night, and leaves us without a ray of comfort in the howling waste!

I am interrupted, and must leave off. You shall soon hear from me again.

No.

No. CXXXVI.

To Mrs. DUNLOP.

Dumfries, 6th December, 1792.

I shall be in Ayrshire, I think, next week; and, if at all possible, I shall certainly, my much-esteemed friend, have the pleasure of visiting at Dunlop-house.

Alas, Madam! how seldom do we meet in this world, that we have reason to congratulate ourselves on accessions of happiness! I have not passed half the ordinary term of an old man's life, and yet I scarcely look over the obituary of a newspaper, that I do not see some names that I have known, and which I and other acquaintances, little thought to meet with there so soon. Every other instance of the mortality of our kind makes us cast an anxious look into the dreadful abyss of uncertainty, and shudder with apprehension for our own fate. But of how different an importance are the lives
of

of different individuals? Nay, of what importance is one period of the same life more than another? A few years ago, I could have lain down in the dust, " careless of the voice of the morning ;" and now not a few, and these most helpless individuals, would, on losing me and my exertions, lose both their, " staff and shield." By the way, these helpless ones have lately got an addition, Mrs. B— having given me a fine girl since I wrote you. There is a charming passage in Thomson's *Edward and Eleanora*—

" The valiant, *in himself*, what can he suffer?
Or what need he regard his *single woes?*" &c.

As I am got in the way of quotations, I shall give you another from the same piece, peculiarly, alas! too peculiarly apposite, my dear Madam, to your present frame of mind:

" Who so unworthy but may proudly deck him
With his fair-weather virtue, that exults
Glad o'er the summer main? the tempest comes,
The rough winds rage aloud; when from the helm
This virtue shrinks, and in a corner lies
Lamenting—Heavens! if privileged from trial,
How cheap a thing were virtue!"

I do not remember to have heard you men- on Thomson's dramas. I pick up favourite uotations, and store them in my mind as ready armour,

armour, offensive or defensive, amid the struggle of this turbulent existence. Of these is one, a very favourite one, from his *Alfred:*

> " Attach thee firmly to the virtuous deeds
> And offices of life; to life itself,
> With all its vain and transient joys, sit loose."

Probably I have quoted some of these to you formerly, as indeed when I write from the heart, I am apt to be guilty of such repetitions. The compass of the heart, in the musical style of expression, is much more bounded than that of the imagination; so the notes of the former are extremely apt to run into one another; but in return for the paucity of its compass, its few notes are much more sweet. I must still give you another quotation, which I am almost sure I have given you before, but I cannot resist the temptation. The subject is religion—speaking of its importance to mankind, the author says,

> " 'Tis this, my friend, that streaks our morning bright,"
> &c. *as in p.* 259.

I see you are in for a double postage, so I shall e'en scribble out t'other sheet. We, in this country here, have many alarms of the reforming, or rather the republican spirit, of your part of the kingdom. Indeed we are a good deal in commotion ourselves. For me, I am *a placeman,* you know; a very humble one indeed,

deed, Heaven knows, but still so much so as to gag me. What my private sentiments are, you will find out without an interpreter.

* * * * * *

I have taken up the subject in another view, and the other day, for a pretty Actress's benefit night, I wrote an Address, which I will give on the other page, called *The Rights of Woman.*

. . . .

THE RIGHTS OF WOMAN.

An Occasional Address spoken by Miss FONTE-NELLE *on her Benefit-Night.*

WHILE Europe's eye is fix'd on mighty things,
The fate of empires and the fall of kings;
While quacks of state must each produce his plan,
And even children lisp *the Rights of Man;*
Amid this mighty fuss, just let me mention,
The Rights of Woman merit some attention.

First, in the sexes' intermix'd connexion,
One sacred Right of Woman is *protection.—*
The tender flower that lifts its head, elate,
Helpless, must fall before the blasts of fate,
Sunk on the earth, defac'd its lovely form,
Unless your shelter ward th' impending storm.—

No. CXXXVII.

To Miss B*****, of York.

21st March, 1793.

MADAM,

Among many things for which I envy those hale, long-lived old fellows before the flood, is this in particular, that when they met with any body after their own heart, they had a charming long prospect of many, many happy meetings with them in after-life.

Now, in this short, stormy, winter day of our fleeting existence, when you now and then, in the Chapter of Accidents, meet an individual whose acquaintance is a real acquisition, there are all the probabilities against you, that you shall never meet with that valued character more. On the other hand, brief as this miserable being is, it is none of the least of the miseries belonging to it, that if there is any miscreant whom you hate, or creature whom you despise, the ill-run of the chances shall be so against you, that in the overtakings, turnings, and jostlings of life, pop, at some unlucky corner, eternally comes the wretch upon you, and will not allow your indignation or contempt a moment's repose. As I am a sturdy believer in the powers of darkness, I take these to be the doings of that old author of mischief, the devil. It is well known that he has some kind of shorthand way of taking down our thoughts, and I make no doubt that he is perfectly acquainted with my sentiments respecting Miss B——; how much I admired her abilities and valued her worth, and how very fortunate I thought myself in her acquaintance. For this last reason, my dear Madam, I must entertain no hopes of the very great pleasure of meeting with you again.

Miss H—— tells me that she is sending a packet to you, and I beg leave to send you the inclosed sonnet, though, to tell you the real truth, the sonnet is a mere pretence, that I may have the opportunity of declaring with how much respectful esteem I have the honour to be, &c.

No.

No. CXXXVIII.

To Miss C****.

August, 1793.

MADAM,

Some rather unlooked-for accidents have prevented my doing myself the honour of a second visit to Arbeigland, as I was so hospitably invited, and so positively meant to have done.—However, I still hope to have that pleasure before the busy months of harvest begin.

I inclose you two of my late pieces, as some kind of return for the pleasure I have received in perusing a certain MS volume of poems in the possession of Captain Riddel. To repay one with an *old song*, is a proverb, whose force, you, Madam, I know, will not allow. What is said of illustrious descent is, I believe, equally true of a talent for poetry: none ever despised

it who had pretensions to it. The fates and characters of the rhyming tribe often employ my thoughts when I am disposed to be melancholy. There is not, among all the martyrologies that ever were penned, so rueful a narrative as the lives of the poets.—In the comparative view of wretches, the criterion is not what they are doomed to suffer, but how they are formed to bear. Take a being of our kind, give him a stronger imagination and a more delicate sensibility, which between them will ever engender a more ungovernable set of passions than are the usual lot of man; implant in him an irresistible impulse to some idle vagary, such as arranging wild flowers in fantastical nosegays, tracing the grasshopper to his haunt by his chirping song, watching the frisks of the little minnows in the sunny pool, or hunting after the intrigues of butterflies—in short, send him adrift after some pursuit which shall eternally mislead him from the paths of lucre, and yet curse him with a keener relish than any man living for the pleasures that lucre can purchase: lastly, fill up the measure of his woes by bestowing on him a spurning sense of his own dignity, and you have created a wight nearly as miserable as a poet. To you, Madam, I need not recount the fairy pleasures the muse bestows to counterbalance this catalogue of evils. Bewitching

witching poetry is like bewitching woman; she has in all ages been accused of misleading mankind from the councils of wisdom and the paths of prudence, involving them in difficulties, baiting them with poverty, branding them with infamy, and plunging them in the whirling vortex of ruin; yet, where is the man but must own that all our happiness on earth is not worthy the name—that even the holy hermit's solitary prospect of paradisiacal bliss is but the glitter of a northern sun rising over a frozen region, compared with the many pleasures, the nameless raptures that we owe to the lovely Queen of the heart of Man!

No.

No. CXXXIX.

To JOHN M'MURDO, Esq.

December, 1793.

SIR,

It is said that we take the greatest liberties with our greatest friends, and I pay myself a very high compliment in the manner in which I am going to apply the remark. I have owed you money longer than ever I owed it to any man.—Here is Ker's account, and here are six guineas; and now, I don't owe a shilling to man—or woman either. But for these damned dirty, dog's-ear'd little pages,* I had done myself the honour to have waited on you long ago. Independent of the obligations your hospitality has laid me under; the consciousness of your superiority

---

* Scottish Bank Notes.

superiority in the rank of man and gentleman, of itself was fully as much as I could ever make head against; but to owe you money too, was more than I could face.

I think I once mentioned something of a collection of Scots songs I have some years been making: I send you a perusal of what I have got together. I could not conveniently spare them above five or six days, and five or six glances of them will probably more than suffice you. A very few of them are my own. When you are tired of them, please leave them with Mr. Clint, of the King's arms. There is not another copy of the collection in the world; and I should be sorry that any unfortunate negligence should deprive me of what has cost me a good deal of pains.

No.

No. CXL.

To Mrs. R*****.

Who was to bespeak a Play one Evening at the Dumfries *Theatre.*

I am thinking to send my *Address* to some periodical publication, but it has not got your sanction, so pray look over it.

As to the Tuesday's play, let me beg of you, my dear Madam, to give us, *The Wonder, a Woman keeps a Secret!* to which please add, *The Spoilt Child*—you will highly oblige me by so doing.

Ah, what an enviable creature you are! There now, this cursed gloomy blue-devil day, you are going to a party of choice spirits—

" To

> " To play the shapes
> Of frolic fancy, and incessant form,
> Those rapid pictures, that assembled train
> Of fleet ideas, never join'd before,
> Where lively *wit* excites to gay surprise;
> Or folly-painting *humour*, grave himself,
> Calls laughter forth, deep-shaking every nerve."

But as you rejoice with them that do rejoice, do also remember to weep with them that weep, and pity your melancholy friend.*

---

* This lady, to whom the bard has so happily and justly applied the above quotation, paid the debt of nature a few months ago. The graces of her person were only equalled by the singular endowments of her mind, and her poetical talents rendered her an interesting friend to Burns, in a part of the world where he was in a great measure excluded from the sweet intercourse of literary society.

London, 21st June, 1809.

No.

No. CXLI.

To a Lady, in favour of a Player's Benefit.

MADAM,

You were so very good as to promise me to honour my friend with your presence on his benefit night. That night is fixed for Friday first: the play a most interesting one! *The way to keep Him.* I have the pleasure to know Mr. G. well. His merit as an actor is generally acknowledged. He has genius and worth which would do honour to patronage: he is a poor and modest man; claims which from their very *silence* have the more forcible power on the generous heart. Alas, for pity! that from the indolence of those who have the good things of this life in their gift, too often does brazen-fronted importunity snatch that boon, the rightful due of retiring, humble want! Of all the qualities we assign to the author and director of Nature, by far the most enviable is—to be able " To wipe away all tears from all eyes." O
what

what insignificant, sordid wretches are they, however chance may have loaded them with wealth, who go to their graves, to their magnificent *mausoleums*, with hardly the consciousness of having made one poor honest heart happy!

But I crave your pardon, Madam; I came to beg, not to preach.

No. CXLII.

EXTRACT OF A LETTER

To Mr. ———.

1794.

I am extremely obliged to you for your kind mention of my interests, in a letter which Mr. S*** shewed me. At present, my situation in life must be in a great measure stationary, at least for two or three years. The statement is this—I am on the supervisors' list; and as we come on there by precedency, in two or three years I shall be at the head of that list, and be appointed *of course*—then, a Friend might be of service to me in getting me into a place of the kingdom which I would like. A supervisor's income varies from about a hundred and twenty, to two hundred a-year; but the business is an incessant drudgery, and would be nearly a complete bar to every species of literary pursuit. The moment I am appointed supervisor

supervisor in the common routine, I may be nominated on the Collectors' list; and this is always a business purely of political patronage. A collectorship varies much from better than two hundred a-year to near a thousand. They also come forward by precedency on the list, and have, besides a handsome income, a life of complete leisure. A life of literary leisure, with a decent competence, is the summit of my wishes. It would be the prudish affectation of silly pride in me, to say that I do not need, or would not be indebted to a political friend; at the same time, Sir, I by no means lay my affairs before you thus, to hook my dependent situation on your benevolence. If, in my progress of life, an opening should occur where the good offices of a gentleman of your public character and political consequence might bring me forward, I will petition your goodness with the same frankness and sincerity as I now do myself the honour to subscribe myself, &c.

No.

No. CXLIII.

To Mrs. R*****.

DEAR MADAM,

I MEANT to have called on you yesternight; but as I edged up to your box door, the first object which greeted my view was one of those lobster-coated puppies, sitting like another dragon, guarding the Hesperian fruit. On the conditions and capitulations you so obligingly offer, I shall certainly make my weather-beaten rustic phiz a part of your box furniture on Tuesday, when we may arrange the business of the visit.

* * * * * * *

Among the profusion of idle compliments, which insidious craft, or unmeaning folly, incessantly offer at your shrine—a shrine, how far exalted above such adoration—permit me, were it but for rarity's sake, to pay you the honest tribute of a warm heart and an independent mind; and to assure you that I am, thou most amiable, and most accomplished of thy sex, with the most respectful esteem, and fervent regard, thine, &c.

No.

No. CXLIV.

TO THE SAME.

I WILL wait on you, my ever-valued friend, but whether in the morning I am not sure. Sunday closes a period of our curst revenue business, and may probably keep me employed with my pen until noon. Fine employment for a poet's pen! There is a species of the human genus that I call *the gin-horse class*: what enviable dogs they are! Round, and round, and round they go,—Mundell's ox, that drives his cotton-mill, is their exact prototype —without an idea or wish beyond their circle; fat, sleek, stupid, patient, quiet, and contented; while here I sit, altogether Novemberish, a d—— melange of fretfulness and melancholy; not enough of the one to rouse me to passion, nor of the other to repose me in torpor; my soul flouncing and fluttering round her tenement, like a wild finch caught amid the horrors of winter, and newly thrust into a cage. Well, I am

I am persuaded that it was of me the Hebrew sage prophesied, when he foretold—" And be-
" hold, on whatsoever this man doth set his
" heart, it shall not prosper!" If my resentment is awaked, it is sure to be where it dare not squeak; and if—

* * * * * * * *

Pray that wisdom and bliss be more frequent visitors of

R. B.

No. CXLV.

TO THE SAME.

I HAVE this moment got the song from S***, and I am sorry to see that he has spoilt it a good deal. It shall be a lesson to me how I lend him any thing again.

I have sent you *Werter*, truly happy to have any the smallest opportunity of obliging you.

'Tis true, Madam, I saw you once since I was at W——; and that once froze the very life-blood of my heart. Your reception of me was such, that a wretch meeting the eye of his judge, about to pronounce sentence of death on him, could only have envied my feelings and situation. But I hate the theme, and never more shall write or speak on it.

One thing I shall proudly say, that I can pay Mrs. —— a higher tribute of esteem, and appreciate her amiable worth more truly, than any man whom I have seen approach her.

No.

No. CXLVI.

TO THE SAME.

I HAVE often told you, my dear friend, that you had a spice of caprice in your composition, and you have as often disavowed it: even, perhaps, while your opinions were, at the moment, irrefragably proving it. Could *any thing* estrange me from a friend such as you?— No! To-morrow I shall have the honour of waiting on you.

Farewel, thou first of friends, and most accomplished of women; even with all thy little caprices!

No.

No. CXLVII.

TO THE SAME.

MADAM,

I RETURN your common-place book: I have perused it with much pleasure, and would have continued my criticisms; but as it seems the critic has forfeited your esteem, his strictures must lose their value.

If it is true that " offences come only from the heart," before you I am guiltless. To admire, esteem, and prize you, as the most accomplished of women, and the first of friends—if these are crimes, I am the most offending thing alive.

In a face where I used to meet the kind complacency of friendly confidence, *now* to find cold neglect and contemptuous scorn—is a wrench that my heart can ill bear. It is, however,

ever, some kind of miserable good luck, that while *de haut-en-bas* rigour may depress an unoffending wretch to the ground, it has a tendency to rouse a stubborn something in his bosom, which, though it cannot heal the wounds of his soul, is at least an opiate to blunt their poignancy.

With the profoundest respect for your abilities; the most sincere esteem and ardent regard for your gentle heart and amiable manners; and the most fervent wish and prayer for your welfare, peace, and bliss, I have the honour to be, Madam, your most devoted humble servant.

No.

No. CXLVIII.

To JOHN SYME, Esq.

You know that, among other high dignities, you have the honour to be my supreme court of critical judicature, from which there is no appeal. I inclose you a song which I composed since I saw you, and I am going to give you the history of it. Do you know, that among much that I admire in the characters and manners of those great folks whom I have now the honour to call my acquaintances, the O***** family, there is nothing charms me more than Mr. O.'s unconcealable attachment to that incomparable woman. Did you ever, my dear Syme, meet with a man who owed more to the Divine Giver of all good things than Mr. O.? A fine fortune; a pleasing exterior; self-evident amiable dispositions, and an ingenuous upright mind, and that informed, too, much beyond the usual run of young fellows of his rank and
fortune;

fortune; and to all this, such a woman!—but of her I shall say nothing at all, in despair of saying any thing adequate. In my song, I have endeavoured to do justice to what would be his feelings, on seeing, in the scene I have drawn, the habitation of his Lucy. As I am a good deal pleased with my performance, I in my first fervour, thought of sending it to Mrs. O———; but, on second thoughts, perhaps what I offer as the honest incense of genuine respect, might, from the well-known character of poverty and poetry, be construed into some modification or other of that servility which my soul abhors.*

---

* The song inclosed was that, *vol.* iv. *p.* 340.
O wat ye wha's in yon town?   E.

No.

No. CXLIX.

To MISS ——.

MADAM,

Nothing short of a kind of absolute necessity could have made me trouble you with this letter. Except my ardent and just esteem for your sense, taste, and worth, every sentiment arising in my breast, as I put pen to paper to you, is painful. The scenes I have past with the friend of my soul and his amiable connexions! the wrench at my heart to think that he is gone, for ever gone from me, never more to meet in the wanderings of a weary world! and the cutting reflection of all, that I had most unfortunately, though most undeservedly, lost the confidence of that soul of worth, ere it took its flight!

These, Madam, are sensations of no ordinary anguish.—However, you also, may be offended

fended with some *imputed* improprieties of mine; sensibility you know I possess, and sincerity none will deny me.

To oppose those prejudices which have been raised against me, is not the business of this letter. Indeed it is a warfare I know not how to wage. The powers of positive vice I can in some degree calculate, and against direct malevolence I can be on my guard; but who can estimate the fatuity of giddy caprice, or ward off the unthinking mischief of percipitate folly?

I have a favour to request of you, Madam; and of your sister Mrs. ——, through your means. You know that, at the wish of my late friend, I made a collection of all my trifles in verse which I had ever written. They are many of them local, some of them puerile and silly, and all of them unfit for the public eye. As I have some little fame at stake, a fame that I trust may live when the hate of those who " watch for my halting," and the contumelious sneer of those whom accident has made my superiors, will with themselves, be gone to the regions of oblivion; I am uneasy now for the fate of those manuscripts—Will Mrs. —— have the goodness to destroy them, or return them to me? As a pledge of friendship they
were

were bestowed; and that circumstance indeed was all their merit. Most unhappily for me, that merit they no longer possess; and I hope that Mrs. ———'s goodness, which I well know, and ever will revere, will not refuse this favour to a man whom she once held in some degree of estimation.

With the sincerest esteem, I have the honour to be, Madam, &c.

No. CL.

To Mr. CUNNINGHAM.

25th February, 1794.

Canst thou minister to a mind diseased? Canst thou speak peace and rest to a soul tost on a sea of troubles, without one friendly star to guide her course, and dreading that the next surge may overwhelm her? Canst thou give to a frame, tremblingly alive as the tortures of suspense, the stability and hardihood of the rock that braves the blast? If thou canst not do the least of these, why wouldst thou disturb me in my miseries with thy inquiries after me?

* * * * * * * *

For these two months I have not been able to lift a pen. My constitution and frame were, *ab origine*, blasted with a deep incurable taint of hypochondria, which poisons my existence. Of late a number of domestic vexations, and some pecuniary share in the ruin of these ***** times; losses which, though trifling, were yet what I could ill-bear, have so irritated me, that my feelings at times could only be envied by a reprobate spirit listening to the sentence that dooms it to perdition.

Are you deep in the language of consolation? I have exhausted in reflection every topic of comfort. *A heart at ease* would have been charmed with my sentiments and reasonings; but as to myself, I was like Judas Iscariot preaching the gospel: he might melt and mould the hearts of those around him, but his own kept its native incorrigibility.

Still there are two great pillars that bear us up, amid the wreck of misfortune and misery. The ONE is composed of the different modifications of a certain noble, subborn something in man, known by the names of courage, fortitude, magnanimity. The OTHER is made up of those feelings and sentiments, which, however the sceptic may deny them, or the enthusiast disfigure them, are yet, I am convinced, original and component parts of the human soul; those *senses of the mind,* if I may be allowed

lowed the expression, which connect us with, and link us to, those awful obscure realities— an all-powerful, and equally beneficent God; and a world to come, beyond death and the grave. The first gives the nerve of combat, while a ray of hope beams on the field :—the last pours the balm of comfort into the wounds which time can never cure.

I do not remember, my dear Cunningham, that you and I ever talked on the subject of religion at all. I know some who laugh at it, as the trick of the crafty FEW, to lead the undiscerning MANY; or at most as an uncertain obscurity, which mankind can never know any thing of, and with which they are fools if they give themselves much to do. Nor would I quarrel with a man for his irreligion, any more than I would for his want of a musical ear. I would regret that he was shut out from what, to me and to others, were such superlative sources of enjoyment. It is in this point of view, and for this reason, that I will deeply imbue the mind of every child of mine with religion. If my son should happen to be a man of feeling, sentiment, and taste, I shall thus add largely to his enjoyments. Let me flatter myself that this sweet little fellow, who is just now running about my desk, will be a man of
a melting,

a melting, ardent, glowing heart; and an imagination, delighted with the painter, and rapt with the poet. Let me figure him wandering out in a sweet evening, to inhale the balmy gales, and enjoy the growing luxuriance of the spring; himself the while in the blooming youth of life. He looks abroad on all nature, and through nature up to nature's God. His soul, by swift delighting degrees, is rapt above this sublunary sphere, until he can be silent no longer, and bursts out into the glorious enthusiasm of Thomson,

> " These, as they change, Almighty Father, these
> Are but the varied God.—The rolling year
> Is full of thee."

And so on in all the spirit and ardour of that charming hymn.

These are no ideal pleasures; they are real delights; and I ask what of the delights among the sons of men are superior, not to say equal, to them? And they have this precious, vast addition, that conscious Virtue stamps them for her own; and lays hold on them to bring herself into the presence of a witnessing, judging, and approving God.

No.

No. CLI.

To Mrs. R*****.

Supposes himself to be writing from the Dead to the Living.

MADAM,

I DARE say this is the first epistle you ever received from this nether world. I write you from the regions of Hell, amid the horrors of the damned. The time and manner of my leaving your earth I do not exactly know, as I took my departure in the heat of a fever of intoxication, contracted at your too hospitable mansion; but, on my arrival here, I was fairly tried, and sentenced to endure the purgatorial tortures of this infernal confine for the space of ninety-nine years, eleven months, and twenty-nine days, and all on account of the impropriety of my conduct yesternight under your roof. Here am I, laid on a bed of pitiless furze,

furze, with my aching head reclined on a pillow of ever-piercing thorn, while an infernal tormentor, wrinkled, and old, and cruel, his name I think is *Recollection*, with a whip of scorpions, forbids peace or rest to approach me, and keeps anguish eternally awake. Still, Madam, if I could in any measure be reinstated in the good opinion of the fair circle whom my conduct last night so much injured, I think it would be an alleviation to my torments. For this reason I trouble you with this letter. To the men of the company I will make no apology.—Your husband, who insisted on my drinking more than I chose, has no right to blame me; and the other gentlemen were partakers of my guilt. But to you, Madam, I have much to apologize. Your good opinion I valued as one of the greatest acquisitions I had made on earth, and I was truly a beast to forfeit it. There was a Miss I——, too, a woman of fine sense, gentle and unassuming manners—do make, on my part, a miserable d—d wretch's best apology to her. A Mrs. G——, a charming woman, did me the honour to be prejudiced in my favour; this makes me hope that I have not outraged her beyond all forgiveness.—To all the other ladies please present my humblest contrition for my conduct, and my petition for their gracious pardon. O, all ye powers of decency

cency and decorum! whisper to them that my errors, though great, were involuntary—that an intoxicated man is the vilest of beasts—that it was not in my nature to be brutal to any one— that to be rude to a woman, when in my senses, was impossible with me—but—

* * * * * *

Regret! Remorse! Shame! ye three hell-hounds that ever dog my steps and bay at my heels, spare me! spare me!

Forgive the offences, and pity the perdition of, Madam, your humble slave.

No. CLII.

To Mrs. DUNLOP.

15th *December*, 1795.

MY DEAR FRIEND,

As I am in a complete Decemberish humour, gloomy, sullen, stupid, as even the deity of Dulness herself could wish, I shall not drawl out a heavy letter with a number of heavier apologies for my late silence. Only one I shall mention, because I know you will sympathize in it: these four months, a sweet little girl, my youngest child, has been so ill, that every day, a week or less, threatened to terminate her existence. There had much need be many pleasures annexed to the states of husband and father, for, God knows, they have many peculiar cares. I cannot describe to you the anxious, sleepless hours, these ties frequently give me. I see a train of helpless little folks; me and my exertions all their stay; and on what
a brittle

a brittle thread does the life of man hang! If I am nipt off at the command of Fate, even in all the vigour of manhood as I am—such things happen every day—gracious God! what would become of my little flock! 'Tis here that I envy your people of fortune.—A father on his death-bed, taking an everlasting leave of his children, has indeed woe enough; but the man of competent fortune leaves his sons and daughters independency and friends; while I—but I shall run distracted if I think any longer on the subject!

To leave talking of the matter so gravely, I shall sing with the old Scots ballad—

" O that I had ne'er been married,
    I would never had nae care;
Now I've gotten wife and bairns,
    They cry crowdie! evermair.

" Crowdie! ance; crowdie! twice;
    Crowdie! three times in a day:
An ye, crowdie! ony mair,
    Ye'll crowdie! a' my meal away."

* * * * * * *

December 24*th.*

We have had a brilliant theatre here this season;

season; only, as all other business has, it experiences a stagnation of trade from the epidemical complaint of the country, *want of cash*. I mention our theatre merely to lug in an occasional *Address* which I wrote for the benefit-night of one of the actresses, and which is as follows—

ADDRESS.

Spoken by Miss FONTENELLE *on her Benefit-night, Dec. 4, 1795, at the Theatre,* DUMFRIES.

STILL anxious to secure your partial favour,
And not less anxious, sure, this night, than ever,
A Prologue, Epilogue, or some such matter,
'Twould vamp my bill, said I, if nothing better;
So, sought a Poet, roosted near the skies,
Told him I came to feast my curious eyes;
Said, nothing like his works was ever printed;
And last, my prologue-business slily hinted.
" Ma'am let me tell you," quoth my man of rhymes,
" I know your bent—these are no laughing times:
Can you—but Miss, I own I have my fears,
Dissolve in pause—and sentimental tears—
With laden sighs, and solemn-rounded sentence,
Rouse from his sluggish slumbers, fell Repentance;
Paint Vengeance as he takes his horrid stand,
Waving on high the desolating brand,
Calling the storms to bear him o'er a guilty land?"

I could

I could no more—askance the creature eyeing,
D'ye think, said I, this face was made for crying?
I'll laugh, that's poz—nay more, the world shall know it;
And so, your servant, gloomy Master Poet!

Firm as my creed, Sirs, 'tis my fixed belief,
That Misery's another word for Grief;
I also think—so may I be a bride!
That so much laughter, so much life enjoy'd.

Thou man of crazy care and ceaseless sigh,
Still under bleak Misfortune's blasting eye;
Doom'd to that sorest task of man alive—
To make three guineas do the work of five:
Laugh in Misfortune's face—the beldam witch!
Say, you'll be merry, tho' you can't be rich.

Thou other man of care, the wretch in love,
Who long with jiltish arts and airs hast strove;
Who, as the boughs all temptingly project,
Measur'st in desperate thought—a rope—thy neck—
Or, where the beetling cliff o'erhangs the deep,
Peerest to meditate the healing leap:
Would'st thou be cur'd, thou silly, moping elf?
Laugh at her follies—laugh e'en at thyself:
Learn to despise those frowns now so terrific,
And love a kinder—that's your grand specific.

To sum up all, be merry, I advise;
And as we're merry, may we still be wise.

. . . .

25th

25th, Christmas Morning.

This, my much-loved friend, is a morning of wishes; accept mine—so heaven hear me as they are sincere! that blessings may attend your steps, and affliction know you not! In the charming words of my favourite author, *The Man of Feeling*, " May the Great Spirit bear up the weight of thy grey hairs, and blunt the arrow that brings them rest!"

Now that I talk of authors, how do you like Cowper? Is not the *Task* a glorious poem? The religion of the *Task*, bating a few scraps of Calvinistic divinity, is the religion of God and Nature; the religion that exalts, that ennobles man. Were not you to send me your *Zeluco*, in return for mine? Tell me how you like my marks and notes through the book. I would not give a farthing for a book, unless I were at liberty to blot it with my criticisms.

I have lately collected, for a friend's perusal, all my letters; I mean those which I first sketched, in a rough draught, and afterwards wrote out fair. On looking over some old musty papers, which, from time to time, I had parcelled by, as trash that were scarce worth preserving, and which yet at the same time I did not care to destroy; I discovered many of these

these rude sketches, and have written, and am writing them out, in a bound MS for my friend's library. As I wrote always to you the rhapsody of the moment, I cannot find a single scroll to you, except one, about the commencement of our acquaintance. If there were any possible conveyance, I would send you a perusal of my book.

No.

No. CLIII.

To Mrs. DUNLOP, *in* LONDON.

Dumfries, 20th December, 1795.

I HAVE been prodigiously disappointed in this London journey of yours. In the first place, when your last to me reached Dumfries, I was in the country, and did not return until too late to answer your letter; in the next place, I thought you would certainly take this route; and now I know not what is become of you, or whether this may reach you at all.—God grant that it may find you and yours in prospering health and good spirits! Do let me hear from you the soonest possible.

As I hope to get a frank from my friend Captain Miller, I shall, every leisure hour, take up the pen, and gossip away whatever comes first, prose or poesy, sermon or song. In this
last

last article I have abounded of late. I have often mentioned to you a superb publication of Scottish songs which is making its appearance in your great metropolis, and where I have the honour to preside over the Scottish verse, as no less a personage than Peter Pindar does over the English. I wrote the following for a favourite air. *See* vol. iv.

. . . .

December 29*th.*

Since I began this letter, I have been appointed to act in the capacity of the supervisor here; and I assure you, what with the load of business, and what with that business being new to me, I could scarcely have commanded ten minutes to have spoken to you, had you been in town, much less to have written you an epistle. This appointment is only temporary, and during the illness of the present incumbent: but I look forward to an early period when I shall be appointed in full form; a consummation devoutly to be wished! My political sins seem to be forgiven me.

. . . .

This is the season (New-year's-day is now my date) of wishing; and mine are most fervently

vently offered up for you! May life to you be a positive blessing while it lasts, for your own sake; and that it may yet be greatly prolonged, is my wish for my own sake, and for the sake of the rest of your friends! What a transient business is life! Very lately I was a boy; but t'other day I was a young man; and I already begin to feel the rigid fibre and stiffening joints of old age coming fast o'er my frame. With all my follies of youth, and, I fear, a few vices of manhood, still I congratulate myself on having had, in early days, religion strongly impressed on my mind. I have nothing to say to any one as to which sect he belongs to, or what creed he believes; but I look on the man, who is firmly persuaded of infinite Wisdom and Goodness superintending and directing every circumstance that can happen in his lot—! felicitate such a man as having a solid foundation for his mental enjoyment; a firm prop and sure stay in the hour of difficulty, trouble, and distress; and a never-failing anchor of hope, when he looks beyond the grave.

. . . .

January 12*th.*

You will have seen our worthy and ingenious friend, the Doctor, long ere this. I hope he he is well, and beg to be remembered to him. I have just been reading over again, I dare say for the hundred and fiftieth time, his *View of Society and Manners;* and still I read it with delight. His humour is perfectly original—it is neither the humour of Addison, nor Swift, nor Sterne, nor of any body but Dr. Moore. By the bye, you have deprived me of *Zeluco;* remember that, when you are disposed to rake up the sins of my neglect from among the ashes of my laziness.

He has paid me a pretty compliment, by quoting me in his last publication.*

* * * * * * * *

---

* Edward.

No.

No. CLIV.

To Mrs. R*****.

20th January, 1796.

I CANNOT express my gratitude to you for allowing me a longer perusal of *Anacharsis*. In fact, I never met with a book that bewitched me so much; and I, as a member of the library, must warmly feel the obligation you have laid us under. Indeed to me, the obligation is stronger than to any other individual of our society; as *Anacharsis* is an indispensable desideratum to a son of the Muses.

The health you wished me in your morning's card, is, I think, flown from me for ever. I have not been able to leave my bed to-day till about an hour ago. These wickedly unlucky advertisements I lent (I did wrong) to a friend, and I am ill able to go in quest of him.

The Muses have not quite forsaken me. The following detached stanzas I intend to interweave in some disastrous tale of a shepherd.

* * * * * * * *

No.

No. CLV.

To Mrs. DUNLOP.

31st January, 1796.

THESE many months you have been two packets in my debt—what sin of ignorance I have committed against so highly valued a friend I am utterly at a loss to guess. Alas! Madam! ill can I afford, at this time, to be deprived of any of the small remnant of my pleasures. I have lately drunk deep of the cup of affliction. The autumn robbed me of my only daughter and darling child, and that at a distance too, and so rapidly, as to put it out of my power to pay the last duties to her. I had scarcely begun to recover from that shock, when I became myself the victim of a most severe rheumatic fever, and long the die spun doubtful; until, after many weeks of a sick bed,

bed, it seems to have turned up life, and I am beginning to crawl across my room, and once indeed, have been before my own door in the street.

> When pleasure fascinates the mental sight,
>   Affliction purifies the visual ray,
> Religion hails the drear, the untried night,
>   And shuts, for ever shuts, life's doubtful day!

No.

No. CLVI.

To Mrs. R*****,

Who had desired him to go to the Birth-Day Assembly on that day, to shew his loyalty.

4th June, 1796.

I AM in such miserable health as to be utterly incapable of shewing my loyalty in any way. Rackt as I am with rheumatisms, I meet every face with a greeting, like that of Balak to Balaam—" Come curse me Jacob; and come defy me Israel!" So say I—Come curse me that east wind; and come defy me the north! Would you have me, in such circumstances, copy you out a love song?

* * * * * * *

I may perhaps see you on Saturday, but I will not be at the ball.—Why should I? " Man delights not me, nor woman either!" Can you supply me with the song, *Let us all be unhappy together*—do if you can, and oblige *le pauvre miserable*,

R. B.

No. CLVII.

To Mr. CUNNINGHAM.

Brow, Sea-bathing quarters, 7th July, 1796.

MY DEAR CUNNINGHAM,

I RECEIVED yours here this moment, and am indeed highly flattered with the approbation of the literary circle you mention; a literary circle inferior to none in the two kingdoms. Alas! my friend, I fear the voice of the bard will soon be heard among you no more! For these eight or ten months I have been ailing, sometimes bed-fast and sometimes not; but these last three months, I have been tortured with an excruciating rheumatism, which has reduced me to nearly the last stage. You actually would not know me if you saw me.— Pale, emaciated, and so feeble as occasionally to need help from my chair—my spirits fled! fled!—but I can no more on the subject—only the medical folks tell me that my last and only chance is bathing, and country quarters, and riding.—The deuce of the matter is this; when an exciseman is off duty, his salary is reduced to 35l. instead of 50l.—What way, in the name of thrift, shall I maintain myself, and keep a horse in country quarters—with a wife and five children at home, on 35l.? I mention this, because I had intended to beg your utmost interest, and that of all the friends you can muster, to move our Commissioners of Excise to grant me the full salary—I dare say you know them all personally. If they do not grant it me, I must lay my account with an exit truly *en poëte*, if I die not of disease, I must perish with hunger.

I have sent you one of the songs; the other my memory does not serve me with, and I have no copy here; but I shall be at home soon, when I will send it you.—Apropos to being at home, Mrs. Burns threatens in a week or two to add one more to my paternal charge, which, if of the right gender, I intend shall be introduced to the world by the respectable designation of *Alexander Cunningham Burns*. My last was *James Glencairn*, so you can have no objection to the company of nobility. Farewell.

No.

No. CLVIII.

To Mrs. BURNS.

MY DEAREST LOVE,

Brow, Thursday.

I DELAYED writing until I could tell you what effect sea-bathing was likely to produce. It would be injustice to deny that it has eased my pains, and, I think, has strengthened me; but my appetite is still extremely bad. No flesh nor fish can I swallow; porridge and milk are the only thing I can taste. I am very happy to hear, by Miss Jess Lewars, that you are all well. My very best and kindest compliments to her, and to all the children. I will see you on Sunday. Your affectionate husband,

R. B.

No. CLIX.

To Mrs. DUNLOP.

Brow, 12th July, 1796.

MADAM,

I HAVE written you so often, without receiving any answer, that I would not trouble you again, but for the circumstances in which I am. An illness which has long hung about me, in all probability will speedily send me beyond that *bourne whence no traveller returns.* Your friendship, with which for many years you honoured me, was a friendship dearest to my soul. Your conversation, and especially your correspondence, were at once highly entertaining and instructive. With what pleasure did I use to break up the seal! The remembrance yet adds one pulse more to my poor palpitating heart. Farewell!!! R. B.

The above is supposed to be the last production of Robert Burns, who died on the 21st of the month, nine days afterwards. He had, however, the pleasure of
receiving

receiving a satisfactory explanation of his friend's silence, and an assurance of the continuance of her friendship to his widow and children; an assurance that has been amply fulfilled.

It is probable that the greater part of her letters to him were destroyed by our Bard about the time that this last was written. He did not foresee that his own letters to her were to appear in print, nor conceive the disappointment that will be felt, that a few of this excellent lady's have not served to enrich and adorn the collection.

E.

END OF THE SECOND VOLUME.

J. M'CREERY, Printer,
Black Horse-court, Fleet-street.

www.bookjungle.com email: sales@bookjungle.com fax: 630-214-0564 mail: Book Jungle PO Box 2226 Champaign, IL 61825

The Codes Of Hammurabi And Moses
W. W. Davies

QTY

The discovery of the Hammurabi Code is one of the greatest achievements of archaeology, and is of paramount interest, not only to the student of the Bible, but also to all those interested in ancient history...

Religion ISBN: *1-59462-338-4* Pages:132 MSRP *$12.95*

The Theory of Moral Sentiments
Adam Smith

QTY

This work from 1749. contains original theories of conscience amd moral judgment and it is the foundation for systemof morals.

Philosophy ISBN: *1-59462-777-0* Pages:536 MSRP *$19.95*

Jessica's First Prayer
Hesba Stretton

QTY

In a screened and secluded corner of one of the many railway-bridges which span the streets of London there could be seen a few years ago, from five o'clock every morning until half past eight, a tidily set-out coffee-stall, consisting of a trestle and board, upon which stood two large tin cans, with a small fire of charcoal burning under each so as to keep the coffee boiling during the early hours of the morning when the work-people were thronging into the city on their way to their daily toil...

Childrens ISBN: *1-59462-373-2* Pages:84 MSRP *$9.95*

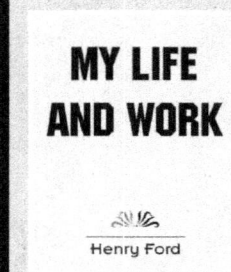

My Life and Work
Henry Ford

QTY

Henry Ford revolutionized the world with his implementation of mass production for the Model T automobile. Gain valuable business insight into his life and work with his own auto-biography... "We have only started on our development of our country we have not as yet, with all our talk of wonderful progress, done more than scratch the surface. The progress has been wonderful enough but..."

Biographies/ ISBN: *1-59462-198-5* Pages:300 MSRP *$21.95*

www.bookjungle.com email: sales@bookjungle.com fax: 630-214-0564 mail: Book Jungle PO Box 2226 Champaign, IL 61825

The Art of Cross-Examination
Francis Wellman

QTY

I presume it is the experience of every author, after his first book is published upon an important subject, to be almost overwhelmed with a wealth of ideas and illustrations which could readily have been included in his book, and which to his own mind, at least, seem to make a second edition inevitable. Such certainly was the case with me; and when the first edition had reached its sixth impression in five months, I rejoiced to learn that it seemed to my publishers that the book had met with a sufficiently favorable reception to justify a second and considerably enlarged edition. ...

Reference   ISBN: *1-59462-647-2*

Pages:412
MSRP *$19.95*

On the Duty of Civil Disobedience
Henry David Thoreau

QTY

Thoreau wrote his famous essay, On the Duty of Civil Disobedience, as a protest against an unjust but popular war and the immoral but popular institution of slave-owning. He did more than write—he declined to pay his taxes, and was hauled off to gaol in consequence. Who can say how much this refusal of his hastened the end of the war and of slavery?

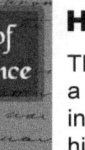

Law   ISBN: *1-59462-747-9*

Pages:48
MSRP *$7.45*

Dream Psychology Psychoanalysis for Beginners
Sigmund Freud

QTY

Sigmund Freud, born Sigismund Schlomo Freud (May 6, 1856 - September 23, 1939), was a Jewish-Austrian neurologist and psychiatrist who co-founded the psychoanalytic school of psychology. Freud is best known for his theories of the unconscious mind, especially involving the mechanism of repression; his redefinition of sexual desire as mobile and directed towards a wide variety of objects; and his therapeutic techniques, especially his understanding of transference in the therapeutic relationship and the presumed value of dreams as sources of insight into unconscious desires.

Psychology   ISBN: *1-59462-905-6*

Pages:196
MSRP *$15.45*

The Miracle of Right Thought
Orison Swett Marden

QTY

Believe with all of your heart that you will do what you were made to do. When the mind has once formed the habit of holding cheerful, happy, prosperous pictures, it will not be easy to form the opposite habit. It does not matter how improbable or how far away this realization may see, or how dark the prospects may be, if we visualize them as best we can, as vividly as possible, hold tenaciously to them and vigorously struggle to attain them, they will gradually become actualized, realized in the life. But a desire, a longing without endeavor, a yearning abandoned or held indifferently will vanish without realization.

Self Help   ISBN: *1-59462-644-8*

Pages:360
MSRP *$25.45*

www.bookjungle.com email: sales@bookjungle.com fax: 630-214-0564 mail: Book Jungle PO Box 2226 Champaign, IL 61825

QTY

	Title	ISBN	Price
☐	**The Rosicrucian Cosmo-Conception Mystic Christianity** by *Max Heindel* The Rosicrucian Cosmo-conception is not dogmatic, neither does it appeal to any other authority than the reason of the student. It is: not controversial, but is: sent forth in the, hope that it may help to clear...	ISBN: 1-59462-188-8 New Age/Religion Pages 646	$38.95
☐	**Abandonment To Divine Providence** by *Jean-Pierre de Caussade* "The Rev. Jean Pierre de Caussade was one of the most remarkable spiritual writers of the Society of Jesus in France in the 18th Century. His death took place at Toulouse in 1751. His works have gone through many editions and have been republished...	ISBN: 1-59462-228-0 Inspirational/Religion Pages 400	$25.95
☐	**Mental Chemistry** by *Charles Haanel* Mental Chemistry allows the change of material conditions by combining and appropriately utilizing the power of the mind. Much like applied chemistry creates something new and unique out of careful combinations of chemicals the mastery of mental chemistry...	ISBN: 1-59462-192-6 New Age Pages 354	$23.95
☐	**The Letters of Robert Browning and Elizabeth Barret Barrett 1845-1846 vol II** by *Robert Browning* and *Elizabeth Barrett*	ISBN: 1-59462-193-4 Biographies Pages 596	$35.95
☐	**Gleanings In Genesis (volume I)** by *Arthur W. Pink* Appropriately has Genesis been termed "the seed plot of the Bible" for in it we have, in germ form, almost all of the great doctrines which are afterwards fully developed in the books of Scripture which follow...	ISBN: 1-59462-130-6 Religion/Inspirational Pages 420	$27.45
☐	**The Master Key** by *L. W. de Laurence* In no branch of human knowledge has there been a more lively increase of the spirit of research during the past few years than in the study of Psychology, Concentration and Mental Discipline. The requests for authentic lessons in Thought Control, Mental Discipline and...	ISBN: 1-59462-001-6 New Age/Business Pages 422	$30.95
☐	**The Lesser Key Of Solomon Goetia** by *L. W. de Laurence* This translation of the first book of the "Lernegton" which is now for the first time made accessible to students of Talismanic Magic was done, after careful collation and edition, from numerous Ancient Manuscripts in Hebrew, Latin, and French...	ISBN: 1-59462-092-X New Age/Occult Pages 92	$9.95
☐	**Rubaiyat Of Omar Khayyam** by *Edward Fitzgerald* Edward Fitzgerald, whom the world has already learned, in spite of his own efforts to remain within the shadow of anonymity, to look upon as one of the rarest poets of the century, was born at Bredfield, in Suffolk, on the 31st of March, 1809. He was the third son of John Purcell...	ISBN: 1-59462-332-5 Music Pages 172	$13.95
☐	**Ancient Law** by *Henry Maine* The chief object of the following pages is to indicate some of the earliest ideas of mankind, as they are reflected in Ancient Law, and to point out the relation of those ideas to modern thought.	ISBN: 1-59462-128-4 Religiom/History Pages 452	$29.95
☐	**Far-Away Stories** by *William J. Locke* "Good wine needs no bush, but a collection of mixed vintages does. And this book is just such a collection. Some of the stories I do not want to remain buried for ever in the museum files of dead magazine-numbers an author's not unpardonable vanity..."	ISBN: 1-59462-129-2 Fiction Pages 272	$19.45
☐	**Life of David Crockett** by *David Crockett* "Colonel David Crockett was one of the most remarkable men of the times in which he lived. Born in humble life, but gifted with a strong will, an indomitable courage, and unremitting perseverance...	ISBN: 1-59462-250-2 Biographies/New Age Pages 424	$27.45
☐	**Lip-Reading** by *Edward Nitchie* Edward B. Nitchie, founder of the New York School for the Hard of Hearing, now the Nitchie School of Lip-Reading, Inc, wrote "LIP-READING Principles and Practice". The development and perfecting of this meritorious work on lip-reading was an undertaking...	ISBN: 1-59462-206-X How-to Pages 400	$25.95
☐	**A Handbook of Suggestive Therapeutics, Applied Hypnotism, Psychic Science** by *Henry Munro*	ISBN: 1-59462-214-0 Health/New Age/Health/Self-help Pages 376	$24.95
☐	**A Doll's House: and Two Other Plays** by *Henrik Ibsen* Henrik Ibsen created this classic when in revolutionary 1848 Rome. Introducing some striking concepts in playwriting for the realist genre, this play has been studied the world over.	ISBN: 1-59462-112-8 Fiction/Classics/Plays 308	$19.95
☐	**The Light of Asia** by *sir Edwin Arnold* In this poetic masterpiece, Edwin Arnold describes the life and teachings of Buddha. The man who was to become known as Buddha to the world was born as Prince Gautama of India but he rejected the worldly riches and abandoned the reigns of power when...	ISBN: 1-59462-204-3 Religion/History/Biographies Pages 170	$13.95
☐	**The Complete Works of Guy de Maupassant** by *Guy de Maupassant* "For days and days, nights and nights, I had dreamed of that first kiss which was to consecrate our engagement, and I knew not on what spot I should put my lips..."	ISBN: 1-59462-157-8 Fiction/Classics Pages 240	$16.95
☐	**The Art of Cross-Examination** by *Francis L. Wellman* Written by a renowned trial lawyer, Wellman imparts his experience and uses case studies to explain how to use psychology to extract desired information through questioning.	ISBN: 1-59462-309-0 How-to/Science/Reference Pages 408	$26.95
☐	**Answered or Unanswered?** by *Louisa Vaughan* Miracles of Faith in China	ISBN: 1-59462-248-5 Religion Pages 112	$10.95
☐	**The Edinburgh Lectures on Mental Science (1909)** by *Thomas* This book contains the substance of a course of lectures recently given by the writer in the Queen Street Hall, Edinburgh. Its purpose is to indicate the Natural Principles governing the relation between Mental Action and Material Conditions...	ISBN: 1-59462-008-3 New Age/Psychology Pages 148	$11.95
☐	**Ayesha** by *H. Rider Haggard* Verily and indeed it is the unexpected that happens! Probably if there was one person upon the earth from whom the Editor of this, and of a certain previous history, did not expect to hear again...	ISBN: 1-59462-301-5 Classics Pages 380	$24.95
☐	**Ayala's Angel** by *Anthony Trollope* The two girls were both pretty, but Lucy who was twenty-one who supposed to be simple and comparatively unattractive, whereas Ayala was credited, as her Bombwhat romantic name might show, with poetic charm and a taste for romance. Ayala when her father died was nineteen...	ISBN: 1-59462-352-X Fiction Pages 484	$29.95
☐	**The American Commonwealth** by *James Bryce* An interpretation of American democratic political theory. It examines political mechanics and society from the perspective of Scotsman James Bryce	ISBN: 1-59462-286-8 Politics Pages 572	$34.45
☐	**Stories of the Pilgrims** by *Margaret P. Pumphrey* This book explores pilgrims religious oppression in England as well as their escape to Holland and eventual crossing to America on the Mayflower, and their early days in New England...	ISBN: 1-59462-116-0 History Pages 268	$17.95

www.bookjungle.com email: sales@bookjungle.com fax: 630-214-0564 mail: Book Jungle PO Box 2226 Champaign, IL 61825

QTY

The Fasting Cure by *Sinclair Upton* ISBN: *1-59462-222-1* **$13.95**
In the Cosmopolitan Magazine for May, 1910, and in the Contemporary Review (London) for April, 1910, I published an article dealing with my experiences in fasting. I have written a great many magazine articles, but never one which attracted so much attention... New Age/Self Help/Health Pages 164

Hebrew Astrology by *Sepharial* ISBN: *1-59462-308-2* **$13.45**
In these days of advanced thinking it is a matter of common observation that we have left many of the old landmarks behind and that we are now pressing forward to greater heights and to a wider horizon than that which represented the mind-content of our progenitors... Astrology Pages 144

Thought Vibration or The Law of Attraction in the Thought World ISBN: *1-59462-127-6* **$12.95**
by *William Walker Atkinson* Psychology/Religion Pages 144

Optimism by *Helen Keller* ISBN: *1-59462-108-X* **$15.95**
Helen Keller was blind, deaf, and mute since 19 months old, yet famously learned how to overcome these handicaps, communicate with the world, and spread her lectures promoting optimism. An inspiring read for everyone... Biographies/Inspirational Pages 84

Sara Crewe by *Frances Burnett* ISBN: *1-59462-360-0* **$9.45**
In the first place, Miss Minchin lived in London. Her home was a large, dull, tall one, in a large, dull square, where all the houses were alike, and all the sparrows were alike, and where all the door-knockers made the same heavy sound... Childrens/Classic Pages 88

The Autobiography of Benjamin Franklin by *Benjamin Franklin* ISBN: *1-59462-135-7* **$24.95**
The Autobiography of Benjamin Franklin has probably been more extensively read than any other American historical work, and no other book of its kind has had such ups and downs of fortune. Franklin lived for many years in England, where he was agent... Biographies/History Pages 332

Name	
Email	
Telephone	
Address	
City, State ZIP	

☐ Credit Card   ☐ Check / Money Order

Credit Card Number	
Expiration Date	
Signature	

Please Mail to: Book Jungle
PO Box 2226
Champaign, IL 61825
or Fax to: 630-214-0564

ORDERING INFORMATION

web: *www.bookjungle.com*
email: *sales@bookjungle.com*
fax: *630-214-0564*
mail: *Book Jungle PO Box 2226 Champaign, IL 61825*
or PayPal *to sales@bookjungle.com*

Please contact us for bulk discounts

DIRECT-ORDER TERMS

20% Discount if You Order Two or More Books
Free Domestic Shipping!
Accepted: Master Card, Visa, Discover, American Express

www.ingramcontent.com/pod-product-compliance
Lightning Source LLC
Chambersburg PA
CBHW082103230426

43671CB00015B/2592